DRUG TRANSIT AND DISTRIBUTION, INTERCEPTION AND CONTROL

DRUG CONTROL IN THE UNITED STATES

2014 STRATEGY AND AN APPRAISAL OF PAST POLICY

DRUG TRANSIT AND DISTRIBUTION, INTERCEPTION AND CONTROL

Additional books in this series can be found on Nova's website under the Series tab.

Additional e-books in this series can be found on Nova's website under the e-book tab.

DRUG TRANSIT AND DISTRIBUTION, INTERCEPTION AND CONTROL

DRUG CONTROL IN THE UNITED STATES

2014 STRATEGY AND AN APPRAISAL OF PAST POLICY

IVAN T. RAINS
EDITOR

nova publishers
New York

For permission to use material from this book please contact us:
Telephone 631-231-7269; Fax 631-231-8175
Web Site: http://www.novapublishers.com

Additional color graphics may be available in the e-book version of this book.

Library of Congress Cataloging-in-Publication Data

ISBN: 978-1-63321-969-4

Published by Nova Science Publishers, Inc. † New York

CONTENTS

PREFACE

This book discusses the 2014 National Drug Control Strategy and functions as a guide for shaping Federal policy, to stop drug production and trafficking, prevent drug use, and provide care for those who are addicted.

Chapter 1 - The 2014 National Drug Control Strategy builds on the foundation laid down by the Administration's previous four Strategies and serves as the Nation's blueprint for reducing drug use and its consequences. Continuing a collaborative, balanced, and science-based approach, the new Strategy provides a review of the progress made over the past four years. It also looks ahead to continuing efforts to reform, rebalance, and renew national drug control policy to address the public health and safety challenges of the 21st century.

The strategy is rooted in the belief that illicit drug use is a public health issue, not just a criminal justice problem. It calls on law enforcement, courts, and doctors to collaborate with each other and for healthcare providers to prevent and treat addictive disorders just like they would treat any other chronic disorder, like diabetes or heart disease.

Beyond its function as a guide for shaping Federal policy, the National Drug Control Strategy is a useful resource for anyone interested in learning what is being done—and what other work can be done— to stop drug production and trafficking, prevent drug use, and provide care for those who are addicted. For parents, teachers, community leaders, law enforcement officers, elected officials, ordinary citizens, and others concerned about the health and safety of our young people, the Strategy is a valuable tool that not only informs but also can serve as a catalyst to spark positive change.

Chapter 2 - In the four decades since President Richard Nixon first declared war on drugs, the U.S. counterdrug strategy has remained virtually unchanged—favoring supply-reduction, law enforcement, and criminal sanctions over demand reduction, treatment, and education. While the annual counterdrug budget has ballooned from $100 million to $25 billion, the availability of most illicit drugs remains at an all-time high. The human cost is staggering—nearly 40,000 drug-related deaths in the United States annually. The societal impact, in purely economic terms, is now estimated to be approximately $200 billion per year. The global illicit drug industry now accounts for 1 percent of all commerce on the planet—approximately $320 billion annually. Legalization is almost certainly not the answer; however, an objective analysis of available data confirms that: 1) the United States has pursued essentially the same flawed supply-reduction strategy for 40 years; and, 2) simply increasing the amount of money invested each year in this strategy will not make it successful. Faced with impending budget cuts and a future of budget austerity, policymakers must replace the longstanding U.S. counterdrug strategy with a pragmatic, science-based, demand-reduction strategy that offers some prospect of reducing the economic and societal impacts of illicit drugs on American society.

In: Drug Control in the United States
Editor: Ivan T. Rains

ISBN: 978-1-63321-969-4

Chapter 1

2014 NATIONAL DRUG CONTROL STRATEGY*

Office of National Drug Control Policy

INTRODUCTION

Throughout 2013, the Administration continued to play a leading role in advancing drug policy reform, beginning with the release of the 2013 *National Drug Control Strategy,* which called for an approach rooted in scientific research on addiction, evidence-based prevention programs, increased access to treatment, a historic emphasis on recovery, and criminal justice reform. In May, the Office of National Drug Control Policy (ONDCP) hosted actor Matthew Perry at the White House to discuss alternatives to incarceration and criminal justice reform. Mr. Perry currently serves as a celebrity ambassador for drug courts, which divert approximately 120,000 nonviolent substance-involved offenders each year to treatment instead of prison. There is a large base of research supporting the effectiveness of drug courts, and Mr. Perry has been instrumental in getting the word out about this important criminal justice and public health program. In June, ONDCP participated in a White House event focusing on 12 "Champions of Change" who have dedicated themselves to helping children of incarcerated parents and their caregivers. This event was linked to the work of the Federal Interagency Reentry Council, which is

* This is an edited, reformatted and augmented version of a document issued by the Executive Office of the President, July 2014.

committed to identifying and eliminating legal obstacles faced by people reentering society after incarceration.

In August, Attorney General Eric Holder announced new changes to the Department of Justice's (DOJ) charging policies regarding mandatory minimum sentences for certain nonviolent, low-level drug offenses. The policy changes are part of DOJ's "Smart on Crime" initiative, a comprehensive review of the criminal justice system aimed at ensuring Federal laws are enforced more fairly, Federal resources are used more efficiently, and focus is placed on top law enforcement priorities. These changes ensure that the most severe mandatory minimum penalties are reserved for serious, high-level, or violent drug traffickers. And, where appropriate, Federal law enforcement encourages alternatives to incarceration such as drug courts, specialty courts, or other diversion programs for non-violent offenses. Also in August, the Administration observed International Overdose Awareness Day with the release of the Department of Health and Human Services (HHS) Opioid Overdose Toolkit. The Toolkit provides information on overdose prevention, treatment, and recovery for first responders, prescribers, and patients. It also promotes the use of naloxone, a life-saving overdose reversal prescription drug that should be in the patrol cars of every law enforcement professional across the Nation for use as appropriate.

In November, another critical component of drug policy reform was introduced when the Administration issued the final rule implementing the Mental Health Parity and Addiction Equity Act of 2008. The rule makes it easier for Americans to get the care they need by prohibiting certain discriminatory practices that limit insurance coverage for behavioral health treatment and services. The "parity rule" ends discrimination against those who suffer from substance use and mental health disorders, significantly expands access to treatment services, and improves the ability of health care providers to identify symptoms and provide treatment before a chronic condition develops. The Affordable Care Act now requires Qualified Health Plans offered through the Health Insurance Marketplaces in every state to include coverage for mental health and substance use disorders as one of the 10 categories of Essential Health Benefits, and the coverage must comply with these Federal parity requirements.

The Administration capped this important year with the first-ever Drug Policy Reform Conference at the White House in December. The conference gathered more than 100 leaders from the prevention, treatment, early intervention, and criminal justice reform communities to discuss innovative, evidence-based approaches to reducing drug use and its consequences. The conference included addresses from senior Administration officials and panel discussions focusing on public health approaches to drug policy, the transition from "tough on crime" to "smart on crime" policies, and efforts to lift the stigma faced by those struggling with substance use disorders and those who are in recovery.

THE IMPORTANCE OF LANGUAGE: REDUCING THE STIGMA SURROUNDING SUBSTANCE USE DISORDERS

Substance use disorders are medical conditions, and reducing the stigma surrounding these medical conditions is a particularly important component of drug policy reform—one in which every American can play a part. As we have worked to help guide the millions of Americans who suffer from substance use disorders into recovery and support the millions more who are already in long-term recovery, we have learned that how we describe or refer to substance use disorders can have an important effect on outcomes. Research demonstrates that the use of stigmatizing words like "addict" can discourage individuals from seeking help.[1] Additionally, using such terms reinforces the idea that someone with a substance use disorder is exhibiting a willful choice rather than suffering from a recognized medical condition.[2]

Researchers also note that identifying an individual with a substance use disorder as a "substance abuser" evokes less sympathy than if the individual is described as having a disease.[3] Avoiding these terms—and thereby reducing the stigma faced by those with substance use disorders—can play an important role in encouraging these individuals to seek help at an earlier stage in the disease.

While we have made significant progress in advancing evidence-based drug policy reform, serious challenges still remain. Among those challenges are the declining perceptions of harm—and associated increases in use—of marijuana among young people. These challenges have gained prominence with the passage of state ballot initiatives in 2012 legalizing marijuana in the states of Colorado and Washington. In August DOJ released guidance reiterating that marijuana remains illegal under Federal law and that Federal law enforcement activities in these two states would continue to be guided by *eight priorities* focused on protecting public health and safety. ONDCP is working with DOJ and other Federal partners to monitor the implementation of these state laws and the public health and safety consequences related to these eight priorities. ONDCP is also working with its Federal partners and stakeholders throughout the country to address other remaining challenges like the problem of opioid use disorders—including both prescription opioids and heroin—and the dynamic problem of new synthetic drugs.

RESPONDING TO THE OPIOID ABUSE EPIDEMIC: HEROIN AND PRESCRIPTION DRUGS

In 2010, opioid pain relievers like oxycodone, hydrocodone, and methadone were involved in more than 16,600 overdose deaths—approximately 45 Americans every day.[i] This startling figure is approximately 4 times greater than the number of deaths just a decade earlier in 2000.[ii] And with reports of increasing heroin use in many American communities, the potential transition from prescription opioid abuse to heroin and injection drug use has become an increasing concern.

Although rates of heroin use remain low compared to rates of use for other drugs, there has been a troubling increase in the number of people using heroin—from 373,000 past year users in 2007 to 669,000 in 2012. A recent report from the Substance Abuse and Mental Health Services Administration (SAMHSA) found that four out of five recent heroin initiates (79.5 percent) had previously used prescription pain relievers non-medically.

These findings underscore the need for a comprehensive approach to address opioid abuse, focusing on both heroin and prescription drug abuse. The Administration is working to increase the use of FDA-approved medications to treat opioid use disorders, to include providing treatment within the criminal justice system. ONDCP is working with the Office of National AIDS Policy, Federal partners, and state and local governments to develop a collaborative approach to address substance use disorders as well as the public health consequences resulting from increased use of syringes. The Administration has increased its focus on overdose prevention and intervention, to include

- educating the public about overdose risks and interventions (such as through the HHS *Opioid Overdose Prevention Toolkit*);

- increasing access to naloxone, an emergency overdose reversal medication; and
- working with states to promote Good Samaritan laws and other measures that can help save lives.

The Administration is also working with law enforcement partners across the country and around the world to disrupt and dismantle criminal organizations involved in the trafficking of heroin. Mexico remains the primary source of heroin to U.S. markets, and U.S. and Mexican agencies continue to build on their strong law enforcement partnership to target transnational criminal organizations involved in heroin trafficking.

Through all of these efforts, the Administration is working to improve data collection on heroin use, production, trafficking, and street-level sales. This effort to improve our understanding of the heroin problem and its relationship with prescription drug abuse was significantly advanced during the "Summit on Heroin and Prescription Drugs," hosted by ONDCP at the White House in June 2014. During the Summit, public health specialists, law enforcement professionals, drug policy experts, community organizations, and Federal, state, and local government officials gathered to discuss the epidemic of opioid abuse in the United States. The discussions at the Summit will inform the Administration's continuing efforts to address this urgent public health and safety issue throughout 2014.

[i] Jones, C.M., Mack, K.A., & Paulozzi, L.J. (2013). Pharmaceutical overdose deaths, United States, 2010. Journal of the American Medical Association, 309(7), 657-9.

[ii] Centers for Disease Control and Prevention, National Center for Health Statistics. Underlying Cause of Death 2000-2010 on CDC WONDER Online Database. Extracted February 2013.

The *Strategy* that follows addresses these challenges and others through a modern, evidence-based approach encompassing prevention, early intervention, treatment, recovery support, criminal justice reform, effective law enforcement, and international cooperation. The overall framework, goals, and agency responsibilities established in the President's first *Strategy* remain in effect, even as we remain ready to adapt our approach based on new developments and emerging trends. With a significant record of accomplishment, an ongoing agenda for reform, and strong partnerships throughout the Government, across the country, and around the world, we will continue our progress toward the President's goals for 2015.

National Drug Control Strategy Goals to Be Attained by 2015

Goal 1: Curtail illicit drug consumption in America

1a. Decrease the 30-day prevalence of drug use among 12-to 17-year-olds by 15 percent
1b. Decrease the lifetime prevalence of 8th graders who have used drugs, alcohol, or tobacco by 15 percent
1c. Decrease the 30-day prevalence of drug use among young adults aged 18–25 by 10 percent
1d. Reduce the number of chronic drug users by 15 percent

Goal 2: Improve the public health and public safety of the American people by reducing the consequences of drug abuse

2a. Reduce drug-induced deaths by 15 percent
2b. Reduce drug-related morbidity by 15 percent
2c. Reduce the prevalence of drugged driving by 10 percent

Data Sources: SAMHSA's National Survey on Drug Use and Health (NSDUH) (1a, 1c); Monitoring the Future (1b); What Americans Spend on Illegal Drugs (1d); Centers for Disease Control and Prevention (CDC) National Vital Statistics System (2a); Substance Abuse and Mental Health Services Administration's (SAMHSA) Drug Abuse Warning Network (DAWN) drug-related emergency room visits, and CDC data on HIV infections attributable to drug use (2b); NSDUH and National Highway Traffic Safety Administration (NHTSA) roadside survey (2c)

Section 1. Strengthen Efforts to Prevent Drug Use in our Communities

One of the Administration's primary drug policy goals is preventing drug use before it begins. The consequences of drug use affect every sector of society and hamper the ability of both young people and adults to reach their full potential. Prevention is a cost-effective and common-sense way to avoid the consequences of drug use among youth.[4]

Substance use prevention efforts can be effective when approaches are comprehensive,[5] address risk and protective factors,[6] and focus on a community's unique challenges.[7] It is also important that prevention efforts focus on parental awareness and involvement,[8] strengthen social norms against drug use,[9],[10] and limit access to illicit substances.[11] Research has shown that every dollar invested in school-based substance use prevention programs has the potential to save up to $18 in costs related to substance use disorders.[12]

This research into the effectiveness of prevention has become even more relevant in light of recent trends in youth drug use. Long term data from the Monitoring the Future study—which surveys 8th, 10th, and 12th graders on their behaviors and attitudes—demonstrate that when the perceptions of harm related to drug use decrease, rates of drug use are more likely to subsequently increase.13 Over the past 5 years, perception of harm regarding marijuana use among 12th graders has decreased,14 signaling potential continued increases in marijuana use.

Improving youth educational achievement is vital to America's success in the global economy of the 21st century, but substance use can serve as a major obstacle to such achievement. Youth who use drugs are often at risk for poor academic performance, truancy, delinquency, and other problems. Studies have shown that among youth who earn mostly Ds and Fs in school, 66 percent had used marijuana, a higher percentage than other risk behaviors studied.15 Heavy cannabis use during the teen years has also been found to result in an average 8 point drop in IQ between childhood and adulthood; by comparison, those who never used marijuana showed no decline in IQ.[16]

Despite these challenges, it is possible to make a positive impact on youth, their families, and communities. A range of Federal efforts have helped make certain that communities, schools, parents, and health professionals have the information they need to implement evidence-based prevention programs and policies. For example, the U.S. Department of Agriculture (USDA) 4-H program has established a peer mentoring program, and the Department of Education is providing professional development and technical assistance through the 21st century Community Learning Centers program, which enables communities to establish or expand centers that provide additional student learning opportunities, such as before- and after-school programs and summer school programs, and provide related services to students' families. ONDCP's Drug-Free Communities (DFC) Support Program provides funding to over 600 community coalitions organized to prevent youth substance use.

Strengthening efforts to prevent drug use in our communities requires a strategic plan to carry out comprehensive policies, programs, and practices. Partnerships have been developed with Federal, state, and local agencies, school health officials, criminal justice agencies, and community-based organizations that are interested in changing the landscape regarding drug use among youth. Federal agencies, tribal nations, states, and local coalitions have worked together to ensure the latest and most accurate information is available for communities to execute their own plans of action. This *Strategy* continues to be a blueprint to inform this process, and progress made throughout 2013 is detailed below.

1. A National Prevention System Must be Grounded at the Community Level

A. Collaborate with States to Support Communities

The President's Proclamation for National Substance Abuse Prevention Month, issued in October 2013, called upon all Americans to promote comprehensive substance abuse prevention efforts within their communities. The Administration works with states and communities to promote the critical role of prevention partnerships. Through support from the Substance Abuse and Mental Health Services Administration (SAMHSA), states utilize the Substance Abuse Prevention and Treatment Block Grant Prevention Set-Aside to implement substance abuse prevention activities in communities across the Nation. In 2013, a total of 49 technical assistance visits in 27 states were completed. Under the Partnership for Success II program, 15 new grants were awarded to states to address priority areas, including underage drinking and prescription drug abuse among high-risk populations. SAMHSA's Center for Substance Abuse Prevention (CSAP) provided support to states through the State Epidemiological Outcomes Workgroups, which are funded at $150,000 per year for states and a range of $75,000 to $100,000 for jurisdictions and tribal entities. These grants help communities develop secure data collection systems to expand prevention capacity, adopt data-driven strategies, and promote evidence-based and outcome-based approaches. The Guide to Community Preventive Services serves as a comprehensive resource to support communities in implementing evidence-based prevention strategies targeting such substance use issues as underage alcohol and tobacco use.

The Administration has worked with national organizations such as the America's Promise Alliance and state-affiliated professional membership groups to advance the message that we must make substance abuse prevention a priority.[17] These groups have helped promote youth prevention messaging through their Federal, state, and local affiliations. The National Education Association Representative Assembly passed a resolution to disseminate prescription drug abuse information among its membership and developed resource materials for educators to reach their youth in schools.

Comprehensive Prevention Efforts in Yukon, Oklahoma

The community of Yukon, Oklahoma is taking a comprehensive and collaborative approach to substance abuse prevention, and survey results show that the approach has been effective.[18] Working out of the Red Rock Behavioral Health Services Agency, and funded by the Oklahoma Department of Mental Health and Substance Abuse Services, the Region Prevention Coordinator has been an active member of the Yu-Can coalition for over 5 years. This is the first coalition in this community that has brought together a broad group of youth-led stakeholders. Its priorities include: implementation of Project Alert, an evidence-based substance abuse prevention curriculum; alcohol compliance checks to reduce alcohol sales to minors; alcohol restrictions at community events; and AlcoholEdu (an Internet-based education tool provided to every high school). To help build capacity for the community and to ensure sustainability, the Yu-Can Coalition receives support from the Oklahoma State Office of Substance Abuse Services, the Yukon Public Schools, a DFC grant, and the area Office of the School Superintendent. The Coalition works with local law enforcement, alcohol retailers, businesses, parents, school groups, and other stakeholders to create sustainable and effective community partnerships.

B. Spread Prevention to the Workplace

The workplace is a prime location to educate employees about making informed decisions about the health and well-being of themselves and their families. The Division of Workplace Programs at SAMHSA disseminates information on building safer, healthier, and more productive workplaces through health risk assessments, brief screenings, early identification, and referral to treatment services. The Division of Workplace Programs also has oversight for drug testing of 400,000 Federal employees in security and safety sensitive positions, including employees regulated by the Nuclear Regulatory Commission. SAMHSA and the U.S. Food and Drug Administration's (FDA) Office of Women's Health launched National Wellness Week in September 2013 to focus on the eight dimensions of wellness and their integration into a person's home and work life. SAMHSA also manages the Preventing Prescription Drug Abuse in the Workplace program to provide technical assistance to Federal and state partners. The Department of Transportation (DOT) regulates a strong industry-based drug and alcohol testing program that conducted approximately 6.1 million drug screenings in 2013. The testing program protects public health and safety by ensuring that safety-sensitive transportation employees in the aviation, trucking, railroad, mass transit, pipeline, and other transportation industries are screened for substance abuse issues and receive help if needed.

2. Prevention Efforts Must Encompass the Range of Settings in Which Young People Grow up

A. Strengthen the Drug-Free Communities Support Program

Coalitions across the country mobilize to address the drug trends unique to their communities. Through the DFC Support Program, community-based coalitions have mobilized more than 9,000 community volunteers across the country. DFC-funded coalitions are required to work with various sectors of a community to identify local drug problems and implement comprehensive strategies to create community-level change. According to the DFC Support Program's national cross-site evaluation, communities with DFC-funded coalitions have experienced consistently lower rates of past 30-day teen substance use as compared to communities without DFC-funded coalitions. For FY 2013, ONDCP announced $19.8 million in new DFC grants to 147 communities and 19 new DFC mentoring grants across the country. The awards are in addition to the existing $59.4 million in DFC continuation grants simultaneously released to 473 currently funded DFC coalitions and 4 DFC mentoring coalitions. The DFC Support Program collaborates with SAMHSA/CSAP to provide grants of up to $625,000 over 5 years to coalitions, with technical assistance provided through the Community Anti-Drug Coalitions of America (CADCA). CADCA's National Coalition Institute also provides technical assistance to states for coalition development, reaching 1,153 participants.

B. Leverage and Evolve the Above the Influence Brand to Support Teen Prevention Efforts

The Above the Influence (ATI) campaign is dedicated to demonstrating the power of young people living "above the influence" of drugs and alcohol. The second annual National ATI Day was held on October 17, 2013 as part of National Substance Abuse Prevention Month. On that day, teens and community organizations across the country participated in various youth-focused events and activities. Campaign partners and young people in four featured markets—California, New York, Florida, and Washington, D.C.—were visited by the ATI team for a special "cross-country" event. Through social media, the teens interacted with participants at the other event sites. Nearly 1,000 teens participated directly in local ATI Day events. Social networks (Facebook, Tumblr, Twitter, and Instagram) further extended participation across the country. Thousands of teen-generated messages on these networks reached an audience exceeding 700,000.

ATI has achieved a greater than 80 percent awareness level among teens. The campaign continues to have a strong presence in the Facebook community, surpassing 1.8 million "likes" and making it one of the largest national teen-targeted Facebook presences among Federal Government or nonprofit youth organizations. Additionally, three independent peer-reviewed studies have confirmed that ATI is effective, relevant to youth, and instrumental to drug prevention efforts in communities across the country.[19,20,21] ONDCP is transitioning the ATI brand to The Partnership for Drug-Free Kids to help ensure its continuation.

C. Support Mentoring Initiatives, Especially among at-Risk Youth

Mentoring young people who are at risk helps reduce drug use among this vulnerable group. Young people who participate in structured activities and identify with mentors who are a consistent presence in their lives have better outcomes for success. The National Guard Youth ChalleNGe Program is a community-based program that leads, trains, and mentors at-risk youth so that they may become productive citizens. Currently, there are 33 ChalleNGe programs in 27 states and the Commonwealth of Puerto Rico. The Department of Justice advances tribal mentoring initiatives by providing grants to federally recognized tribes to develop and implement culturally sensitive programs in the five following categories: prevention services to impact risk factors for delinquency, interventions for court-involved youth, improvements to the juvenile justice system, alcohol and substance abuse prevention programs, and mental health program services.

The USDA 4-H program prepares young people to be leaders in their communities and take an active role in improving the lives of fellow young people. ONDCP partnered with USDA 4-H to host a webinar that provided 60 USDA staff members tools to implement ATI activities and to encourage their youth partners to participate in the campaign.

ADVOCATE FOR ACTION: JUDGE ARTHUR L. BURNETT, SR.

Retired Judge Arthur L. Burnett, Sr. is being honored as an Advocate for Action for his role in founding the National African American Drug Policy Coalition (NAADPC) program for youth drug prevention. Judge Burnett designed and implemented a program through which African American professionals visit schools and talk to young people about the harmful effects of drug use on individual health and academic success. Under his leadership, the NAADPC works 7 days a week to prevent youth drug and alcohol use across the country. NAADPC provides tutors, counselors, and mentors from a coalition of African American professionals numbering over one million. Judge Burnett personally appears in schools across the country to provide inspirational talks about avoiding youth alcohol and drug use. His talks emphasize the value of good citizenship and the potential for individuals from humble backgrounds to be a part of the American dream. In the course of his work, Judge Burnett also provides expert advice on drug and juvenile delinquency judicial issues to Members of Congress.

The Department of Education's You for Youth (Y4Y) portal provides online professional development and technical assistance resources, such as substance abuse prevention strategies, for professionals working with students through the 21st century Community Learning Centers program.

D. Mobilize Parents to Educate Youth to Reject Drug Use

Parents need to be equipped with information and skills to communicate effectively with their youth. National Substance Abuse Prevention Month, declared by the President in October 2013, included activities with a focus on parents. Parent resource materials are available to ensure that parents receive the support and tools they need to engage their youth. ONDCP works with the National Institute on Drug Abuse (NIDA) to get parents to participate in their research-based prevention tools—including the Family Check-Up, which focuses on parenting skills and interactive scenarios. NIDA's updated web page for parents and educators provides resources for caregivers and teachers. In 2013 CADCA hosted online chats and provided state-level trainings to 385 attendees in 7 states. SAMHSA released its *Talk. They Hear You.* campaign especially for parents of youth aged 9-15 to provide messages for parent-youth conversations. In 2013, the campaign's public service announcements (PSAs) were seen 809 million times via earned media through national television networks, PSA placements, and other placements, including malls and airports.

3. Develop and Disseminate Information on Youth Drug, Alcohol, and Tobacco Use

A. Support Substance Abuse Prevention on College Campuses

The Department of Education supports the National Center on Safe Supportive Learning Environments (NCSSLE), which provides technical assistance, training, and resources on substance abuse prevention to institutions of higher education to benefit college and university students. SAMHSA has launched technology-based products to prevent high risk drinking among college students. The Federal Government, through its Interagency Coordinating Council on Preventing Underage Drinking, collaborates with colleges and universities and provides training and technical assistance. Comprehensive resources developed with input from 15 Federal agencies are maintained on a web portal that includes materials to support prevention efforts.

B. Expand Research on Understudied Substances and other Drug-related Issues

The ONDCP Prevention Interagency Work Group has focused on working with Federal partners to develop an agenda to address research gaps, such as newly emerging drugs of abuse. NIDA's prevention research program focuses on risks for drug use and other problem behaviors that may occur throughout a child's development. Leading researchers have formulated a *prevention cooperative* that will publish outcomes from prevention research conferences as well as action items for continued dialogue and collaboration between researchers and practitioners.

C. Prepare a Report on the Health Risks of Youth Substance Use

It is important to keep information current and disseminate information to address behavioral risk factors that increase the incidence of drug use. In 2012, HHS released *Preventing Tobacco use Among Youth and Young Adults: A Report of the Surgeon General.* The HHS Interagency Workgroup on Adolescent Health has disseminated materials to its partners to include drug use information and best practices. The National Prevention Council identified four strategic directions designed to improve overall health and wellness and includes preventing drug use and excessive alcohol use among its targeted priorities. The Centers for Disease Control and Prevention (CDC) document *Work in Adolescent Health: Selected Tools for Moving Research into Practice* provides a snapshot of adolescent health tools that include HIV/AIDS prevention, a particularly important issue given that rates of infectious diseases such as HIV, viral hepatitis, sexually transmitted diseases, and tuberculosis are substantially higher among persons who use drugs illicitly than among persons who do not use drugs illicitly.[22]

4. Criminal Justice Agencies and Prevention Organizations Must Collaborate

A. Enable Law Enforcement Officers to Participate in Community Prevention Programs in Schools, Community Coalitions, Civic Organizations, and Faith-Based Organizations

Participation by law enforcement professionals in prevention activities in schools, community settings, and organizations that involve youth is an effective way to support prevention efforts. Twenty of the 28 High Intensity

Drug Trafficking Areas (HIDTAs) are engaged in activities that connect law enforcement with community-based prevention efforts through mentoring, role modeling, and life skills education. The Houston HIDTA has increased its coalition efforts and includes over 15 new partners.

The Drug Enforcement Administration (DEA) is committed to partnering with community prevention programs, providing education materials and trainings to targeted law enforcement groups and continuing its annual Red Ribbon Week prevention events.

The Federal Bureau of Investigation's (FBI) Community Outreach Program (COP) seeks to enhance public trust and confidence in the FBI in order to enlist the cooperation and support of the community in preventing crime. The COP also provides information to the public in support of crime prevention efforts and opens new lines of communication to help make the FBI more responsive to community concerns. In these ways, the COP plays an increasingly broader role in improving the FBI's understanding of the communities it serves.

The National Association of School Resource Officers is refining its curriculum training to ensure officers in school settings are getting the most updated information on best practices in substance use prevention. At its annual conference, over 800 participants identified preventing youth substance use as a priority.

B. Strengthen Prevention Efforts along the Southwest Border

The *National Southwest Border Counternarcotics Strategy* includes a focus on supporting communities in the Southwest border region. The *Strategy* emphasizes elevating support for coalitions to enhance their prevention efforts with existing community-based organizations and agencies. Relationships are being developed among HIDTA grantee sites, local DFCs, and community-based non-profit groups to ensure collaboration to address regional issues. The National Prevention Network Conference, held in Oklahoma City in August of 2013 with nearly 700 attendees, provided information and opportunities for further dialogue with local coalitions in the southwest region. Work with the U.S.-Mexico Border Commission has expanded to include dissemination of prevention information to its member organizations and has reached 42 key drug demand reduction professionals in the region.

HOUSTON HIDTA PREVENTION EFFORTS

Newly established in mid-2013, the Houston HIDTA Drug Prevention and Awareness Initiative (DPAI) was designed to present a concerted and collaborative drug prevention and awareness effort for the Houston community. DPAI involves a partnership with the DEA Demand Reduction Unit and the Houston mayor's office Crackdown Coalition, merging behavioral health professionals, law enforcement officials, and professionals in prevention and treatment. This coalition has broad representation and works together to increase awareness of drug trafficking and community drug use trends. The Houston HIDTA co-sponsored the 2013 Coalition's 4th Annual Community Drug Awareness Day at Rice University, with an audience of approximately 240 people. The event received positive reviews from the community and afforded the Houston HIDTA the opportunity to be involved in prevention work. Plans are underway to provide forums on specific college campuses to engage at least 1,000 students in 2014. The Houston HIDTA has also partnered with the Success Through Addiction Recovery (STAR) program, which bridges the gap between criminal justice and therapeutic approaches for defendants with drug dependencies.

SECTION 2. SEEK EARLY INTERVENTION OPPORTUNITIES IN HEALTH CARE

A systematic approach within health care systems for the early identification of substance use disorders among patients is critical to reducing drug use and its consequences. As research findings emerge and are translated into practice, the benefits of investing in early intervention for substance use disorders are becoming ever more apparent. Research suggests that investing in early intervention services can contribute to a reduction in health care costs and help ensure the improved health and well-being of patients.[23] Health care reform under the Affordable Care Act extends access to and parity for substance use and mental health disorder services for an estimated 62 million Americans.[24]

Early intervention helps individuals recognize when they are at risk of substance use disorders and need help to identify and change high-risk behaviors into healthy patterns. Health care providers use approaches such as

Screening, Brief Intervention, and Referral to Treatment (SBIRT) to identify individuals with problematic substance use behaviors before they progress to substance use disorders. SBIRT can be implemented in primary care settings and hospitals, allowing quick responses to substance use disorders and providing care for more people.

Research indicates that the younger a person begins using alcohol or drugs, the more likely that individual is to develop a substance use disorder later in life.[25,26] According to the 2013 Monitoring the Future study, by the time students reach the 12th grade, 50 percent of these youth had used illicit drugs in their lifetime, with over 45 percent having used marijuana.[27] Given these findings, the Administration is giving special attention to substance use disorders among adolescents and young adults. Using SBIRT, health care providers can identify and intervene early with adolescents and young adults who engage in high-risk behaviors (See Figure 1).

Brief Interventions Reduce Adolescent Substance Abuse

NIDA research on brief interventions show that two hour-long sessions a week apart reduce symptoms of substance abuse or dependence.

Drug- and alcohol-involved middle and high school students markedly reduced their substance use following two 60-minute sessions that combined motivational interviewing (MI) and cognitive behavioral therapy.

The students also reported significantly fewer substance-related symptoms of substance use disorders during the 6 months after the intervention compared with the 6 months before it.

Adding a separate 1-hour MI-based session with a parent or primary caregiver enhanced the beneficial effects.

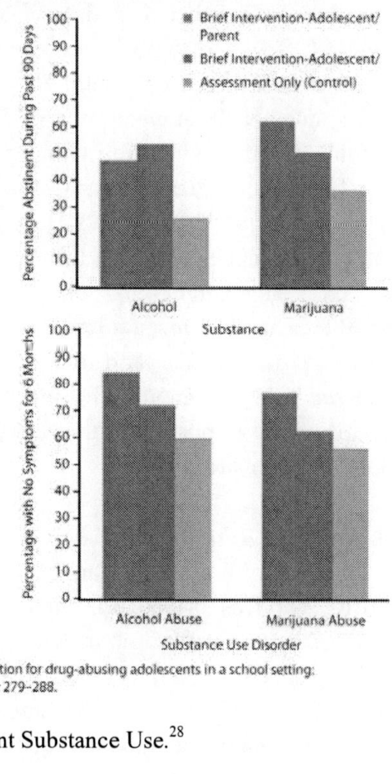

Winters, K.C., Fahnhorst, T., Botzet, A., Lee, S. & Lalona, B. (2012) Brief intervention for drug-abusing adolescents in a school setting: Outcomes and mediating factors. *Journal of Substance Abuse Treatment 42(3)*: 279–288.

Figure 1. Brief Interventions Reduce Adolescent Substance Use.[28]

Substance use behaviors initiated early in life are often carried into older adulthood. For example, the rate of current illicit drug use among adults aged 50 to 64 has increased significantly from 2002 to 2012. This trend represents the aging of the "baby boomer" generation, which has consistently exhibited higher levels of illicit drug use than older age groups.[29] This underscores the importance of prevention and intervention early in life, while also highlighting an additional population for which screening and brief intervention services can still be useful.

1. Catching Substance Use Disorders Early Saves Lives and Money

A. Expand and Evaluate Screening for Substance Use in All Health Care Settings

In 2013, SAMHSA funded SBIRT grants to Vermont, Ohio, South Carolina, New Mexico, and New York. An Addiction Technology Transfer Center (ATTC) for SBIRT was established to provide resources to SAMHSA grantees and health care entities. The ATTC conducted an SBIRT webinar series; developed an electronic SBIRT newsletter; provided SBIRT resources, training products, and information; and maintained two learning communities.

Throughout 2013, the Health Resources and Services Administration (HRSA) partnered with SAMHSA through the SAMHSA/HRSA Center for Integrated Health Solutions to provide SBIRT technical assistance to HRSA-funded health centers. A series of webinars were conducted using model SBIRT programs for adolescents, employee assistance programs, criminal justice professionals, and the military. A Technical Assistance Protocol released in 2013 on SBIRT from a state's administrative and organizational perspective was posted on the SAMHSA/HRSA Center for Integrated Health Solutions website.

B. Increase Adoption and Use of SBIRT Codes

SBIRT billing codes can be used to reimburse health care providers for SBIRT services. Medicaid, Medicare, and commercial insurers have these codes for provider reimbursement. In 2013, SAMHSA conducted webinar trainings and provided technical assistance for SBIRT grantees to integrate the codes for billing and reimbursement for SBIRT services into their systems. These webinars use model SBIRT health care programs that successfully integrate methods for generating revenue for services. Conducting these webinars helps address provider challenges, such as unfamiliarity with the codes in billing departments and the need to initiate new processes for billing submission. SBIRT specifications must be made a part of the newly developed electronic medical records (EMR) billing system. In 2014, SAMHSA will conduct additional webinars on the effective use of SBIRT codes.

C. Enhance Health Care Providers' Skills in Screening and Brief Intervention

With SBIRT, substance abuse screening is incorporated into mainstream health care settings, such as college health clinics, hospitals, trauma centers, and dental clinics, as well as tribal and military health care settings. Practitioners screen patients to assess substance use, then, based on the screening results, provide the appropriate intervention. In 2013, 17 SBIRT medical residency grantees trained 6,600 physicians. Of these grantees, 14 programs trained 11,800 other health professionals. Also in 2013, 16 state SBIRT programs trained clinical staff and other health care professionals.

Throughout 2013, SAMHSA offered webinars or online courses using the medical residency program curriculum. To demonstrate SBIRT in action, best practice examples were used in these trainings and disseminated to medical and behavioral health practitioners. In addition, a webinar series was conducted on lessons learned from successful former and current SBIRT grantees. SAMHSA developed an SBIRT Medical Residency Training Implementation Guide for dissemination to current and future grantees. The SBIRT Technical Assistance Publication was released, providing information and guidance for the implementation of SBIRT in diverse health care settings.

D. Identify and Make Available Additional Training in Evidence-based Practices for Substance Use Disorder Assessment and Care to Health Care Professionals Providing Care to Military Health System Beneficiaries

In 2013, the Department of Defense (DoD) instituted a web-based training program called *Do No Harm*. The training includes scenario-based clinical vignettes for military treatment personnel on prescription drug misuse. In 2014, performance metrics will be developed to evaluate the program.

ADVOCATE FOR ACTION: DR. JOAN STANDORA

For 40 years, Joan Standora, Ph.D. has worked tirelessly to improve clinical, administrative, and educational practices in the substance use disorder field. Early in her career, Dr. Standora developed an expressive therapy program in a methadone-maintenance residential program and received a NIDA grant for a program serving mothers with substance use disorders and their children. In 1998, she became the first clinical director of New York City's Manhattan Treatment Court. Dr. Standora established protocols and policies, supervised staff, and conducted outreach to providers for the drug court participants. Dr. Standora was instrumental in establishing the New York City Regional Drug Court/Treatment Consortium. Dr. Standora then became the Executive Clinical Director at a Bronx-based treatment program, instituting staff trainings focusing on substance use disorders among clients from low-income minority communities plagued by poor health care and unemployment. In 2000, Dr. Standora developed and implemented a substance abuse counselor education program at the City University of New York's Kingsborough Community College. The program became a degree program in 2003, approved by both New York State's Education Department and the Office of Alcoholism and Substance Abuse Services (OASAS). In 2010, Dr. Standora received a grant from the Department of Labor (DOL) through OASAS to retrain 25 unemployed workers as substance abuse counselors as part of the American Recovery and Reinvestment Act of 2009. In 2013, Dr. Standora received a grant to enroll persons over the age of 50 as a community college workforce education project for professionals in the substance use disorder field. She currently directs the degree program in chemical dependency counseling at the City University of New York.

Throughout 2013, DoD focused its efforts to improve access to behavioral health in primary care. DoD has assigned 470 behavioral health professionals to primary care clinics to increase access to behavioral health screening and intervention in less stigmatizing environments. Through the Patient Centered Medical Home, DoD will provide consultation on mental health and substance use issues to staff members in primary care. Next year, DoD plans to incorporate SBIRT training for Army primary care providers.

SECTION 3. INTEGRATE TREATMENT FOR SUBSTANCE USE DISORDERS INTO HEALTH CARE AND EXPAND SUPPORT FOR RECOVERY

Recovering from a substance use disorder is often a long process, one that may require help from health care professionals such as doctors, physician assistants, nurses, counselors, social workers, recovery peer support counselors, and other specialists. Across the Nation, teams of health care professionals and recovery support service providers work with patients to reduce the prevalence of substance use disorders by providing treatment and recovery support. This effort includes the use of innovative technologies to help individuals access substance use disorder services. These technologies range from electronic health records to mobile health applications to telehealth technologies. They support health care reform by delivering evidence-based care, coordinating care, engaging the patient in shared decision making, and monitoring progress and outcomes. As substance use disorder services can be received in many locations, efforts should be made to support interoperable technologies that provide seamless care provision across all settings of care and types of provider.

In addition to encouraging health care professionals to use innovative technologies to help patients with substance use disorders, the Administration encourages the use of the FDA's approved medications to treat opioid use disorders: methadone, naltrexone (Vivitrol-a once-monthly extended-release injectable formulation), and buprenorphine. Under a health care provider's care, medication is often an essential element of opioid use disorder treatment. According to NIDA, "medication assisted treatment of opioid addiction increases patient retention and decreases drug use, infectious disease transmission, and criminal activity."[30] Used properly, the medication does not continue an addiction nor create a new one. Rather, it can stabilize individuals, permitting them to pursue and sustain recovery.[31] The Administration continues to underscore the importance of educating practitioners across all medical fields about medications for the treatment of opioid use disorders.

Another area of importance is providing effective care for persons living with substance use disorders and infectious diseases such as HIV and viral hepatitis. Increased prevention efforts must be focused and brought to scale for populations at highest risk. Science-based interventions are vital, to include testing and treatment, prevention education, comprehensive substance use disorder treatment, and new prevention technologies such as pre-exposure prophylaxis. To better facilitate access to appropriate care for HIV, viral hepatitis, and substance use disorders, support is needed for screening in general health care and specialty treatment settings. The 2012 Summary Guidance from CDC and HHS describes the rationale for and importance of integrated prevention services for infectious diseases among persons who use drugs illicitly and provides information on effective models and evaluation of integrated services.[32]

Stigma, rooted in the misperception that a substance use disorder is a personal moral failing rather than a brain disease, is a major obstacle to drug policy reform. The Administration is committed to addressing laws, policies, and practices that often prevent people in recovery from accessing housing, education, and employment. The Administration is also committed to ensuring that substance use disorders are recognized as chronic conditions that often require ongoing support after treatment. Nowhere is this of greater importance than among adolescents and young adults who are in or seeking recovery. In the coming year, the Administration will continue to work to support promising approaches to expand access to housing and employment among recovering persons with felony convictions.

Community-based recovery support service providers are an indispensable part of the substance use disorder services infrastructure. These providers help people sustain recovery by providing a stable and welcoming peer recovery community through which recovery coaching, training, employment, housing, and other services are provided. The Administration celebrates and champions recovery throughout the year and gives it special recognition every September when the White House issues a Presidential Proclamation for National Alcohol and Drug Addiction Recovery Month. In 2013, the Administration actively used social media as part of these efforts. In addition to hosting Twitter chats, ONDCP established the Americans in Recovery Facebook page, providing a place for people in recovery to share their stories and learn about relevant Federal policies and programs.

1. Addiction Treatment Must be an Integrated, Accessible Part of Mainstream Health Care

A. Expand Addiction Specialty Services in Health Centers

The Affordable Care Act will increase the availability of treatment for people with substance use disorders. With an increased demand for substance use disorder treatment will come a need for an increase in the skilled health care workforce. To begin to address this demand, the SAMHSA-HRSA Center for Integrated Health Solutions organized a year-long learning network in three states, involving two health centers from each state, to establish medication-assisted treatment services within health centers. In addition, the SAMHSA-HRSA Center for Integrated Health Solutions created an online course for substance use disorder treatment providers specific to the experience and skills needed to succeed in a primary care environment.

B. Increase Addiction Treatment Services within the Indian Health Service

In 2013, the Indian Health Service's (IHS) Tele-Behavioral Health Center of Excellence, along with the SAMHSA-HRSA Center for Integrated Health Solutions, conducted webinar training on substance use disorders for more than 2,400 service providers in the IHS, as well as tribal and urban Indian health care providers. In addition, the IHS Scholarship Program provided funding for 17 behavioral health scholars in clinical psychology, social work, and substance abuse counseling.

C. Expand the Innovations of the Department of Veterans Affairs Substance Use Disorder

Treatment Approach to Other Federal Health Care Systems The Veterans Health Administration is America's largest integrated health care system, serving 8.7 million veterans a year at more than 1,700 sites of care.[33] The Department of Veterans Affairs' (VA) commitment to expand access to behavioral health care is an important component of its work with veterans and their family members. To assist veterans who experience posttraumatic stress disorder (PTSD), depression, substance use disorders, suicidality, chronic pain, insomnia, and nicotine dependence, the VA provides evidence-based psychotherapies and psychopharmacology interventions specified in clinical practice guidelines for mental health and substance use disorders. To ensure these services are known to veterans and their families, the VA developed and implemented Make the Connection. *Make the Connection* is a public awareness and outreach campaign connecting veterans and their friends and family members with information, resources, and solutions related to issues affecting their health, well-being, and relationships. The initiative aims to:

1. Reduce the stigma many veterans and their families associate with seeking mental health support;
2. Highlight the particular strengths of veterans who have sought support and are living a richer life today as a result: resilience, courage, perseverance, leadership, and mission focus; and
3. Feature more than 300 veterans and their family members who have contributed personal, candid testimonials about seeking treatment for challenges ranging from physical injury, flashbacks, traumatic brain injury, posttraumatic stress disorder, and depression.

ONDCP continues to work with the VA to ensure continuing education for health care practitioners on proper prescribing and disposal of prescription drugs, with a focus on opioid analgesics. More information can be found under "*Policy Focus: Preventing and Addressing Prescription Drug Abuse.*"

D. Enhance Public and Private Insurance Coverage of Addiction Treatment

In 2013, SAMHSA conducted a state-by-state analysis to determine state readiness and progress related to health care reform. Analysis results were used to identify technical assistance and other resources that state behavioral health agencies needed to fully implement the Affordable Care Act requirements. Subsequently, SAMHSA convened the 10th State Systems Development Program Conference titled "Mental Health and Substance Abuse Prevention and Treatment Block Grants: Cornerstones of Behavioral Health Services," which provided information to state mental health and substance abuse treatment authorities about enhanced coverage of substance use disorder treatment under the Affordable Care Act.

E. Inform Public Health Systems on Implementation of Needle Exchange Programs

Addressing the connection between substance use disorders and infectious diseases such as HIV and viral hepatitis remains a priority for both ONDCP and the Office of National AIDS Policy. The reported increase in injection drug use among young people in some parts of the country—particularly in rural and suburban settings—means that state and local governments need to develop a collaborative approach to address substance use disorders as well as the public health issues that result from increased use of syringes. The Administration is committed to informing public health systems on the implementation of needle exchange programs that protect the public, reduce infections, and encourage involvement in substance use disorder treatment. Although the Consolidated Appropriations Act of 2012 reinstated a ban on most Federal funding for syringe services programs, 30 states, the District of Columbia, the Commonwealth of Puerto Rico, and several Indian Nations currently have their own sterile syringe exchange programs.[34]

2. Patients with Substance Use Disorders and Their Families Must Receive High-Quality Care

A. Support the Development of New Medications for Addiction

Progress continues to be made in leveraging public-private partnerships to help bring substance use disorder medications to market. Over the past year, NIDA has established formal collaborations with several pharmaceutical companies. Accumulated knowledge and recent discoveries have revealed numerous potential new approaches to medications development. To achieve the goal of accelerating medications development, NIDA is focusing on the scientific opportunities in genetics research, high-resolution mapping of targeted brain areas, the development of vaccines against substance use disorders (see text box), and combination medications similar to promising strategies used for treating other diseases such as cancer and HIV/AIDS.

B. Integrate and Coordinate Substance Use Disorder Services under the Affordable Care Act (3.2.B.)

Health homes were established under the Affordable Care Act to coordinate care for people with Medicaid who have chronic conditions such as mental health disorders, substance use disorders, asthma, diabetes, heart disease, and obesity. Health home providers integrate and coordinate all primary, acute, behavioral health, and long-term services, as well as support services to treat the whole person. Ensuring implementation of the health home program involves effective integration of the treatment of substance use disorders into primary care, and SAMHSA and CMS have developed a state consultation plan for states submitting proposals for State Plan Amendments to create health home programs. As of December 31, 2013, 14 states had approved State Plan Amendments that include plans for screening of substance abuse and referral to treatment. An additional 15 states are developing a health home proposal.

BUILDING AN ANTI-DRUG VACCINE

Vaccines have a unique role to play in a comprehensive strategy to help people overcome substance use disorders. A successful vaccine will make it easier for individuals with substance use disorders to establish and maintain abstinence. It will reduce the chances that isolated lapses into drug use escalate into protracted relapses. Ideally, a single dose will remain effective for months or longer, eliminating the potential for missed doses and consequent gaps in protection that sometimes occur with shorter-acting agents.

Anti-drug vaccines take advantage of a tissue filter that surrounds the blood vessels in the brain. The filter, called the blood-brain barrier, protects the brain from exposure to many potentially harmful substances circulating in the blood. The barrier normally does not block out drug molecules, which easily pass through it despite being harmful.

If an individual has been vaccinated, the antibodies produced by the vaccine bind to the drug molecules in the bloodstream. The compound drug-antibody molecules are too big to go through the blood brain barrier. The drug cannot enter the brain and cannot produce psychoactive effects or lead to the development of a substance use disorder. An anti-drug vaccine will be clinically useful if the antibody response it induces is sufficiently strong and long-lasting.

A video from NIDA on anti-drug vaccines can be viewed here.

C. Promulgate the National Quality Forum Standards for Addiction Treatment

Mental health and substance use disorder clinical quality measures support health care quality, promoting effective, safe, efficient, patient-centered, equitable, and timely care. In 2013, ONDCP, HHS, and other Federal partners recommended behavioral health related clinical quality measures to be included in the Centers for Medicare and Medicaid Services (CMS) Medicare and Medicaid EHR Incentive Program, also known as the "Meaningful Use Program." The Meaningful Use Program provides Federal incentives to help health care providers adopt electronic health records. These measures are to be endorsed by the Office of the National Coordinator for Health Information Technology and CMS.

Also in 2013, ONDCP, SAMHSA, and NIDA facilitated the development of the Composite Measure for Substance Use Screening for inclusion in the CMS Electronic Health Records Meaningful Use Incentive Program. This measure includes screening and brief counseling for the use of tobacco, alcohol, illicit drugs, and misuse of prescription drugs.

D. Equip Health Care Providers and First Responders to Recognize and Manage Overdoses

Naloxone is a lifesaving overdose-reversal medication. First responders and community-based programs can use naloxone to save the lives of those overdosing from heroin or prescription medicines made with opioids. In 2013, SAMHSA launched an *Opioid Overdose Toolkit.* For further information about this toolkit, see "*Policy Focus: Preventing and Addressing Prescription Drug Abuse.*"

E. Integrate Substance Use Treatment and HIV Prevention and Care, Including in the Criminal Justice System

Approximately half of all teens who enter the juvenile justice system need treatment for substance use disorders.[35] The remaining half would benefit from a drug abuse prevention intervention. To address this situation, in 2013, NIDA launched Juvenile Justice Translational Research on Interventions for Adolescents in the Legal System (JJ-TRIALS). As part of this JJ-TRIALS cooperative, seven research centers will work together to determine how juvenile justice programs can effectively adopt science- based prevention and treatment services for drug abuse and HIV. Awardees will develop and execute collaborative multisite studies across a variety of juvenile justice settings, including juvenile probation and drug courts. This initiative is particularly important given the connection between illicit drug use and infectious diseases such as HIV, viral hepatitis, sexually transmitted diseases, and tuberculosis.[36]

3. Celebrate and Support Recovery from Addiction

A. Review Laws and Regulations that Impede Recovery from Addiction

In 2013, ONDCP and the Department of Education developed and released a document clarifying restrictions on eligibility for Federal student aid related to convictions for the possession or sale of illegal drugs. Titled FAFSA Facts, the document explains how drug-related convictions affect student loan eligibility; clarifies the period of time a person is considered to be receiving Federal student aid; and details steps people can take to regain eligibility for Federal student aid. ONDCP and the Department of Housing and Urban Development (HUD) completed a document profiling promising practices among Public Housing Authorities that provide housing and support to people returning to the community from incarceration—many are in recovery from substance use disorders. For further discussion about housing for reentering offenders, see Section 4.

ADVOCATE FOR ACTION: SCOTT STRODE

Scott Strode has dedicated his life to helping individuals with substance use disorders find and maintain their recovery through sport, a dedication that has earned the attention of national media organizations such as CNN, which honored him as a CNN Hero. Scott founded Phoenix Multisport in 2007 to foster a safe, supportive, physically active community for individuals recovering from alcohol and substance abuse and for those who choose to live a sober life. Through pursuits such as climbing, hiking, running, strength training, yoga, road/mountain biking, CrossFit, and other activities, Phoenix seeks to help its members develop and maintain the emotional strength they need to stay sober. All activities are free. The only requirement is that individuals have at least 48 hours of continued sobriety to participate. They also must adhere to Phoenix Multisport's code of conduct, which says that anything that is not nurturing is not welcome. Since 2007, over 11,000 individuals have attended Phoenix Multisport events in Colorado, where they find a safe, sober community of friends to help support them in their recovery. Scott is devoted to changing how the world views those with substance use disorders. By living sober and rising from the ashes of one's substance use disorder, Scott believes that one's life has new meaning and should be celebrated. Scott and the staff at Phoenix Multisport welcome newly-recovering individuals to join them for a free activity or workout. It is Scott's hope that Phoenix Multisport will expand to other areas of the country to reach even more of those in need.

B. Foster the Expansion of Community-Based Recovery Support Programs, Including Recovery Schools, Peer-led Programs, Mutual Aid Groups, and Recovery Community Organizations

Under its new Peer-to-Peer Targeted Capacity Expansion grant program, SAMHSA has awarded grants to 15 recovery community organizations (RCOs) and five facilitating organizations that serve as fiduciary agents for emerging RCOs. An RCO is a community-based, non-profit organization led by members of the recovery community. These organizations serve the community by providing a range of peer-led services, such as peer recovery coaching, employment and housing support, training, ongoing access to a community of recovering peers, and advocacy. By funding established and emerging RCOs, the grants expand and enhance access to a wide array of community-based peer recovery support services. Many of these services were initially developed under the Recovery Community Services Program, which also funded RCOs.

In 2013, the ONDCP Recovery-Oriented Systems of Care Learning Community for states, tribes, and local governments continued its operations with teams from 14 jurisdictions. Additionally, SAMHSA conducted an online policy academy for states interested in implementing the Recovery-Oriented Systems of Care framework. The Administration continues to highlight the needs of adolescents and young adults in recovery, including recovery high schools and collegiate recovery programs.

SECTION 4. BREAK THE CYCLE OF DRUG USE, CRIME, DELINQUENCY, AND INCARCERATION

At the end of 2012, nearly 7 million adults were involved in the criminal justice system—either on probation, parole, or incarcerated in jail or prison.[37] The United States has the largest per capita prison population in the world,[38] a costly statistic in terms of both money and societal impact. In too many cases, individuals with substance use disorders are sent to jail or prison when drug treatment—or alternatives such as drug courts—can achieve better outcomes at reduced costs. The long-lasting and far reaching consequences of criminal justice involvement are an impediment to employment, housing, and education, all necessary for a strong recovery and successful reentry into the community.

Since the release of the President's first *Strategy*, the Administration has emphasized the importance of a full range of interventions for individuals with substance use disorders at every stage of the criminal justice system. States are currently implementing such approaches and programs as pre-trial diversion, the use of risk assessment tools, drug courts, enhanced probation and parole protocols, the expansion of treatment (including medication-assisted treatment), and reentry support. At the Federal level, DOJ's Smart on Crime Initiative pursues such reform efforts as modifications to charging policies for low-level nonviolent offenders, sentencing reform, and addressing persistent demographic disparities.

If incarceration is necessary, appropriate treatment and other supportive services should be provided to help incarcerated individuals fully recover from their substance use disorder and maintain their recovery after their sentence is complete. A study conducted in the California Department of Corrections and Rehabilitation found that inmates who participated in an in-prison treatment program and completed an aftercare program had the lowest 3-year recidivism rates—31.3 percent—when compared to those who did not receive treatment and only received some aftercare (78.8 percent).[39]

Like all diseases, substance use disorders should be treated with every evidence-based, medically appropriate tool available, including the use of medications for the treatment of opioid disorders. Several jurisdictions have encountered success with the use of medication-assisted treatment for justice-involved individuals. For example, methadone has long been used to maintain abstinence from heroin while people are incarcerated, but newer medications like buprenorphine and Vivitrol have also shown promise in controlling opioid use disorders. When combined with behavioral therapy, connecting offenders with a maintenance program after their release can help them sustain recovery.

The Administration has made significant strides in assisting formerly incarcerated individuals success- fully transition back into their communities. The Federal Interagency Reentry Council,[40] consisting of 20 Federal partners, continues to identify and reduce barriers to employment, education, and housing, helping justice-involved individuals who have served their sentences.

Across the country, state and local authorities are also taking action to help formerly incarcerated individuals reenter the community, with some jurisdictions instituting "ban the box" initiatives that ask employers to remove questions about prior criminal convictions from initial employment applications.

The Administration, with the help of experts, practitioners, researchers, policymakers, and private citizens, is poised to effect systemic change. Implementing evidence-based interventions for individuals within the criminal justice system; saving the most resource-intensive programs for those with the most need and the highest risk of recidivism; and providing opportunities for gainful employment, housing, and education are all part of the Administration's reform efforts. Many of these efforts have already met with great success, and the items below outline the actions the Administration will continue to take to break the cycle of drug use, crime, delinquency, and incarceration.

1. Provide Communities with the Capacity to Prevent Drug-Related Crime

A. Organize Communitywide Efforts to Reduce Open-Air Drug Markets and Gang Activity via Drug Market Intervention Approaches

The Drug Market Intervention (DMI) model has proven effective in shutting down open-air drug markets through community-based solutions and direct engagement with the community. The Bureau of Justice Assistance (BJA) is working with RAND to evaluate the success of the DMI training and technical assistance initiative. Previously, BJA funded technical assistance to several cities, including Roanoke, VA, which has reported great success in the implementation of DMI. Since the beginning of their DMI efforts, the Roanoke Police Department reports a 71 percent reduction in crime, as well as an interest from businesses to develop in the area.

B. Engage Faith-Based and Neighborhood Community Organizations to Prevent Drug- Related Crime

The National Youth Violence Prevention Forum is a White House-led initiative commissioned by the President in 2010, linking cities and Federal agencies to implement strategies and programs to prevent youth and gang violence in the United States. The 10 cities of the Forum[41] sent leaders and youth to Washington, D.C. in September 2013 to share their work and exchange ideas at the Summit on Preventing Youth Violence. The 2013 Summit focused on the issue of sustaining and growing the cities' efforts beyond the availability of Federal funds.

C. Support Innovative Criminal Justice Research Programs

In 2011, BJA funded the Honest Opportunity Probation with Enforcement Demonstration Field Experiment (HOPE DFE) in four jurisdictions.[42] This program is modeled on Hawaii's successful probation program that combines drug testing with swift, certain sanctions to reduce probation violations. In 2013, the HOPE Training and Technical Assistance team hosted a peer-to-peer training session for the judges, probation administrators, and project coordinators involved in the HOPE DFE to assist them in more closely approximating the successful model used in Hawaii. BJA anticipates that the four pilot sites will expand to serve more probationers prior to the conclusion of the program. The BJA training and technical assistance team is also developing materials to assist in other jurisdictions that might be interested in implementing a "swift and certain" model; these documents are expected to be released in 2016. The National Institute of Justice (NIJ) is conducting an evaluation to determine the effectiveness of the HOPE model at the four sites. The final evaluation results are expected in summer 2016.

2. Develop Infrastructure to Promote Alternatives to Incarceration When Appropriate

A. Enhance and Promote Diversion Strategies

BJA is working with the Center for Court Innovation to develop the Misdemeanor Evidence-Based Assessment project, a screening tool for offenders in New York that can be used at the earliest possible moment in the processing of a court case. Before arraignment, the tool will be administered to provide information on key needs to both attorneys and the judge. Ultimately, the project will supply an evidence-based assessment tool that can be administered by case managers, pre-trial services staff, or prosecutors and will allow individuals to be matched with appropriate interventions. The tool will be created and ready for validation beginning in early 2015, with initial results available in mid-2015.

B. Support Drug Courts and Other Problem-Solving Courts

The Administration supports the use of drug courts and other problem-solving courts—including family dependency courts, tribal healing to wellness courts, and veterans treatment courts—to meet the unique needs of offenders with substance use disorders. BJA has received feedback from its drug court grantees regarding the need for additional training and technical assistance to educate practitioners on evidence-based services. As a result of this feedback, BJA has convened a new grantee orientation call to better acquaint grantees with available trainings and services.

ONDCP issued a training and technical assistance grant to the National Association of Drug Court Professionals (NADCP) to provide, among other things, training to drug court practitioners on emerging issues at national conferences. Specifically, NADCP has provided training sessions on integrating these issues into drug court practice, including medication-assisted treatment for individuals with opioid use disorders, recovery support systems, addressing the problem of synthetic drugs, and interventions for pregnant and postpartum women. ONDCP also worked with NIDA to provide training on the use of medication-assisted treatment in justice settings to criminal justice practitioners in the American Correctional Association.

Jurisdictions across the country are exploring opportunities to develop community courts, which focus on improving the quality of life for the localities in which they sit. The courts rely on community-based public/private partnerships to deliver wrap-around services to clients while also protecting the safety of the community. In 2012, BJA and the Center for Court Innovation named three regional mentor community courts, including the South Dallas Community Court.43 Since the inception of this project, the Dallas program has hosted more than a dozen teams from cities across the United States and from other countries; Dallas is assisting in the planning stages for community courts in Houston, Atlanta, Detroit, and Canada.

C. Support Systemic Change in Evidence-Based Sentencing through Training and Outreach

To improve the criminal justice system at all levels, change agents must be identified and informed of new evidence, perspectives, and innovations. In partnership with NADCP and Treatment Alternatives for Safe Communities (TASC), ONDCP is funding training sessions to help law enforcement officers and executives understand the science of addiction and how this understanding could inform practices and policies. In 2013, TASC convened a task force of law enforcement professionals and police organizations to develop training materials. The task force comprised representatives from the Police Executive Research Forum, the International Association of Chiefs of Police, and Major Cities Chiefs; experts from the criminal justice and law enforcement fields; and senior and mid-level managers from police departments in Chicago, IL, Philadelphia, PA, Montgomery County, MD, the Cherokee Nation, Austin, TX, Overland Park, KS, and Hennepin County, MN. In spring 2014, TASC convened a roundtable of police chiefs, sheriffs, and national law enforcement organizations to discuss the science of addiction, training for officers, and law enforcement's role in criminal justice reform. Curricula developed through these two meetings will be piloted over the course of 2014.

ADVOCATES FOR ACTION: MELODY HEAPS AND PAMELA RODRIGUEZ

Melody Heaps and Pamela Rodriguez are partners and leaders in advancing system-wide justice interventions for people with substance use disorders. For more than 30 years, they have shared a collective commitment to collaborative solutions that improve both public health and public safety.

Melody founded TASC in Chicago in 1976 as a nonprofit agency focused on alternatives to incarceration. She would go on to lead TASC to become a nationally recognized organization before she retired from her role as president and CEO in 2009. She remains president emeritus of TASC and is an advisor to TASC's Center for Health and Justice, which offers public policy and consulting services nationally and internationally.

Melody began her career during the civil rights movement and served on Martin Luther King, Jr.'s staff during the Chicago campaign. From these roots grew a lifelong professional commitment to addressing the complex and interrelated issues of drugs, poverty, and crime. Under her leadership, TASC matured from a small pilot project in Cook County, Illinois to a statewide organization providing direct services for 25,000 individuals annually.

Pamela Rodriguez has served as TASC's president and CEO since 2009, having previously directed every aspect of the agency's operations. Under her leadership, TASC has continued to grow and thrive, including an expanded focus on diversion programs early in the justice continuum to reduce recidivism and the collateral consequences of justice involvement.

An expert in connecting research to clinical practice, Pam was appointed in 2007 to serve as a practitioner model of the Federal Coordinating Council on Juvenile Justice and Delinquency Prevention. She is active in numerous bodies to increase alternatives to incarceration, improve juvenile justice, and decrease the disproportionate incarceration of people of color.

Together, Melody and Pam have played significant roles at local, state, and national levels in the development and expansion of community-based diversion programs and treatment alternatives to incarceration to create healthier and safer communities.

D. Foster Equitable Drug Sentencing

In 2013, DOJ announced the Smart on Crime initiative to ensure that law enforcement resources are best prioritized to protect public safety. In a memorandum to United States Attorneys (USAs) issued in August 2013, the Attorney General reaffirmed that, when making charging decisions, prosecutors "must take into account numerous factors, such as a defendant's conduct and criminal history and the circumstances relating to the commission of the offense...and Federal resources and priorities." Pursuant to this policy, USAs should "decline to pursue charges triggering a mandatory minimum sentence" in certain circumstances. This guidance may prove to lessen "unduly harsh sentences and perceived or actual disparities" in the justice system.[44]

E. Promote Best Practices as Alternatives to Incarceration

To study the impact of legislation promoting alternatives to incarceration for nonviolent drug offenders, the National Institute of Justice funded a policy analysis of the 2009 New York state drug law reform legislation that removed previously mandated prison sentences and created treatment diversion alternatives. The Vera Institute of Justice examined the impact of this legislation on felony drug cases based on arrest charges in New York City and found an increase in judicial diversion and a decrease in criminal sentences to incarceration, as well as fewer rearrests on both misdemeanor and felony charges. However, implementation varied widely across counties. Furthermore, savings to law enforcement, corrections, and victims resulting from decreased recidivism were outweighed by an increase in treatment costs related to increased use of residential over outpatient services.[45]

ONDCP is working through a grant to NADCP to collaborate with national criminal justice leaders and experts on alternatives to incarceration. The project will yield a repository of evidence-based practices that practitioners can use to choose the best intervention for each offender. The model takes into account each offender's risk of violating the terms of their supervision or dropping out of treatment and their need for treatment services. In 2014, NADCP will develop and pilot training sessions both to trainers, who can in turn train others, and to end-users.

F. Improve Intervention and Treatment Services for Female Offenders in the Juvenile and Criminal Justice Systems

The National Institute of Corrections (NIC) is working with Federal and non-governmental partners to improve programmatic responses to the needs of female offenders. For example, the Center for Gender and Justice has developed the "Gender Responsive Policy and Practices Assessment," an evidence-based, gender-informed tool for correctional agencies to assess their current practices for women and assist in planning for future improvements to policy, practice, and programming; development of budget requests; and strategic planning. The tool has been piloted in a jail, a prison, and two community corrections agencies, and will be available online by the end of the fiscal year.

NIC has also revised "Women Offenders: Developing an Agency-Wide Approach," a curriculum for correctional administrators to assist them in adapting their programs to improve outcomes for female offenders. The curriculum, which consists of in-person classroom training, webinars, and follow-up coaching provided by experts in the field, was piloted with 24 correctional administrators in August 2013 and will be offered again in 2014.

G. Examine Interventions and Treatment Services for Veterans within the Criminal Justice System

The VA has built the Veteran Reentry Search Service (VRSS), a Web-based system that will allow prison, jail, and court staff to quickly and accurately identify veterans among their inmate or defendant populations. VRSS will also prompt VA field staff to conduct outreach to the identified veterans to help connect them to benefits.

VA produced a brief outreach video titled *Suits* that encourages incarcerated veterans to use their time wisely by taking an active role in the reentry planning process and informs them how to contact a VA outreach specialist for help. The video, directed by an Operation Iraqi Freedom veteran, has been distributed to all state and Federal prisons, as well as more than 500 local jails.

H. Connect Incarcerated Veterans with Critical Substance Abuse and Reentry Services

The VA has reached more than 100,000 justice-involved veterans through direct outreach in prisons, jails, and criminal courts—including through the estimated 168 veterans treatment courts—to connect them with needed mental health, substance abuse, and other clinical services.[46]

Veterans, particularly those who are homeless, at risk of becoming homeless, or have prior criminal justice system involvement, have a significant and often unmet need for legal services. Although VA cannot provide legal services directly, local legal service providers have been given space in VA medical centers so that they can work with veterans where they receive health care. In some cases, assistance with prior criminal activity is available.

I. Address the Issue of Drug Use and Drug-Related Crime for American Indian/Alaskan Natives

In June 2013, President Obama signed an Executive Order creating the White House Council on Native American Affairs. The Executive Order called on all Federal agencies with equities in Indian Country to work together and with tribal nations. Among the priorities identified by tribal leadership and the White House are, "supporting greater access to and control over…health care" and, "improv[ing] the effectiveness and efficiency of tribal justice systems."47 Improving health and justice in Indian Country requires an emphasis on reducing drug use and its consequences, and the Administration is working to ensure resources and technical assistance are available to tribes seeking help on their lands and among their people.

Further, SAMHSA's Office of Indian Alcohol and Substance Abuse is working with tribes to develop "Tribal Action Plans," strategic documents that identify ways to prevent and treat substance use as part of a comprehensive approach to public health.

3. Use Community Corrections Programs to Monitor and Support Drug- Involved Offenders

A. Support Drug Testing with Certain and Swift Sanctions in Probation and Parole Systems

Drug testing with swift and certain sanctions, such as short periods of incarceration, has shown promise as a way to reduce probation and parole violations, and the Administration supports further research into its potential for broader applicability. Currently, NIJ is conducting two field studies. The first field experiment is a drug testing and graduated sanctions program, assessing the implementation process of such a program in a large urban probation department. The Decide Your Time (DYT) Program is an intensive supervision protocol developed by the Delaware Department of Corrections for new probationers and parolees who test positive for drugs.[48] The field experiment randomly assigned 400 offenders who tested positive at intake to the DYT protocol and compared recidivism outcomes for 200 participants to those for 200 offenders in the default standard probation. The final evaluation results are expected in 2014.

The second project, based at Pepperdine University, investigates long-term recidivism and relapse outcomes for the 2007-2009 cohorts of the Hawaii HOPE program. Researchers are using administrative court and probation records to determine recidivism outcomes and testing oral fluid and hair for a sample of those probationers to examine drug use in the context of how fidelity to the program model may affect these outcomes.

B. Consider Mechanisms for Assessing and Intensifying Community Corrections

The Department of Justice is working on community corrections improvement through its "Smart Supervision" initiative. BJA provided funding for jurisdictions to implement risk/needs assessments in probation departments aimed at matching individuals with the appropriate level of supervision— making more cost-effective decisions while preserving public safety. BJA will issue additional awards in 2014 and will expand the project to include parole. The project also has a research aspect, analyzing the type of offense and offender as well as the assessments of relative risk of re-offense and need for social services and supports.

C. Align the Criminal Justice and Public Health Systems to Intervene with Heavy Users

SAMHSA is providing funding to improve treatment interventions in problem-solving courts, expanding the number of courts and improving the effectiveness of existing courts. In 2013, SAMHSA issued 42 drug court awards: 10 Joint Adult Drug Court Grants with BJA; 29 Adult, Juvenile, and Family Drug Court Grants; and three Early Diversion Grants.

The new "Early Diversion" grants were a joint solicitation between SAMHSA's Center for Substance Abuse Treatment and its Center for Mental Health Services, focusing on diverting people with severe behavioral health issues away from the criminal justice system and toward community-based service alternatives by developing effective partnerships among law enforcement, behavioral health care providers, and service providers. One of the grantees, the Knoxville Early Diversion Program, is developing a specialized diversion team. The team, comprising police liaisons and case managers, will work with police officers to identify individuals in need of behavioral health services and connect them with community resources instead of arresting them.

D. Tackling Co-Occurring Disorders Using a Community-Based Response

Substance use and mental health disorders often co-occur, and in many instances require treatment for both disorders. In the general population, adults with a serious mental illness were more likely to experience dependence on or abuse of drugs or alcohol in the past year than those without any mental illness.[49] For offenders with a diagnosable substance use disorder, early intervention can make the difference between recurring criminal behavior and sustained recovery and mental well-being. SAMHSA requires grantees to ensure that community-based programs in its portfolio include effective screening for co-occurring disorders and appropriate treatment approaches. In 2013, SAMHSA's grantees screened more than 20,000 clients for co-occurring mental health and substance use disorders.[50]

E. Improve and Advance Substance Abuse Treatment in Prisons

The Federal Bureau of Prisons (BOP) is expanding access to evidence-based treatment for substance use disorders. In 2013, BOP implemented 18 new Residential Drug Abuse Treatment programs to reach more than 1,500 additional inmates, including two newly available Spanish-language treatment programs in Texas and Florida.

BOP has completed its portion of a demonstration project regarding the use of medication-assisted treatment in a community corrections environment. The project established a network of stakeholders that brought together community corrections, treatment agency staff, and other essential persons to better serve Federal offenders participating in Transitional Drug Abuse Treatment. The study demonstrated the benefits of establishing a network, and through this project, the Bureau determined medication-assisted treatment could be a viable treatment option for Federal offenders in a community corrections environment. BOP is now reviewing the possibility of conducting a trial study in which inmates would receive medication-assisted treatment for substance use disorders during the final weeks of their incarceration and then continue the medication-assisted treatment in the Residential Reentry Center. Based upon the outcome of the trial study, the Bureau will determine if a broader implementation of medication-assisted treatment should be pursued.

At the state level, BJA funds the Residential Substance Abuse Treatment program (RSAT) to help states create treatment programs for people in their custody that approximate residential treatment available in the community. Several grantees have used these funds to adopt and advance evidence-based treatment within their facilities. In Barnstable County, Massachusetts, the Sheriff, with support from community health officials, has started using Vivitrol—a medication for the treatment of opioid use disorders—to assist individuals in their return to their communities. The medication is only one aspect of their treatment: it helps prevent relapse while the individual with the substance use disorder works to make lasting behavioral changes. For each person in the RSAT program, there is a thorough risk and needs assessment to assist in planning for reentry. The Sheriff has already reported some success in this program, which started in 2012: of the 37 inmates treated, 59 percent remain in recovery and 2 people have stopped using Vivitrol to maintain their recovery.

In a further step to expand access to treatment for those in the criminal justice system, in March 2014 the Attorney General announced a new component of the Department of Justice's Smart on Crime initiative, through which the Bureau of Prisons (BOP) will impose new requirements on Federal halfway houses that help inmates transition back into society. Under the proposed new requirements, these halfway houses will have to provide a specialized form of treatment to prisoners, including those with mental health and substance use disorders.[51]

4. Create Supportive Communities to Sustain Recovery for the Reentry Population

A. Expand Reentry Support and Services through the Second Chance Act and Other Federal Grants

The Federal Interagency Reentry Council is helping reentering offenders compete for appropriate work opportunities. In the past year, the Office of Personnel Management, DOL, and the Equal Employment Opportunity Commission have issued guidance and best practices on the appropriate use of criminal histories in hiring procedures.[52,53,54]

B. Develop Ex-Offender Adult Reentry Programs

Several Federal programs are working to provide appropriate supportive services for individuals returning to their communities after a period of incarceration. For example, SAMHSA has funded 13 Offender Reentry Programs, which allow grantees to develop multidisciplinary approaches to planning, developing, and providing transitional services. These services include connecting ex-offenders with community-based substance abuse treatment and related reentry services before their release from jail or prison. In Chattanooga, TN, the program begins with reentry planning while offenders are still incarcerated to help them quickly adjust to daily life post-release. The Transitioning to Recovery program provides screening, assessments, and planning for offenders with substance use disorders and helps them stay engaged in treatment and recovery support services post-release through the use of intensive clinical case management.

C. Facilitate Access to Housing for Reentering Offenders

Access to safe, stable, affordable housing can be among the most significant barriers for individuals wishing to reenter their communities. An evaluation of Second Chance Act grantees, released in August 2013, noted housing instability as one of the foremost challenges for clients receiving reentry services. The Administration for Children and Families (ACF) has funded grants aimed at helping reentering fathers improve the quality and stability of family relationships by improving overall stability, such as housing and employment assistance. ACF is working with the Urban Institute on the Ex-Prisoner Reentry Strategies Study to evaluate the pilot grants and provide future guidance for other programs that improve chances of successful reentry for fathers and improved family relationships.

HUD is working with ONDCP to identify local public housing authorities who have implemented successful models for helping reentering offenders find safe and stable housing. More information about this project can be found in Section 3.

D. Provide Work-Related Training and Assistance to Reentering Offenders

DOL issues several grants that help prepare youth and adult ex-offenders for the workforce and remove barriers to employment. These include grants on Training to Work, Strategies Targeting Characteristics Common to Female Ex-Offenders, and Face Forward. As of mid-2013, the 1-year recidivism rate for adults involved in DOL-funded reentry programs was 13 percent.[55]

In 2013, DOL awarded two new grants to New York and Massachusetts to improve employment outcomes for formerly incarcerated individuals. The New York State Pay for Success Project: Employment to Break the Cycle of Recidivism will serve 1,000 individuals who are recently released from prison and have high employment needs with life skills assistance, transitional jobs, job placement, and post-placement support. The Massachusetts Juvenile Employment and Recidivism Initiative will reach more than 500 young men aging out of the juvenile justice system. These young men will have access to education and pre-vocational training as part of the grant program's long-term engagement in supportive services.

E. Encourage States Receiving Federal Funds for Corrections Programs to Provide Assistance to the Bureau of Justice Statistics in Conducting Annual Recidivism Studies

The Bureau of Justice Statistics (BJS) is working with data from state and Federal criminal history repositories to determine national estimates of recidivism. BJS has spent several years developing a software system that requests, captures, and processes large samples of rap sheets into research databases. The first product of this new technology is a report published in April 2014 describing the recidivism patterns of persons released from state prisons in 30 states in 2005.[56] Currently, BJS is working to develop statistically sound comparisons with its prior recidivism study of prisoners released in 1994, taking into account compositional differences in the demographic and criminal history attributes of the 1994 and 2005 release cohorts and changes in the nature and quality of information captured on rap sheets.

5. Improve Treatment for Youth Involved with the Juvenile Justice System

A. Develop and Disseminate More Effective Models of Addressing Substance Abuse and Mental Health Problems among Youth in the Juvenile Justice System

The Office of Juvenile Justice and Delinquency Prevention has issued several grants to expand interventions for justice-involved young people, including two training and technical assistance grants for juvenile substance abuse and family drug courts and program grants to seven family drug courts across the Nation. Family drug courts focus on treating substance use disorders among parents involved in the criminal justice system so they may be reunited with their children and provide safe, healthy home environments. For example, the Idaho Family Drug Court Enhancement Project will use the grant to expand the capacity of the drug courts from 40 to 60 participants per year, increase the percentage of children reunited with their parents, and provide comprehensive services to improve retention in the drug court program and success in recovery. Substance abuse and mental health assessments, improved case management, and recovery coaching services are among the wraparound supports the courts will provide.

In 2014, OJJDP will fund the implementation of the Reclaiming Futures model in up to three new sites. This model calls for a multi-disciplinary approach to working with juveniles in the justice system and integrates evidence-based treatment approaches that are appropriate to the adolescent populations served.

SECTION 5. DISRUPT DOMESTIC DRUG TRAFFICKING AND PRODUCTION

Drug trafficking organizations and the criminal activity associated with them can be found in every part of the United States. Whether they are operating watercraft along the California coast, using illicit crossborder tunnels along the Southwest border, or even using public lands for drug cultivation, these organizations unlawfully smuggle and distribute both illegal and diverted legal drugs in our communities. Trafficking and use of illicit drugs continue to constitute dynamic and challenging threats to the United States. Drug use not only poses risks to public health, but also is linked to violence and, in some cases, the financing of terrorism. Methamphetamine availability is on the increase because of sustained production in Mexico and ongoing small-scale domestic production. Additionally, marijuana availability appears to be growing because of sustained high levels of production in Mexico along with domestic cultivation.

Federal, state, local, and tribal law enforcement agencies play an integral role in the Administration's balanced approach to reducing drug use and its consequences. Maximizing Federal support for interagency law enforcement drug task forces is critical to leveraging limited resources. Law enforcement agencies and the intelligence community have strengthened cooperative efforts to address challenges related to information sharing and exchanging intelligence. Sharing information ensures law enforcement agencies are working together on targeted threats and taking full advantage of available resources. New and continued information sharing initiatives have led to substantial improvements in the combined intelligence capabilities of law enforcement.

Continued focus on security along the Mexican and Canadian borders also plays a significant role in reducing drug trafficking, use, and its consequences. Although still a serious concern, since 2008, crime in each of the four Southwest border states (California, Arizona, New Mexico, and Texas) has decreased significantly.[57] Transnational criminal organizations operating on both sides of the U.S.-Canada border also exploit the international boundary to smuggle proceeds from illegal drugs sold in the United States and Canada and to transport drugs such as marijuana, MDMA (ecstasy), methamphetamine, and cocaine between the two countries. Meanwhile, illicit proceeds cross the border in both directions, along with members of gangs and other organized crime groups, traffickers, facilitators, and couriers.

The Administration recognizes that communities across the country face distinct drug-related challenges. The abuse of non-controlled synthetic designer drugs such as synthetic cannabinoids, commonly referred to as "K2" and "Spice," and synthetic cathinones, commonly referred to as "bath salts," rapidly increased during the past several years, with serious public health and safety consequences. The Nation's law enforcement community must continue to focus on existing threats and collect information and data to address emerging threats. New economic developments in areas with limited resources like those occurring in the Bakken oilfields of Montana and North Dakota are resulting in an increase in drug-related criminal activity that requires a multi-agency approach.

WORKING WITH PUERTO RICO TO ADDRESS DRUG-RELATED CHALLENGES

South American transnational criminal organizations are increasingly trafficking larger and more numerous drug shipments through the Caribbean region. As a result, drug trafficking remains a significant threat to Puerto Rico and the U.S. Virgin Islands (USVI). An increase in violent crime has contributed to social problems in Puerto Rico and the USVI. Continuing the work started by the Puerto Rico Interagency Public Safety Working Group (added to the President's Task Force on Puerto Rico's Status) in 2012, ONDCP is working with the Puerto Rico/USVI HIDTA and in close cooperation with DOJ, the Department of Homeland Security (DHS), and other Federal and local partners to confront the ongoing threat to public safety.

Federal, commonwealth, and local law enforcement agencies in Puerto Rico continue to conduct operations derived from real time intelligence. The Caribbean Corridor Strike Force (CCSF) is a Federal multi-agency strike force involving the United States Attorney's Office for the District of Puerto Rico, DEA, the Federal Bureau of Investigation (FBI), U.S. Immigration and Customs Enforcement (ICE)/Homeland Security Investigations (HSI), Coast Guard Investigative Service, U.S. Customs and Border Protection (CBP), and the Puerto Rico Police Department. The CCSF, which seeks to disrupt maritime drug trafficking in the Caribbean, relies on tactical assets from local law enforcement agencies, CBP, the United States Coast Guard (USCG), the DoD Joint Interagency Task Force (JIATF) South, and the naval forces of partner nations. Since its inception in 2005, CCSF operations have resulted in the seizure of 42,902 kilograms of cocaine, 1,655 kilograms of marijuana, 241 kilograms of heroin, and $15,296,554 in cash. CCSF activities have also resulted in the arrest of 293 individuals.[58]

The Illegal Firearms and Violent Crime Reduction Initiative, which involves the Bureau of Alcohol, Tobacco, Firearms, and Explosives (ATF), DEA, FBI, U.S. Attorney's Office, ICE/HSI, United States Postal Inspection Service, and the Puerto Rico Department of Justice, has been in effect since November 2011 in five judicial regions in Puerto Rico. The main objective of the initiative is to halt the use of illegal firearms by immediately detaining persons prohibited from possessing them (including convicted felons). To date, the initiative has resulted in 896 arrests and the seizure of 739 firearms and more than 20,000 rounds of ammunition. Notably, more than a third of those arrested had prior convictions.

It remains important that Federal, state, local, and tribal law enforcement agencies work together with prevention and treatment specialists to provide a balanced, holistic approach to reducing drug use and its consequences.

1. Federal Enforcement Initiatives Must be Coordinated with State, Local, and Tribal Partners

A. Maximize Federal Support for Drug Law Enforcement Task Forces

Federal funding for drug law enforcement task forces enables state and local law enforcement agencies to participate in joint investigations, promotes local and regional coordination, and helps minimize duplication of effort. In 2012, HIDTA-funded initiatives disrupted or dismantled 3,030 drug trafficking organizations, removing significant quantities of drugs from the market and seizing over $819.0 million in cash and $1.1 billion in non-cash assets from drug traffickers ($1.9 billion total).[59] State and local law enforcement agencies are active participants in Organized Crime Drug Enforcement Task Forces (OCDETF) Strike Forces. As of November 15, 2013, state and local law enforcement agencies were participating in 4,643 out of 5,098 OCDETF investigations (91.1 percent).[60]

At the Nation's borders, the Border Enforcement Security Task Forces (BESTs) have expanded to a total of 35 locations in 16 states and in Puerto Rico. From their inception in 2005 through August 2013, BEST units had collectively initiated more than 10,654 cases that resulted in the seizure of over $130 million in cash, 110,711 pounds of cocaine, 1.03 million pounds of marijuana, and 15,062 weapons.[61]

Currently there are 163 FBI-led Violent Gang Safe Streets Task Forces (VGSSTF), which are vehicles to join Federal, state, and local law enforcement agencies to effectively combat violent crime. The VGSSTF concept expands cooperation and communication among Federal, state, and local law enforcement agencies, increasing productivity and avoiding duplication of investigative effort. In Fiscal Year 2013, VGSSTF funded initiatives disrupted or dismantled over 2,300 violent gangs, the majority of which were involved in some form of criminal drug activity.

B. Improve Intelligence Exchange and Information Sharing

Systematic collection, analysis, and secure dissemination of accurate and timely intelligence are critical to thwarting the activities of criminal organizations. The HIDTA Investigative Support Centers and Domestic Highway Enforcement (DHE) program have used the DHS Homeland Security Information Network (HSIN) to share intelligence products and requests for information with their partners, including state and major urban area fusion centers (fusion centers), Regional Information Sharing System centers, the El Paso Intelligence Center (EPIC), and the OCDETF Fusion Center (OFC). In FY 2013 the OFC generated 4,079 unique actionable intelligence products that were disseminated to 15,890 investigators in the field. These actionable intelligence products provided analysis on 17,129 targets. This number represents a 21 percent increase over FY 2012.

As recommended in an April 2013 Government Accountability Office report, the HIDTAs are working to ensure that there is interoperability among the three deconfliction systems currently being used: the Secure Automated Fast Event Tracking Network (SAFETNET); RISS Officer Safety Event Deconfliction System (RISSafe); and Case Explorer (CE). The HIDTAs have worked with officials from DHS, DOJ, the office of the Program Manager for the Information Sharing Environment, and the Office of the Director of National Intelligence to integrate the three deconfliction systems.

Along the Nation's highways, the HIDTA DHE program integrates intelligence from border/source enforcement efforts and transit/destination investigation activity. Increased awareness from the HIDTA DHE program resulted in the submission of 6,533 incidents reported as traffic stops to EPIC's National Seizure System (NSS) in Calendar Year 2013, which resulted in 8,660 seizures reported to the NSS.

C. Ensure State and Local Law Enforcement Access to Federal Information on Mexico-Based Traffickers

Current intelligence on Mexico-based traffickers must be readily available to state, local, and tribal law enforcement. State, local, and tribal law enforcement agencies are many times the first to encounter suspects associated with Mexico-based traffickers. The EPIC Strategic Analysis Section provides all-source strategic intelligence, including the Gatekeeper Project[62] assessments, in support of Federal, state, local, and tribal law enforcement activities along the U.S.-Mexico border.

The Financial Crimes Enforcement Network (FinCEN) provides 140 state and local law enforcement agencies with direct access to financial data through its Internet portal and directly supports state and local investigative efforts through its participation in the Southwest Border Anti-Money Laundering Alliance, with which it shares finished intelligence products. FinCEN recently changed its organizational structure to more effectively map, target, and disrupt the financial networks of drug trafficking organizations, support Federal, state, and local law enforcement actions, and more strategically apply its own enforcement and regulatory authorities. FinCEN and the Treasury Department continue to partner with other governments to target illicit financial networks, transnational criminal organizations, drug trafficking organizations, and other criminal actors.

D. Promote Law Enforcement Collaboration along Drug Trafficking Corridors via "Gateway/Destination" Initiatives

Law enforcement information sharing is essential to reducing the drug-related violence that often occurs along drug, money, and weapon trafficking corridors. Increased technology integration at more border ports of entry has forced smugglers to seek other alternatives to smuggle illicit drugs, such as illicit cross-border tunnels, ultra-light aircraft, and the use of panga boats along the California coast. Transnational criminal organizations use these vessels primarily to smuggle marijuana around the land border through the waters off the Southern California coast (from San Diego to as far north as Monterey County).

DEA continues to provide access to the De-Confliction & Information Coordination Endeavor (DICE), a web-based software tool for use by HIDTAs and other state, local, tribal, and Federal law enforcement agencies that provides the ability to de-conflict information such as phone numbers, Push-to-Talk IDs, email addresses, license plates, and other types of data. Through DICE, state and local law enforcement receive notifications involving overlaps of data among investigations. DICE is sponsored by over 102 DEA field division, district, and resident offices, and at the most recent count, DICE has over 17,600 active users (33 percent are state, local, or tribal and 67 percent are Federal law enforcement).

E. Assist Tribal Authorities to Combat Trafficking on Tribal Lands

Seven HIDTA programs collaborate on enforcement operations and training with tribal nations. In Arizona, for example, the HIDTA has provided training and equipment to tribal law enforcement while also coordinating a task force interdiction effort with state, local, and tribal agencies. In the summer of 2013, the Native American Targeted Investigation of Violent Enterprises (NATIVE) Task Force was created as a new HIDTA Initiative for the Arizona HIDTA. NATIVE is a cooperative Federal and tribal task force targeting smuggling operations throughout the Tohono O'odham Nation. NATIVE includes law enforcement personnel from the Tohono O'odham Police Department, ICE/HSI Shadow Wolves, and the Bureau of Indian Affairs Drug Enforcement Division.

In 2013, the FBI conducted a Violent Crime Threat Assessment on the Navajo Nation (AZ) and subsequently held meetings to discuss the scope of the threat and available resources. Additionally, in January 2013 the FBI and DOJ Office of Legal Education sponsored a Criminal Enterprise training course at the National Advocacy Center with approximately 53 attendees, most of whom were tribal police officers.

F. Ensure Comprehensive Review of Domestic Drug Threat

ONDCP's Office of Intelligence will collaborate with its intelligence community colleagues in DHS, DOJ, the Office of the Director of National Intelligence, and other relevant agencies to ensure that national policy makers are provided with the best possible domestic all-source counterdrug intelligence analysis. In support of this endeavor, DEA completed and distributed the *National Drug Threat Assessment* in June 2013. ONDCP's Office of Intelligence will continue to collaborate with DEA and other applicable intelligence community, law enforcement, and domestic health agencies on successive iterations of the *National Drug Threat Assessment,* while also continuing to further develop and refine the requirements for domestic, strategic, all-source drug intelligence analysis and improving the quality, scope, sophistication, and usefulness of products presented to policy makers.

2. U.S. Borders Must be Secured

A. Implement the National Southwest Border Counternarcotics Strategy

The Southwest border is a major arrival zone for illicit drugs, weapons, and money, and the implementation of the *National Southwest Border Counternarcotics Strategy* is critical to addressing these threats. DHS has increased the funding it provides to state and local law enforcement to address border-related crime through the Operation STONEGARDEN[63] grant program. In 2013, $55 million in Federal funds was awarded to states bordering Mexico, Canada, (including Alaska), and states and territories with international water borders. Based on risk, cross-border traffic, and border-related threat intelligence, 80 percent of Operation STONEGARDEN awards between 2011 and 2013 went to Southwest border states. The Southwest Border HIDTA consists of five Regional HIDTAs in Texas, New Mexico, Arizona, and California and has continued to effectively facilitate programs that provide a forum for interagency cooperation at the state, local, tribal, and Federal level.

B. Implement National Plan for Outbound Interdiction of Currency and Weapons

The enormous amount of money generated by drug sales in the United States and its outward flow fuels the operations of violent drug trafficking organizations. In FY 2013, OCDETF Program Co-located Strike Forces expanded the participation of state and Federal agencies in several key locations, enhancing their ability to address the outbound flow of currency and weapons. The San Diego OCDETF Strike Force added the ICE/HSI Marine Task Force, as well as a multi-agency Anti-Money Laundering Group. The Arizona OCDETF Strike Force completed its expansion to Tucson and added a full FBI enforcement group. The New Mexico office of the El Paso Strike Force also secured FBI participation in FY 2013. The Houston/South Texas OCDETF Strike Force expanded to add an additional office in San Antonio.

In addition, DEA expanded the National License Plate Reader Initiative. The National License Plate Reader Initiative is a complex camera and alerting system strategically located along the Southwest border that DEA uses to monitor and interdict roadway conveyances suspected of transporting bulk cash and other contraband.

ATF has increased its capability to identify, disrupt, and dismantle organized efforts to traffic firearms from the United States to Mexico. In September of 2010, Mexico's Attorney General signed a Memorandum of

Understanding to trace seized firearms through the Spanish version of ATF's successful eTrace program. As of December 31, 2012, approximately 350 Mexican law enforcement personnel had received training and access to Spanish eTrace, and several additional training sessions were presented in 2013-2014.

C. Coordinate Efforts to Secure the Northern Border against Drug-Related Threats

In January 2012, following an extensive consultation process, the Administration released the first *National Northern Border Counternarcotics Strategy*, a framework for ongoing efforts to reduce the drug threats on both sides of the U.S.-Canada border. The *Strategy* builds upon the understanding of shared responsibility articulated in *Beyond the Border: A Joint Vision for Perimeter Security and Economic Competitiveness.* The *Strategy* also recognizes the reality that transnational criminal organizations operating on both sides of the U.S.-Canada border exploit the international boundary to smuggle proceeds from illegal drugs sold in the United States and Canada and to transport drugs such as marijuana, MDMA (ecstasy), methamphetamine, and cocaine between the two countries. To increase each country's individual security and economic prosperity, the United States and Canada must appropriately plan, train, and act together to address threats at the earliest point possible and work toward optimizing joint border management goals.

Currently, ONDCP, in consultation with interagency partners, Canadian counterparts, and other stake-holders, is drafting an update to the *Strategy*, to be released in 2014. As in the previous *Strategy*, numerous departments and agencies will be charged with implementing the more than 40 specific action items. A report on the progress of implementing the action items and identified performance measures will also be released in 2014.

D. Deny Use of Ports of Entry and Routes of Ingress and Egress between the Ports

Air and maritime ports represent a unique challenge with regard to drug-related threats. In FY 2013, DOJ and DHS continued to engage in operations that coordinated U.S. Federal, state, local, and tribal law enforcement agencies with international (Government of Mexico) forces to disrupt and dismantle transnational criminal organizations. Some of the operations are year-round efforts employing a whole-of-government approach. Also in 2013, all required bi-national documents were completed under the U.S.-Canada Integrated Cross-border Maritime Law Enforcement Operations "ShipRider" agreement, and regular activities began in USCG Districts 1, 9, and 13. This agreement reduces the ability of drug traffickers to use the international border to evade pursuit.

Efforts will continue to promote collaboration and increase effectiveness by co-locating coordination centers and local fusion centers with OCDETF Southwest Border Strike Forces and BESTs. DHS has 14 of its 35 BESTs located on the Southwest border. These teams include participation from ICE/HSI, CBP, DEA, ATF, the U.S. Attorney's Office, the USCG, state and local law enforcement agencies, and, in some locations, Mexican law enforcement liaisons.

E. Disrupt Surveillance Operations of Drug Trafficking Organizations

Along the Southwest border, drug trafficking organizations employ large numbers of strategically placed spotters who closely observe the enforcement activities of CBP officers and agents, canines, and inspection technology. In turn, these spotters provide guidance to traffickers entering the United States. Traffickers also use advanced technology to intercept law enforcement communications.

Law enforcement agencies employ countermeasures to target the tactics and methods of transnational criminal organizations and to locate and apprehend spotters as they conspire to traffic and smuggle drugs, money, weapons, and humans. While the details of such countermeasures are understandably sensitive, they may include frequent and random personnel rotations, as well as employment of counter-surveillance techniques and activities designed to locate, identify, apprehend, and prosecute spotters.

The FBI created the National Border Corruption Task Forces (BCTFs) in cooperation with the DOJ Public Integrity Section, CBP-Internal Affairs, and Transportation Security Administration (TSA) Office of Inspection. The mission of the BCTFs is to enhance communication, coordination, and cooperation among Federal, state, and local government agencies representing the law enforcement, intelligence, and homeland security communities to more effectively combat corruption at our Nation's borders and ports of entry. There are 23 local BCTFs within 15 FBI field offices. This includes 15 BCTFs operating on the Southwest border and three BCTFs on the Northern border. Currently, there are 91 FBI agents and 103 task force officers from various agencies assigned to the BCTFs. The mission of the BCTFs is to enhance communication, coordination, and cooperation among Federal, state, local, and tribal government agencies representing the law enforcement, intelligence, and homeland security communities to more effectively combat corruption at our

Nation's borders and ports of entry. In Fiscal Year 2013, these task forces were responsible for 47 arrests, 41 indictments, and 40 convictions.

3. Focus National Efforts on Specific Drug Problems

A. Counter Domestic Methamphetamine Production

The Administration remains committed to reducing the production, trafficking, and use of methamphetamine. In 2012, more than 8,300 methamphetamine laboratories were seized nationwide. The number of laboratories seized was more than double that in 2007, although seizures remained low in states such as Oregon and Mississippi, where pseudoephedrine is available only by prescription. Nationwide, the laboratories seized during the last few years are smaller and produce significantly smaller quantities; however, the danger posed by these small toxic labs and the drugs they produce remains significant.

We have seen progress in decreasing the prevalence of methamphetamine use in the United States: according to NSDUH, the number of past month methamphetamine users has declined 40 percent since 2006. However, availability indicators reflect that the supply of Mexican methamphetamine is increasing in the United States. Price and purity data and increased methamphetamine seizures across the Southwest border indicate rising domestic availability, most of which is the result of high levels of methamphetamine production in Mexico. Seizures of Mexican methamphetamine coming across the Southwest border have increased over sixfold between 2008 (2,282.6 kilograms) and 2013 (14,400 kilograms).

To address these threats, the HIDTA program's National Methamphetamine and Pharmaceuticals Initiative (NMPI) provides assistance through coordination, information sharing, and training for prosecutors, investigators, intelligence analysts, and chemists to: enhance the identification of criminal targets; increase the number of chemical/pharmaceutical drug related investigations and prosecutions; and curtail foreign chemical and precursor sources that are used by domestic illicit drug manufacturers.

B. Identify Interior Corridors of Drug Movement and Deny Traffickers Use of America's Highways

Drug traffickers use our Nation's roads and highways to move large amounts of drugs, currency, weapons, and other illicit contraband. The HIDTA DHE program has funded specialized equipment, training, intelligence-sharing activities, and operational capabilities to address this threat. The DHE strategy is based on collaborative, intelligence-led policing to enhance law enforcement efforts on interstate highways specifically identified as drug trafficking corridors. In FY 2012, DHE task forces removed $432.4 million worth of drugs and disrupted or dismantled 32 drug trafficking organizations. Drug-related cash seizures totaled $58.6 million and other drug-related assets seized were valued at $3.2 million.

To enhance DHE enforcement effectiveness, EPIC System Portal (ESP) account holders are able to access HSIN via the ESP. The website allows DHE informational reports and current trends associated with drug trafficking to be accessed by law enforcement officers across the Nation. DHE Coordinators also host 100 Information Sharing Corridor Web meetings per year. Information collected during the corridor meetings is posted live to DHE HSIN. There are more than 500 vetted users from Federal, state, and local law enforcement agencies, with 3,000 searchable corridor drug trafficking documents posted.

C. Address Marijuana Cultivation and its Threat to Public Safety and the Environment

Disrupting the cultivation of marijuana on the Nation's public lands and its attendant public safety and environmental dangers is a priority for the Administration's enforcement of the Controlled Substances Act.[64] Federal enforcement efforts also prioritize the prevention of violence and the use of firearms in the cultivation and distribution of marijuana. Grow sites—even those on public lands—often are protected by booby traps and armed guards. DEA reports that in 2012 more than 10,000 weapons were seized from marijuana cultivation sites, more than double the number seized in 2011.[65]

The cultivation of marijuana frequently entails the diversion of water resources, the clearing of native brush, and the use of banned pesticides. During the 2013 eradication season, the California Campaign Against Marijuana Planting (CAMP) reported that eradication teams seized 44.3 miles of water line and dismantled 89 dams or illegal reservoirs that had been constructed to irrigate marijuana gardens. Of the 284 grow sites and nearly 1 million marijuana plants seized by CAMP teams in 2013, 114 grow sites and more than half a million plants were on public lands. Eradication efforts on public lands are assisted by the National Guard Counterdrug Program, which provides helicopter flight hours, analyst support, and program management.

The HIDTA program seeks to address the issue of marijuana cultivation on public lands through the National Marijuana Initiative (NMI), a law enforcement support initiative that seeks to detect, deter, and disrupt domestic marijuana cultivation and trafficking by coordinating investigations and interdiction operations. The NMI's efforts are coordinated with the Public Lands Drug Control Committee (PLDCC), a Federal interagency group that aligns policies and coordinates programs to support marijuana eradication operations, investigations, and related intelligence and information sharing.

MARIJUANA CULTIVATION: A THREAT TO WILDLIFE

Illicit marijuana cultivation threatens the wildlife inhabiting National Forests and other public lands. Information compiled by CAMP shows that in the 2013 eradication season, law enforcement officers seized 6.8 metric tons of fertilizer, 307 pounds of common pesticides, and 3.1 gallons of extremely hazardous restricted poisons from grow sites. These materials indiscriminately kill wildlife, leach into the soil, and ultimately contaminate the water table, potentially causing irreparable damage.[66] In July 2013, researchers with the University of California-Davis and the Hoopa Valley Tribe found evidence that marijuana cultivators were deliberately poisoning wildlife on public lands.[67] At a marijuana cultivation site, law enforcement officers discovered poisoned hot dogs hung from fishing hooks. Approximately 10 meters away, law enforcement found a dead adult male fisher, a rare forest carnivore declared a candidate species for listing under the Endangered Species Act. A full necropsy conducted by a board-certified veterinary pathologist revealed that the animal died from acute carbamate insecticide (methomyl) poisoning associated with contaminated bait.

Previously, researchers had documented the presence of poisonous chemicals and toxicants at marijuana cultivation sites inhabited by fishers; however, the July incident was the first confirmed intentional poisoning of a fisher with an insecticide associated with a marijuana cultivation site. Researchers will continue to study the effects of marijuana cultivation on fishers. Additional research, funded primarily by the U.S. Fish and Wildlife Service, is planned to determine whether rat poisons used around marijuana grow sites are responsible for the deaths of rare spotted owls.

D. Target Indoor Marijuana Production

Pressure from marijuana eradication efforts has caused many cultivators to abandon large outdoor cannabis plots in favor of indoor cultivation that is easier to conceal. In 2012, researchers documented public health risks associated with indoor marijuana grow operations, including elevated mold spore levels high enough to require respiratory protection for investigators entering the site. Researchers also found pesticides and fertilizers within the reach of children residing in the homes where the grow sites were operating. The detection of these indoor grows has proven challenging for law enforcement. In 2013, DEA and partner agencies seized more than 2,754 indoor grow operations, with 361,727 plants eradicated.[68]

E. Partner with Local Law Enforcement Agencies to Combat Street, Prison, and Motorcycle Drug Gangs

The California Gang Intelligence Initiative (CGII) is a joint intelligence collection and analysis task force consisting of the FBI Safe Streets Gang Unit, BOP, California Department of Corrections and Rehabilitation (CDCR), and the National Gang Intelligence Center (NGIC) to identify, analyze, and disseminate intelligence within the CDCR and BOP relevant to California prison gang leadership, members, associates, and facilitators that enable gangs and gang activity to extend beyond the prison setting and into the community. CGII continues to serve as a resource for law enforcement agencies across the Nation for alternative avenues of case support, intelligence collection, and potential source recruitment. Currently, CGII is composed of 23 FBI personnel, one BOP Special Agent, and 20 CDCR personnel.

The FBI, through personnel assigned to NGIC, ensures gang intelligence products are released to Federal, state, local, and tribal law enforcement through Law Enforcement Online (LEO) and NGIC Online. FBI works closely with the National Alliance of Gang Investigators Association (NAGIA), which represents over 20,000 gang investigators across the country. Requests for information on gangs are disseminated to the NAGIA membership and are addressed through Requests for Information submitted to the FBI's Safe Streets Gang Task Forces, as well as to the other government agencies represented at NGIC.

The FBI works with local and international law enforcement partners to address the growing population of individuals joining or associated with Outlaw Motorcycle Gangs (OMGs), organizations whose members use their motorcycle clubs as conduits for criminal enterprises. OMGs are using their members to sell and traffic in heroin, cocaine, large quantities of marijuana, and methamphetamine. The oil-producing Bakken region has experienced a large influx of OMGs attempting to establish "ownership" of the territory, facilitating the illegal drug trade and prostitution. The FBI, working in concert with its local and international partners, is continuing to aggressively investigate the activities of these groups.

F. Disrupt Illicit Financial Networks by Exploiting Cash Seizures

The National Bulk Cash Smuggling Center (BCSC) provides its Federal, state, and local law enforcement partners with real-time intelligence, investigative support, and expertise in addressing the illicit transportation and smuggling of bulk cash. Since its inception in 2009, the BCSC has initiated more than 700 criminal investigations for referral and has played an active role in more than 550 criminal arrests and currency seizures totaling $206.6 million.

DEA works to identify co-conspirators, shell corporations, and assets used by drug trafficking organizations around the world, and evidence and intelligence gleaned from its investigations often provide critical information on terrorist financing. Towards the end of FY 2013, EPIC consolidated three units involved in financial intelligence into the Financial Intelligence Unit to better focus on supporting the financial aspects of investigations in response to customer requests. EPIC's Bulk Currency Team, within the Financial Intelligence Unit, conducts research on bulk currency seizures, providing intelligence information to law enforcement agencies for tactical and operational support. As of August 31, 2013, DEA had successfully denied drug traffickers $2.1 billion in illicit revenue. From FY 2005 through August 31, 2013, DEA had denied over $24 billion in revenue to drug traffickers.

In 2013, DEA conducted 5 financial investigation training seminars for 87 Federal, state, and local law enforcement officials. In addition, OCDETF conducted 9 financial training seminars in FY 2013 for 595 attendees.

The OFC Pro-Active Asset Targeting Team was established in September 2010 and identifies criminal case connections through review and analysis of FinCEN's suspicious activity reports. As of September 2013, the OFC Proactive Asset Targeting Team identified 13,206 bank accounts, 4,139 vehicles, and 5,820 businesses with suspicious activity and seized assets totaling more than $56 million.

Through direct support to law enforcement conducting drug investigations, the National Guard Counter Threat Finance (CTF) Program supported over 566 money laundering investigations. Subjects of investigation included outlaw motorcycle gangs on the Northern border, transnational criminal organizations on the Southwest border, and financial institutions and front companies with links to terrorist financing, precursor chemical diversion, drug trafficking, and money laundering. Within this target set, National Guard

CTF Analysts identified over 1373 targets and 639 money laundering methods previously unknown to law enforcement.

G. Interdict Drug Trafficking through Mail and Parcel Services

CBP, TSA, and the United States Postal Service are working with the Universal Postal Union and others in the international postal community to enhance the screening of international mail prior to its conveyance to the United States. The parties are developing the foundations for providing advance electronic data on international mail packages to allow CBP and TSA to perform risk-based targeting prior to foreign departure and entry into the domestic mail supply chain. This strategy will enhance CBP's ability to identify, interdict, and disrupt the movement of illicit drugs and stem the persistent threat posed by the smuggling of counterfeit pharmaceuticals and "gray market" goods. This approach is also linked to the *Long Term Strategy for the Screening of International Mail* and the *Global Supply Chain Strategy.*

The Laboratories and Scientific Services Directorate (LSSD) is the scientific arm of CBP. Over 15 years ago, LSSD implemented Operation Safeguard to prevent counterfeit and illicit pharmaceuticals from entering the United States. Operation Safeguard now includes participation from numerous other agencies, including the U.S. Postal Inspection Service, ICE/HSI, and the FDA. While each agency has its own compliance and enforcement objectives for Operation Safeguard, the collective efforts are coordinated by LSSD to maximize efficiency and effectiveness. Operation Safeguard activities are conducted monthly at International Mail Facilities and Express Consignment Centers throughout the United States. Each onsite examination period lasts several days and entails the inspection of hundreds of parcels containing pharmaceuticals and designer drugs. In Fiscal Year 2013, parcels containing over 2,000 different pharmaceutical products were processed and analyzed.

H. Establish Interagency Task Force on Drug Endangered Children

Over a decade ago, the Drug Endangered Children (DEC) movement was founded to address the growing phenomenon of children living in environments made unsafe and unhealthy by drug activity. Some actions had been taken at the state level, but prior to the establishment of the Federal Interagency DEC Task Force, a cohesive and coordinated Federal response was lacking. Initiated as part of the 2010 *National Drug Control Strategy,* the DEC Task Force gathered and produced educational resources (model protocols, programming, promising practices, and downloadable checklists) to aid law enforcement, child welfare workers, health and education professionals, and children's advocates nationwide. In addition, the DEC Task Force expanded the definition of drug endangered children to include children living in an environment where drugs, including pharmaceuticals, are illegally used, possessed, trafficked, diverted, and/or manufactured. In 2012, the DHS Federal Law Enforcement Training Center (FLETC) assembled experts from the National DEC Training and Advocacy Center, the National Alliance for Drug Endangered Children, criminal justice professionals, and FLETC staff to begin development of two courses on drug endangered children for Federal, state, local, tribal, and international law enforcement agencies. Both training programs were developed in 2013 and approved as Center Advanced Programs. The Introduction to Drug Endangered Children Training Program was piloted in August 2013. The Drug Endangered Children Investigations Training Program was approved but has not yet been piloted. DEA continues to raise awareness and provide training on DEC issues for domestic and international law enforcement professionals, educators, social service professionals, first responders, and community leaders.

ADVOCATE FOR ACTION: JUDGE ROBERT RUSSELL

In January 2008, Judge Robert Russell created and began presiding over the first Veterans Treatment Court in the United States. The Veterans Treatment Court is a hybrid Drug Court/Mental Health Court model for justice-involved veterans that features regular court appearances (a bi-weekly minimum in the early phases of the program), mandatory attendance at treatment sessions, and frequent and random testing for substance use (drug and/or alcohol). The Veterans Treatment Court acts as a "one-stop shop" at the courthouse, with a team of Federal, state, and local veterans agencies and organizations working together to link veterans with the programs, benefits, and services they have earned. For his dedication and perseverance in helping this country's veterans, the Vietnam Veterans of America has awarded Judge Russell with the Vietnam Veterans of America Achievement Medal and the Veterans of Foreign Wars of the United States has awarded Judge Russell with the James E. Van Zandt Citizenship Award.

Judge Russell has been a pioneer in the drug treatment court movement and remains a strong leader to this day. In December 1995, Judge Russell created the Buffalo Drug Treatment Court and continues to serve as the Presiding Judge. In addition, in December 2002, he established and began serving over Buffalo's Mental Health Treatment Court.

Judge Russell is the Past Chairman of the Board of Directors of NADCP and the Past President of the New York State Association of Drug Treatment Court Professionals, Inc. He also serves on the National Advisory Board of the Judges' Criminal Justice and Mental Health Leadership Initiative. He is the recipient of several Awards of Merit from the American Bar Association, New York State Bar Association, and the Erie County Bar Association.

I. Respond to the Emerging Threat of Synthetic Drugs

Communities across the United States are facing new challenges related to the threat of synthetic drugs, an umbrella term that includes synthetic cannabinoids ("herbal incense"), synthetic cathinones ("bath salts"), and synthetic hallucinogens like the "2-C" and "NBOMe" series compounds. In 2013, poison control centers logged more than 2,600 exposures[69] to synthetic cannabinoids[70] and nearly 1,000 exposures to synthetic cathinones. While the Administration and state drug control agencies have moved quickly to control many of these substances, producers and traffickers have proven adept at altering the chemical composition of the drugs to exploit gaps in controls. Policy makers and legislators at both the national and state levels must remain vigilant to ensure this threat is contained.

J. Coordinate the Interagency Response to Emerging Drug Related Criminal Activity in Locations with Limited Law Enforcement Resources

The development of the Bakken oil fields of northeastern Montana, northwestern North Dakota, and southern Saskatchewan has caused a sharp spike in both population and income levels. Between 2005 and 2012, the population in the Williston Basin region—driven by the addition of more than 20,000 jobs—grew an estimated 17 percent. This influx of highly paid oil field workers into an area with limited opportunities for spending their income has created a market for drugs and contributed to an overall increase in crime. The FBI Uniform Crime Report shows that crimes in the Williston Basin region increased 32 percent from 2005 through 2011, and violent crimes (which include murder, aggravated assault, forcible rape, and robbery) increased 121 percent. These dramatic increases have overwhelmed state, local, and tribal law enforcement agencies working with limited resources.[71]

In response to this burgeoning threat, FBI and other Federal agencies have partnered with state, local, and tribal law enforcement agencies to conduct task force operations in the Bakken region. Collaborative efforts among Federal, state, local, and tribal partners in June 2013 resulted in the arrest of 22 people and, in October 2013, a coordinated effort led to 4 arrests in North Dakota and 12 in Montana. In both efforts, the charges predominantly were related to drugs, specifically heroin and methamphetamine, which have become increasingly available in the Bakken region. The National Guard assists these efforts by providing intelligence support, including collection, analysis, and dissemination of intelligence data submitted by Federal, state, and local agencies.

In December 2013, ONDCP and the White House Domestic Policy Council (DPC) convened an interagency meeting to explore a comprehensive Federal response to deal with the complex justice, public health, and social issues that have arisen in the area. Moving forward, the Administration will continue to work on law enforcement, quality of life, women's safety, and tribal issues.

Section 6. Strengthen International Partnerships and Reduce the Availability of Foreign-Produced Drugs in the United States

The United States is engaged internationally in bilateral and regional partnerships that are critical aspects of our efforts to reduce drug use and its consequences. Central to these partnerships is a balanced and effective strategy that assists our international partners to reduce the supply of drugs and the demand for those drugs in their communities. Supply reduction enables governments to more effectively address the entire range of negative consequences associated with drug use. The impact of supply reduction policy can be seen most clearly through the dramatic reduction in cocaine supply and demand over the last decade.

Activities far from our shores, such as interdiction on the high seas or cooperating with foreign governments around the world, are too often seen as part of a distant struggle. In reality these efforts have a direct impact within the United States. Available information indicates that cocaine consumed in the United States is almost exclusively derived from Colombian-sourced cultivation and production. Since 2006, cocaine production in Colombia has been reduced, while large multi-ton seizures have been made within South America and the transit zone. The combined effect of eradication, alternative development, law enforcement, and maritime interdiction efforts has contributed to a sharp reduction in cocaine availability in U.S. communities. There also have been significant reductions in cocaine use, treatment admissions, emergency room visits, and overdose deaths. A balanced approach to both demand and supply reduction is essential; and while we have made significant progress in the area of cocaine, recent increases in domestic heroin and methamphetamine use necessitate continued attention and collaboration.

Interdiction operations in the transit zone have been essential to supply reduction efforts. Interdiction can be understood by examining the interdiction continuum (Figure 2). The interdiction continuum reduces the availability of illicit drugs in our communities while providing valuable intelligence that contributes to drug seizures, arrests, prosecutions, and the ultimate disruption and dismantling of international drug trafficking organizations. A successful interdiction continuum, involving cooperation across the interagency, is self-sustaining. Seizures produce new intelligence and advance investigations into major transnational criminal networks. These activities lead to more actionable intelligence on future events, producing follow-on seizures and contributing to a cycle of success.

The U.S. cocaine market has been dramatically transformed, but the threat still remains. Prioritization of resources—affecting our assistance to foreign partners and our interdiction efforts in the transit zone—complicate our efforts to sustain the momentum of the last decade in driving down cocaine supply, consumption, and consequences. Additionally, increases in heroin and methamphetamine trafficking remind us of the threats posed by other drugs. The Administration will examine options to address these challenges in the coming year.

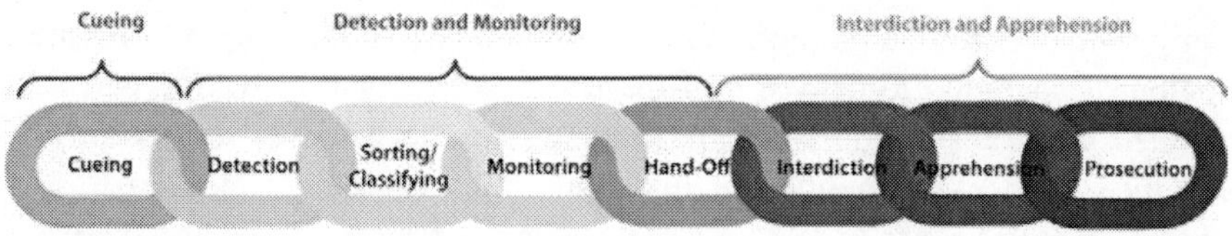

Figure 2. The Interdiction Continuum.

U.S. international initiatives also include expanding global prevention and treatment initiatives through collaboration with partner nations and multilateral organizations. By establishing international partnerships on demand reduction, evidence-based practices will become the standard for global prevention, treatment, and recovery programs. This international collaboration will serve to reduce both the supply and demand for drugs within the global community.

There is more work to be done to consolidate previous efforts. The United States and its partners need to make more efficient use of resources by coordinating activities to disrupt the operations of criminal networks, best accomplished by employing all relevant agencies and their respective legal authorities and operational capabilities.

1. Collaborate with International Partners to Disrupt the Drug Trade

A. Conduct Joint Counterdrug Operations with International Partners

Collaboration with partner nations remains a cornerstone of the *Strategy*. Such collaboration is often reflected in counterdrug operations, such as the DEA-led Operation All Inclusive, the ninth iteration of which took place in 2013. Sixty-seven land, air, maritime, financial, and chemical operations were conducted from intelligence generated by Operation All Inclusive; these operations resulted in the arrest of 1,097 individuals, including two Consolidated Priority Organization Targets (CPOTs), and the seizure of 80 metric tons of cocaine, 1,562 kilograms of methamphetamine, 200 kilograms of heroin, 122 metric tons of precursor chemicals, $19 million in U.S. currency, and 1,163 weapons. In 2013 USCG aircrews from the Helicopter Interdiction Tactical Squadron (HITRON) conducted cross-deck operations with Airborne Use of Force (AUF) capable helicopters on Dutch and British naval vessels, and a USCG Law Enforcement Detachment completed a proof of concept deployment in which Dutch small boats were authorized to conduct surface use-of-force operations, providing additional capability in the Eastern

Caribbean. Additionally, in 2013 Operation MARTILLO, a 14-nation combined operation to deny use of Central America as a trafficking corridor, resulted in the disruption of the trafficking of more than 132 metric tons of cocaine, 41 thousand pounds of marijuana, $3.5 million in bulk cash, 315 arrests, and the seizure of 107 vessels, vehicles, and aircraft. The pressures put upon trafficking organizations by Operation MARTILLO resulted in a 38 percent decrease in illicit air trafficking activity and decreases of 29 percent and 57 percent of the illicit maritime activities in the Western Caribbean and Eastern Pacific littoral routes, respectively.

B. Work with Partner Nations and OAS/CICAD to Strengthen Counterdrug Institutions in the Western Hemisphere

The United States delegation to the Organization of American States Inter-American Drug Abuse Control Commission (OAS/CICAD) continued to share U.S. drug policy research and best practices with Western Hemisphere partners in 2013. The U.S. Government continued to work within the OAS/CICAD Intergovernmental Working Group to update and enhance the Multilateral Evaluation Mechanism (MEM). The MEM evaluates implementation of drug control efforts by CICAD member states and provides recommendations for improvement. DEA and USCG also participated in CICAD Expert Working Groups on anti-money laundering, chemicals and pharmaceuticals, and maritime interdiction, all of which produce guides and model regulations and legislation for use by OAS countries. The United States will work to promote the priorities developed by the Brazilian Chair of the OAS/CICAD Demand Reduction Experts Group, focusing on training health care system professionals on Screening and Brief Intervention strategies and enhancing the treatment/rehabilitation skills of addiction counselors.

C. Work with Partners in Europe, Africa, and Asia to Disrupt Drug Flows in the Trans-Atlantic and Trans-Pacific Regions

The Departments of State, Homeland Security, Justice, and Defense continued to coordinate interagency efforts to promote bilateral and regional cooperation against drug trafficking and transnational organized crime in Europe, Africa, and Asia in 2013. Efforts to promote coordination among donor nations regarding drug trafficking and transnational crime in West Africa were the focus of a U.S.-hosted January 2013 G8 Roma-Lyon Group meeting. The United States coordinates an array of drug issues through semi-annual drug policy discussions in Brussels with the European Commission and member state representatives. The USCG is a member of both the 20-member

North Atlantic Coast Guard Forum and the six-member North Pacific Coast Guard Forum, two distinct international organizations that promote multilateral cooperation among member coast guards. In 2013, JIATF West, DEA, and INL continued to partner through the Narcotics Enforcement Training Team (NETT), which focuses on the development of partner nation counterdrug investigative units that operate with U.S. law enforcement. Current efforts are concentrating on assisting Thailand in building the capability to conduct comprehensive investigations against transnational criminal organizations.

Another initiative that promotes bilateral and regional cooperation against drug trafficking and transnational organized crime is the DEA-sponsored International Drug Enforcement Conference (IDEC), a global forum that provides an opportunity for senior drug law enforcement officials to meet, deliberate, and determine the most effective strategies to disrupt and dismantle drug trafficking organizations. The strategies behind many past and future operations are discussed in regional, multilateral, and bilateral meetings that are at the core of IDEC's activities.

D. Coordinate with Global Partners to Prevent Synthetic Drug Production and Precursor Chemical Diversion

The United States continued its efforts to limit the availability of methamphetamine precursor chemicals in 2013. Methamphetamine manufacturers, operating primarily in Mexico, continued to gain access to sufficient amounts of chemical precursors to produce and transship large amounts of high purity, high potency methamphetamine. Data from the Southwest border show an increase of over 500 percent in methamphetamine seizures from 2008 to 2013.[72] Ready availability at declining price per pure gram could elevate the risk for increased methamphetamine use in the United States. Within the Western Hemisphere, DEA and the State Department are working with Mexico and Central American nations to identify, seize, and destroy chemical precursors and to equip Central American partners with the appropriate legal frameworks to effectively tackle the challenge. In 2013, JIATF West continued its valuable work identifying global methamphetamine precursor diversion networks. China and India remain the primary sources for precursor chemicals used by both Asian and Latin American methamphetamine producers. JIATF West's efforts include conducting network analysis in support of law enforcement efforts, increasing analytical capacity, and enhancing partnerships within the Asia-Pacific region.

ADVOCATE FOR ACTION: COMMANDER HARRY SCHMIDT

CDR Harry Schmidt is being recognized as an Advocate for Action for his tireless work to strengthen international partnerships against transnational organized crime and illicit trafficking. CDR Schmidt led the expansion of the Multilateral Maritime Counterdrug Summit from eight to 17 partner nations in the Western Hemisphere transit zone, sharing operational and legal expertise to improve transnational cooperation and coordination in the apprehension and prosecution of major drug smugglers. The program has been so successful that the Department of State asked CDR Schmidt to replicate the Summit as part of the Caribbean Basin Security Initiative; the first meeting was held in March 2014. CDR Schmidt also initiated and developed the concept for *Coast Guard Support to Interdiction and Prosecution*, an initiative through which three-person USCG teams will be embedded within select U.S. embassies in the Western Hemisphere transit zone. These teams will assist regional partners in case documentation, evidence handling, and prosecution of maritime drug smuggling cases. Through these and other ongoing efforts, CDR Schmidt is helping to strengthen international partnerships to reduce drug production, trafficking, use, and their consequences.

E. Address International Production and Trafficking of New Synthetic Drugs

During the past 5 years new synthetic drugs, also referred to as new psychoactive substances (NPS), have posed an increasing public health threat to the United States. These substances, including synthetic cannabinoids ("Spice,""K2") and synthetic cathinones ("bath salts"), pose a severe risk to those that consume them. Although DEA, through emergency scheduling, and the Congress, via statutory changes, have banned many of these substances, new variants are continually manufactured and distributed, posing a serious challenge to Federal, state, and local authorities seeking to protect public health and safety. DEA has been working closely with bilateral and multilateral partners to increase controls on synthetic drugs. China, a source for most of these new substances, controlled 11 of these substances on January 1, 2014. The Administration will continue to work to ensure an effective global response to this rising concern.

F. Expand Global Prevention and Treatment Initiatives Bilaterally and Through Cooperation with the United Nations, the Organization of American States, the Colombo Plan, and Other Multilateral Organizations

Under the leadership of the Department of State, U.S. international demand reduction initiatives continue to mature. In 2013, 29 new anti-drug community coalitions were established throughout the world (Bolivia, Brazil, Cape Verde, Colombia, Costa Rica, Ghana, Kenya, Philippines, Senegal, Tajikistan, and Iraq). ONDCP is working with international organizations to expand the development of prevention, treatment, and recovery services in areas that have not had access to demand reduction resources. These initiatives to build demand reduction capacity work in concert with broader efforts to promote law and order and strengthen governance structures. In 2014, ONDCP will work to share U.S. experiences in recovery support and overdose prevention and will emphasize the value of collaboration among public health and law enforcement agencies.

G. Expand Internationally a Comprehensive Package of Health Interventions for Injection Drug Users

The President's Emergency Plan for AIDS Relief (PEPFAR) partners with a number of countries and multilateral organizations to provide needed health and drug treatment services for injection drug users. Countries that receive PEPFAR funds provide an array of interventions, such as community-based outreach, counseling and testing, medication-assisted treatment, antiretroviral therapy, and prevention, diagnosis, and management of viral hepatitis and tuberculosis. These evidence-based interventions, along with supportive national laws, policies, and regulations, have been identified by the World Health Organization, UN Office on Drugs and Crime, and UNAIDS as essential interventions for the treatment of opioid use disorders and the prevention of HIV and other blood-borne diseases. In 2013 efforts to maintain or expand medication-assisted treatment continued in Tanzania, Kenya, Vietnam, Ukraine, and Cambodia.

H. Support the Strategy to Combat Transnational Organized Crime

Illicit narcotics provide a means for transnational criminal organizations to obtain wealth, power, and influence, resulting in the destabilization and corruption of vulnerable nations, communities, and institutions. In 2011, the President released the *Strategy to Combat Transnational Organized Crime,* a commitment to build, balance, and integrate U.S. efforts against the expanding national security threat posed by transnational organized crime (TOC). The *Strategy* lays out 56 action items that support five overarching policy objectives:

- Protecting Americans from the negative effects of TOC;
- Helping partner countries strengthen governance and transparency, break the corruptive power of TOC, and sever state-crime alliances;
- Breaking the economic power of transnational criminal networks while protecting strategic markets and the U.S. financial system;
- Defeating TOC networks that pose the greatest threat to national security; and
- Building international, multilateral, and public-private partnerships to defeat TOC.

Overseeing the implementation of this interagency effort is the National Security Council/ONDCP co-chaired Interagency Policy Committee on Illicit Drugs and Transnational Criminal Threats. Under this implementation framework, a number of actions have been taken that advance the goals of both the *Strategy to Combat Transnational Organized Crime* and the *National Drug Control Strategy,* to include a new sanctions program to block the property of and prohibit transactions with significant transnational criminal networks, a new rewards program for information that leads to the arrest and conviction of key transnational criminals, and the formation of an Interagency Threat Mitigation Working Group that has identified those TOC networks that present a sufficiently high national security threat.

2. Support the Drug Control Efforts of Major Drug Source and Transit Countries

SUPPORTING DRUG CONTROL IN KEY REGIONS OF THE WORLD

The *National Drug Control Strategy* remains focused on helping partner nations improve citizen security through programs that strengthen democratic institutions and help reduce drug production, trafficking, and use. Within drug source and transit countries, the center of gravity of past strategies focused on providing specific assistance to disrupt the infrastructure, cultivation, and production efforts of drug trafficking organizations and to break up trafficking routes and networks. While this remains important, the U.S. Government must continue to enter into strong and collaborative partnerships with affected nations to expand our common security goals and create safe communities. We must go beyond traditional relationships and assist friendly nations, where needed, to modernize their security forces, reform their justice systems, support human rights training, and provide alternative development assistance in a safe environment, while at the same time continuing to address the threat posed by the supply side of the illicit trafficking market. This approach aims to build permanent partner nation capacity to provide under governed areas with modern and capable law enforcement and security forces and to provide justice sector reforms to address rising domestic crime, gang activity, and money laundering. In a time of declining resources, it is more important than ever that plans, programs, and activities be coordinated. This is a global undertaking, but particular efforts will be made, under the Department of State's coordination, to ensure integration, coordination, and the achievement of measurable outcomes in Afghanistan and through the Caribbean Basin Security Initiative (CBSI), the Central America Regional Security Initiative (CARSI), the Merida Initiative, the Colombia Strategic Development Initiative, and the West Africa Cooperative Security Initiative (WACSI).

A. Strengthen Strategic Partnerships with Mexico

U.S.-Mexico bilateral cooperation remains strong and focuses on common goals identified and supported through the Merida Initiative and other bilateral efforts. In 2013, the Department of State continued its existing programs, including training of Mexican state and municipal law enforcement professionals. The Department of State's Bureau of International Narcotics and Law Enforcement Affairs (INL) trained nearly 3,500 state and municipal police officers during 2013. INL also provided training, technical assistance, and equipment to the Mexican states of Chihuahua and Sonora to establish joint agency information-sharing task forces, which have already provided key assistance in the arrest of suspects in several cases. INL continues to work with Mexican states to address common needs and promote collaboration among intra-state law enforcement forces. The North American Maritime Security Initiative (NAMSI), a partnership among the United States, Canada, and Mexico, continues to foster cooperation on maritime law enforcement and prosecutions.

The Information Analysis Center (IAC) is responsible for ensuring close coordination of resources between the Government of Mexico (GOM) and the United States in cross border operations along the shared border with Mexico. At the IAC, CBP Office of Air and Marine (OAM), through air surveillance data sharing, enhances partner nation capability and provides the Government of Mexico a means to organically resolve suspect air targets in Northern Mexico; in turn, OAM is capable of fusing radar data from both Mexican and select U.S. sites along the Southwest border. CBP's Air and Marine Operations Center located on March Air Reserve Base provides direct intercept support to the Government of Mexico through the detection, tracking, and sharing of information on suspect radar tracks both within Mexican airspace and approaching Mexico's southern sovereign airspace.

B. Build the Afghan Licit Economy

Illicit drug cultivation, production, trafficking, and consumption flourish in Afghanistan, particularly in parts of the south and southwest where instability is high and state institutions are weak or non-existent. The Afghan drug trade saps the capacity of the Afghan people and undermines governance and democratic institutions. The United States Government estimates that poppy cultivation increased by 10 percent to 198,000 ha in 2013. Total eradication carried out in 2013 was 7,348 hectares (ha), a decline compared to the 9,672 ha eradicated in 2012, but still well above the 2010 level of 2,316 ha and the 2011 level of 3,810 ha.

The U.S. Government's and Afghan Government's counternarcotics strategies call for a multifaceted, long-term approach, well-integrated into broader efforts to build good governance and a licit economy. In 2014, the United States will continue to support Afghanistan's capacity to interdict illicit trafficking within its borders (including through support to the Afghan Special Mission Wing) and bring those traffickers to justice within the Afghan criminal justice system. The United States will also seek collaboration with international partners; support eradication, alternative livelihoods, counternarcotics public information, and demand reduction; and work to disrupt, degrade, and diminish drug trafficking and drug-financed threats in Afghanistan and the region.

In FY 2013, U.S. Government alternative development programs in Afghanistan continued to focus on licit income generation and job creation by improving commercial agriculture, specifically in poppy production-prone areas. In FY 2013, 8,446 ha of licit alternative crops supported by U.S. Government programs were under cultivation in Afghanistan—significantly exceeding the target of 3,285 ha, with 156,209 households benefiting from agriculture and alternative livelihood interventions. This represented a 172 percent increase over the target number of households (57,231), due to better than average precipitation, improved farming techniques, and expansion of extension services. The number of new direct jobs (measured as full-time equivalent) created by U.S. Government-sponsored alternative development programs totaled 4,565, exceeding the target of 3,500.

C. Build the Law Enforcement and Criminal Justice Capacities of Source Countries in the Western Hemisphere to Sustain Progress against Illicit Drug Production and Trafficking

U.S. diplomatic, law enforcement, and security efforts seek to reduce the threat of drugs and organized crime in the hemisphere through interagency counternarcotics assistance and rule of law programs. Multilateral efforts supported by DEA, CBP, State, USAID, and other agencies will assist source and transit countries to promote regional coordination, modernize and enhance the capabilities of their security forces, and reform justice systems to more effectively prosecute criminals. In 2013, the USCG and Department of State co-hosted two Maritime Multilateral Counterdrug Summits with Western Hemisphere partners to exchange best practices on regional interoperability, interdiction operations, and legal issues. The Department of State's assistance to Panama in introducing the Computer Statistics (COMPSTAT) model of modern policing—also implemented in Costa Rica—is an example of the cooperative efforts that can improve technology and management techniques to proactively track crime, develop preventative techniques, and promote community policing. Alternatives to incarceration and increased access to treatment and recovery support also hold the potential to reduce recidivism rates and optimize the use of limited resources.

D. Continue Implementation of the Caribbean Basin Security Initiative

The focus of CBSI is to develop and maintain the capability and capacity of our Caribbean partners to significantly reduce illicit trafficking, increase public safety and security, and promote social justice, enabling them to exercise their sovereign rights and responsibilities. This initiative takes on renewed emphasis given a small but observable uptick in illicit trafficking through the region. During 2013, the USCG, U.S. Southern Command, and the Department of State collaborated to expand the Technical Assistance Field Team (TAFT) to support CBSI. TAFT's mission is to professionalize and improve the operational readiness of 13 Caribbean maritime forces through technical assistance visits.

Beyond CBSI, JIATF South and U.S. Southern Command are assisting the Caribbean Community (CARICOM) with the development and integration of the first-ever *CARICOM Counter Illicit Trafficking Strategy*, which will, when implemented, provide the framework for collaborative multilateral law enforcement responses to regional trafficking threats that will enable direct coordination between JIATF South and the operations centers of the many CARICOM countries.

E. Promote Alternative Livelihoods for Coca and Opium Farmers

In 2013, USAID continued to lead U.S. Government efforts in support of alternative development projects in Colombia and Peru. In Colombia in 2012, USAID's alternative development activities helped contribute to the reduction of the number of hectares cultivated with coca to 78,000 ha. USAID leveraged approximately $15 million in public and private sector funds—by helping achieve approval of nearly 70 project proposals to the Ministry of Agriculture for grants to farmer associations to adapt their production technology to market demand, including for health and organic certifications. In addition, USAID initiated 110 rapid response infrastructure projects (schools, health clinics, sports facilities, tertiary roads) with a total value of $48 million.

In Peru, the regional leader in potential pure cocaine production (305 metric tons in 2013,) the partnership between the U.S. Government and the Humala administration has resulted in a proactive and ambitious strategy that seeks to find alternatives to the drug trade. Peru eradicated a record 23,785 coca ha in 2013. Working hand-in-hand with INL and the Government of Peru, USAID has responded with a comprehensive set of alternative development interventions, including entering the Monzón valley for the first time. USAID helped strengthen the capacity of the Peruvian counternarcotics agency and, working together in collaboration, reached a total of 14,778 farmers with technical assistance and collectively maintained a total of 35,317 ha of licit crops, of which 5,467 were newly planted. Licit sales from USAID-assisted farmers in cacao, oil palm, and coffee production totaled $31.9 million at farm-gate prices and generated 14,574 full-time equivalent jobs, 18 percent of which are held by women.

F. Support the Central America Regional Security Initiative

Through CARSI, the United States works with partner nations to strengthen institutions to counter the effects of organized crime, uphold the rule of law, and protect human rights. Institution building is coupled with prevention programs that dissuade at-risk youth from turning to crime and gangs, and community policing programs engage local communities on citizen security issues. Programs cater to each nation's capabilities and include: model police precincts; youth outreach and vocational training centers; crime prevention in vulnerable communities; training of specialized investigative units; public-private partnerships focused on crime prevention; capacity building for judicial actors; assistance for police academy reform; operations support; and border security capability development. In 2013, CARSI leveraged regional expertise and experience by incorporating regional actors as well as multinational organizations.

Through the U.S.-Colombia Action Plan on Regional Security Cooperation, the United States and Colombia have formalized support to targeted third countries. In 2013, this security assistance included 39 capacity-building activities in four Central American countries focused on multiple areas, such as asset forfeiture, investigations, polygraphs, and interdiction. In 2014, the United States and Colombia will increase security assistance to 152 capacity-building activities in six countries in Central America and the Caribbean. In 2014, these initiatives will expand to include officials from the Dominican Republic and Costa Rica.

G. Leverage Capacities of Partner Nations and International Organizations to Help Coordinate Programs in the Western Hemisphere

In April 2013, representatives from the nations of the Central American Integration System (SICA) gathered in Washington, D.C. for the North America-SICA Security Dialogue in an effort to coordinate international support for Central America. Colombia and Mexico in particular have shown significant leadership and commitment in this area. With support from the Department of State, SICA organized a technical-level workshop to address threats related to precursor chemicals, held in Guatemala City in September 2013. ONDCP met regularly with ambassadors from SICA countries to discuss counternarcotics issues, including the development of a precursor chemical control plan, the United States narcotics certification/majors list process, and demand reduction programs in the United States. The focus in 2014 will be to promote efforts by Mexico and Colombia to share lessons learned and best practices with regional partners.

H. Consolidate the Gains Made in Colombia

The United States made substantial progress in its counternarcotics and security partnership with Colombia during 2013 through the nationalization of aviation programs, expansion of international security cooperation, and reductions in the cultivation of coca. Colombia's coca cultivation fell to 78,000 ha in 2012—a 53 percent decline since 2007. Colombia's production potential also decreased from 190 to 175 metric tons during 2012. The Department of State and DoD will work with Colombian partners to support increased eradication and to develop alternative eradication methods to address the changing patterns of cultivation.

3. Attack Key Vulnerabilities of Transnational Criminal Organizations

A. Improve Our Knowledge of the Vulnerabilities of Transnational Criminal Organizations

Information on the organization and operations of transnational criminal groups is the cornerstone of efficient, targeted efforts to disrupt and dismantle those organizations that pose the greatest threat to the United States and its partners. Information sharing among the intelligence, law enforcement, and defense communities continues to pay dividends in identifying threats and areas in which organizations might be targeted most effectively, sustaining the cycle of success. In FY 2013 the Administration continued to identify the issues of drugs and transnational organized crime as national intelligence priorities; conducted major studies on the transportation and illicit finance operations of illicit trafficking groups; and continued bilateral cooperation with key partner nations, including Mexico and Colombia. The U.S. Government in 2014 will continue to refine its intelligence collection and analysis on the operations and hierarchy of key transnational criminal organizations.

B. Disrupt Illicit Drug Trafficking in the Transit Zone

Targeting bulk shipments of illegal drugs before they reach U.S. borders has the greatest effect on reducing their flow toward the United States, relieves pressure on partner nations, and reduces illicit revenue streams that fund transnational criminal organizations. During FY 2013, 184 metric tons of cocaine were seized or disrupted in the transit zone out of a total documented flow of 646 metric tons, as recorded in the Consolidated Counterdrug Database (CCDB).[73] This represents a 28.5 percent removal rate, which, while below the annual target for 2013 (36 percent), is consistent with the historical average of 25 percent over the past decade and well above the removal rate in 2012 (23.8 percent). The availability of U.S. interdiction assets remains a persistent concern. As depicted in Figure 2, reduced numbers of interdiction assets in the transit zone can have a negative effect on the entire interdiction continuum. The interagency community will examine options to counter the continuing drug trafficking threat in the transit zone.

C. Target the Illicit Finances of Drug Trafficking Organizations

U.S. agencies aggressively targeted the illicit financial activities of drug trafficking and transnational criminal organizations in FY 2013. The Office of Foreign Assets Control designated numerous additional entities linked to Mexico's Sinaloa Cartel and to Zetas leader Miguel Angel Trevino Morales under the Foreign Narcotics Kingpin Act, freezing their assets and financial transactions under U.S. jurisdiction. OFAC also successfully accomplished derivative designations on persons and entities linked to the Yakuza families of Japan and the South-Asian crime syndicate known as "D-Company," headed by Indian national Dawood Ibrahim. The multiagency Financial Crimes Task Force's investigations of illicit money service businesses led to multiple indictments and convictions for money laundering. The DEA, ICE/HSI National Bulk Cash Smuggling Center, and Treasury's FinCEN continued to work with state and local law enforcement entities along the Southwest border to improve information sharing at all levels and to enhance state and local authorities' ability to identify illicit financial activities.

D. Target Cartel Leadership

U.S. Federal agencies and partner nations continue to identify and exploit the vulnerabilities of criminal organizations responsible for drug trafficking and money laundering. Years of bilateral cooperation between the United States and Mexico has bolstered Mexico's capacity for arresting cartel leadership.

Notably, Mexican authorities arrested the previously mentioned Zeta organization leader Miguel Angel Trevino Morales in July 2013, the leader of the rival Gulf Cartel Mario Ramirez Trevino the following month, and in February 2014, Mexican authorities captured Joaquin "Chapo" Guzman Loera, the leader of the infamous Sinaloa Cartel. Bilateral cooperation with Colombia led to the extradition of kingpin Daniel "El Loco" Barrera to the United States in July to face trafficking and money laundering charges.

Over the next year, OCDETF member agencies will continue to share information, identify CPOTs, and work cooperatively to disrupt and dismantle them.

Section 7. Improve Information Systems for Analysis, Assessment, and Local Management

Federal drug control programs and policies must be based upon sound evidence. The credibility of that evidence rests upon the quality of the methods with which the data are compiled and analyzed. Formulation of the *National Drug Control Strategy* relies upon scientifically rigorous studies published in peer-reviewed journals and government reports; rigor and transparency are essential to establishing credibility. Data collected and analyzed with such methods are routinely used in the formulation and evaluation of drug control programs and policies.

For example, in recent years the United States has experienced the emergence and spread of non-controlled synthetic drugs, in particular synthetic cannabinoids and cathinones. Synthetic cannabinoids, colloquially but incorrectly referred to as synthetic marijuana, are chemical compounds laced on plant materials and then smoked. They affect the same brain receptors as marijuana and are said by some users to provide similar effects. However, many users experience effects that include anxiety, confusion, paranoia, dysphoria, intense hallucinations, panic attacks, and aggressive behavior—often with life-threatening consequences. Synthetic cathinones, commonly referred to as "bath salts," are man-made drugs designed to have stimulant effects similar to amphetamines, cocaine, methamphetamine, and MDMA.

These synthetic designer drugs are typically labelled as "not for human consumption" in an attempt to avoid law enforcement.

The use of these substances for their psychoactive effect first arose in Europe during the past decade. Media reports and domestic law enforcement seizures were the first indication of their spread to the United States. Shortly thereafter, some U.S. data systems began to track their use and consequences. In 2011, researchers for the Monitoring the Future study began to ask high school seniors whether they had used synthetic cannabinoids in the past year. Surprisingly, 11.4 percent of them responded in the affirmative, making it the second most used illicit drug behind marijuana.

This estimate was unchanged in 2012, but declined to 7.9 percnet in 2013—similar to the rate of past year use of amphetamines (8.7%). The use of synthetic cathinones among seniors was much lower—1.4 percent in 2012, the first year they were included in the survey, and unchanged in 2013.[74]

The American Association of Poison Control Centers in 2010 began tracking calls to regional centers related to synthetic drugs. That year there were 2,906 calls concerning synthetic cannabinoids; in 2011, the calls more than doubled to 6,968. By 2013, such calls had fallen to 2,643.[75] A similar pattern was observed for bath salts: there were 306 calls in 2010, rising dramatically to 6,137 in 2011, and dropping nearly as dramatically to 995 in 2013.[76]

Users of synthetic cannabinoids have suffered serious health problems that have sent them to the emergency department (ED). The Drug Abuse Warning Network began reporting such cases in 2010, with 11,406 such visits. These visits more than doubled in 2011 with 28,531 synthetic cannabinoid-related ED visits.[77]

As a result of the emergence of these dangerous synthetic substances, Congress enacted the Synthetic Drug Abuse Prevention Act of 2012, as part of the 2012 FDA Safety and Innovation Act. The Act permanently places 26 different synthetic cannabinoids, cathinones, and phenethylamines into Schedule I of the Controlled Substances Act. In 2011, DEA exercised its emergency scheduling authority to control five of these synthetic cannabinoids and three synthetic cathinones.[78] By 2012, all of these substances were permanently designated as Schedule I substances.[79] At least 41 states and Puerto Rico have taken action to control one or more synthetic cannabinoids.[80] Prior to 2010, synthetic cannabinoids were not controlled by any state, nor were they controlled at the Federal level. In addition, at least 43 states and Puerto Rico have taken action to control one or more synthetic cathinones.[81]

As policies and programs are implemented to further address synthetic drugs, the Administration will continue to support research to evaluate their effects and assess the threat.

This research is being conducted using rigorous methods and the highest professional standards. Results will be disseminated via peer-reviewed journal articles and government reports.

Much of the evidence base used by policymakers to assess the effectiveness of drug policies and programs is derived from several key Federal data systems, including the following:

- National Survey on Drug Use and Health (NSDUH),
- Drug Abuse Warning Network (DAWN)
- Treatment Episode Data Set (TEDS),
- Monitoring the Future (MTF) study,
- System to Retrieve Information on Drug Evidence (STRIDE),
- National Seizure System (NSS),
- Consolidated Counterdrug Database (CCDB),
- Arrestee Drug Abuse Monitoring II (ADAM) program, and the
- National Vital Statistics System (NVSS).

The status of the Administration's efforts to achieve the *Strategy*'s goals and evaluate programs is assessed with the data from these systems and many more. These data systems—while observing appropriate privacy policies and protections—also provide the information that populates the *National Drug Control Strategy: Data Supplement*, a compendium of the leading indicators of drug use, drug supply, and related consequences. At a time of limited resources, the role of this information in informing Federal drug policy and ensuring its efficiency and efficacy is increasingly important.

These data systems are not static; they require continual review and updating to ensure their methods incorporate the latest scientific advancements in survey design and data collection.

The following paragraphs provide an update on progress that has been made over the past year in ensuring that these data systems continue to provide accurate and timely data on drug use and its consequences.

1. Existing Federal Data Systems Need to be Sustained and Enhanced

A. Enhance the Drug Abuse Warning Network Emergency Department Data System

In 2011, SAMHSA began the process of replacing the Drug Abuse Warning Network with the SAMHSA Emergency Department Surveillance System (SEDSS). DAWN data collection was discontinued at the end of 2011 (however, analytical reports continue to be published). At the same time, planning for SEDSS commenced as a joint undertaking between SAMHSA and the CDC's National Center for Health Statistics. Under SEDSS, data on drug involvement in ED visits would continue to be collected. NCHS's existing National Hospital Care Survey is being modified to enable collection of these data. This solution is not without trade-offs. While the costs of obtaining the data will be constrained, the data on drug-involvement in ED visits will not be as detailed under the new system as it was under DAWN due to sample constraints. However, the new system will provide data on such visits not previously available, including patient disposition following the ED visit. Funding issues have delayed the expansion of data collection for the SEDSS until 2014. In 2013, with the benefit of additional funding, the ED recruitment process and data collection instrument were pilot tested.

B. Better Assess Price and Purity of Illicit Drugs on the Street

Drug prices are also of great interest to communities, as they provide a snapshot of what drugs are available and how easy they are to obtain. Currently, DEA tracks the price of drugs as part of ongoing casework (STRIDE) or through a few recurring drug purchase programs. From these DEA data, national trends for drug prices and purities are developed for the four major drugs (cocaine, heroin, marijuana, and methamphetamine) in various market levels and are published annually in the *National Drug Control Strategy: Data Supplement.*

An analysis was recently conducted comparing forensic laboratory price trends with law enforcement surveys to determine correlation. These data will be published in the next ONDCP report on illicit drug price and purity. The results indicate there is a mixed level of correlation between price trends and law enforcement survey results, pointing to the necessity of conducting drug purchase programs to obtain accurate price trends.

DEA pursued several possibilities for improved assessment of street drug prices and purities. DEA contacted counterparts at state/local forensic labs seeking specimens for subsequent analysis. However, unlike DEA, the state/local labs do not retain drug samples; specimens are returned to the acquiring law enforcement agencies, which will not release them for various reasons, ranging from legal restrictions to the desire to maintain all evidence until adjudication. A limited set of state and local forensic laboratories do conduct purity analyses on their submitted drug specimens. DEA's National Forensic Laboratory Information System has recorded purity information from these labs. ONDCP and DEA are collaborating to determine the most feasible mechanism for exploiting these data for monitoring trends and comparing geographic fluctuations.

C. Strengthen Drug Information Systems Focused on Arrestees and Incarcerated Individuals

Although national surveys provide invaluable data on overall drug use prevalence, there is special value in studying drug use among the criminal justice population. The ADAM program estimates the prevalence of drug use and related information among booked arrestees in selected U.S. counties and is the only Federal drug survey to include a biologic indicator (urine sample) of recent drug use. The National Institute of Justice conducted ADAM from 2000 through 2003; ONDCP has conducted it (as ADAM II) since 2007; however, due to budget constraints, 2013 was the last year for which ADAM data would be collected. In 2013, ONDCP published the findings from the 2012 ADAM and conducted data collection for 2013. The final annual report is scheduled for publication in 2014.[82]

In 2013, ONDCP implemented a pilot program, the Community Drug Early Warning System (CDEWS), to reassess urine samples collected from individuals under the supervision of the criminal justice system (e.g., drug courts, parolees, and probationers) in the Washington, D.C. and Richmond, Virginia areas. The reassessment tested for drugs that were not originally tested for by the various criminal justice programs. Results suggest that significant proportions of individuals tested positive for synthetic cannabinoids.[83] ONDCP is funding a second round of CDEWS, with results to be published in 2014.

2. New Data Systems and Analytical Methods to Address Gaps Should be Developed and Implemented

A. Transition Drug Seizure Tracking to the National Seizure System

Tabulation of drug seizures is the foundation for reporting statistics on the trends, activities, and patterns related to drug supply reduction policy. EPIC has completed its integration of historical seizure data from the Federal-wide Drug Seizure System with the latest NSS data. Federal agencies are collaborating on improving the consolidation and de-duplication of drug seizure data electronically to provide more accurate and timely tabulations. A template for a strategic drug seizure report with standardized, defined fields will be available by late spring 2014. Each agency's seizure data will be mapped into the NSS for use in strategic reports. The strategic reports will provide decision makers with statistics on temporal and geographic trends in drug seizures.

B. Enhance the Various Data that Inform Our Common Understanding of Global Illicit Drug Markets

Federal agencies continue to refine and enhance the *Interagency Assessment of Cocaine Movement* (IACM)—an annual assessment of the global flow of cocaine—bringing additional Federal and international partners into the analytic process. Incorporating additional information from agencies ranging from CBP to the Australian Federal Police provides additional insight into the global market for cocaine. The IACM relies on U.S. Government estimates of illicit drug production and on the CCDB, which also continues to improve its collection of data on illicit heroin and other opioid movements and the trafficking of precursor chemicals for illicit drugs. Agencies will continue efforts to improve the efficiency and comprehensive nature of CCDB's data collection. At a time of limited resources, the role of the CCDB and other data systems in providing understanding of illicit drug supply trends is increasingly important. Other critical data systems include: the DEA's scientific studies of illicit crop yield and illicit drug lab efficiency, known as Operation Breakthrough; the Cocaine Signature Program; Heroin Signature Program; Methamphetamine Profiling Program; and Heroin Domestic Monitor Program. Evaluating the origin and purity of illicit drugs and the price information in STRIDE also remains essential. Several of these data systems are currently operating under severe budget constraints. These key data sets need to be maintained in order to enable critical research, assessment, and evaluation to continue.

C. In Coordination with Our International Partners, Improve Capacity for More Accurately, Rapidly, and Transparently Estimating the Cultivation and Yield of Marijuana, Opium, and Coca in the World

U.S. Government analysts continue to collaborate with UNODC on improving estimate methodology, sharing best practices, and evaluating potentially useful new techniques. DEA made progress in its studies to inform U.S. Government estimates of illicit drug crop cultivation and production, with analyses in Colombia and Peru. Funding for annual U.S. Government estimates of illicit cultivation of coca, marijuana, and poppy, and production of cocaine and heroin, should be supported to maintain these critical estimates of potential illicit drug production. Continued work with partners around the world, including in Mexico, on yield studies should be supported with adequate funding to further enhance estimates of illicit drug yields and properly inform actions in the *Strategy*.

OPERATION BREAKTHROUGH

Through Operation Breakthrough, DEA supports the *Strategy* by examining illicit drug cultivation and drug production in major source regions. These scientific studies have provided U.S. policy makers and international partners with unique scientific data and strategic analysis on the nature and magnitude of the evolving threats posed by illicit crop cultivation and drug production. For example, coca yield studies in Colombia have documented the success of the Colombian Government's coca eradication operations in reducing coca yields in major coca growing areas. DEA scientific studies specifically provide four of the five data sets (crop yield, alkaloid content, base lab efficiency, and hydrochloride lab efficiency) required for the U.S. Government to produce science-based cocaine and heroin production estimates.

B. Measures of Drug Use and Related Problems Must be Useful at the State and Community Level

A. Develop a Community Early Warning and Monitoring System that Tracks Substance Use and Problem Indicators at the Local Level

Progress in reducing the Nation's drug problem is made at the local level through the efforts of community coalitions, treatment providers, recovery support services providers, law enforcement, and others. SAMHSA, with the assistance of its Federal partners, is developing a system of local drug indicators. In FY 2013, SAMHSA signed an agreement with the US Department of Agriculture's National Institute of Food and Agriculture (USDA/NIFA) to engage their community extension network in identifying community measures, community behavioral health surveillance programs, and strategies currently used by communities to track and monitor substance abuse at the community level. USDA/NIFA has awarded a 1-year grant to Michigan State University to promote this work. Expected deliverables in 2014 will identify data opportunities, develop new data collection strategies, and develop learning tools to teach communities about behavioral health surveillance and monitoring.

ADVOCATE FOR ACTION: DR. KENNETH SILVERMAN

Dr. Kenneth Silverman is a researcher and Professor of Psychiatry and Behavioral Sciences at Johns Hopkins University's School of Medicine and is also Director of the Bayview Medical Center's Center for Learning and Health. Dr. Silverman's research concerns the Therapeutic Workplace, an employment-based intervention for behavioral change. Through the Therapeutic Workplace, unemployed adults living in poverty earn the opportunity to work and earn wages by meeting treatment goals. Goals may include abstinence verified through drug monitoring, as well as adherence to Vivitrol (injectable naltrexone), a medication to prevent narcotic relapse. Pay is contingent on attendance, work speed, and accuracy. Workplace participants are trained in data entry skills using a web-based computerized program that automates teaching and accelerates learning. Enrollees also learn professional demeanor. While Dr. Silverman's approach is similar to other employee drug testing programs, patient recovery is the priority. If drug use occurs, every effort is made to keep the bond between employee and employer intact, so work can resume once abstinence is reestablished. Studies show incentives are among the most effective tools for initiating and sustaining abstinence, but they can be costly. Using wages from employment to pay for incentive interventions is a unique solution for treating people with chronic substance use disorders who may be at risk for relapse even after years of abstinence. In clinical trials, patients with long histories of unemployment and severe substance use disorders, including intravenous heroin and cocaine use, have been able to achieve long-term recovery through the Therapeutic Workplace.

POLICY FOCUS: REDUCING DRUGGED DRIVING

Alcohol-impaired driving has been a focus of road safety for decades, and rates of drunk driving on the roads have declined due to improved laws, enforcement, and sustained public awareness campaigns that have changed the social norm around drunk driving.[84] However, drugs other than alcohol—illicit as well as prescribed and over-the-counter—can affect driving performance with the potential to alter behavior. In the 2010 *National Drug Control Strategy,* the President set a goal of reducing drugged driving in America by 10 percent by 2015. The Administration continues to collaborate with state and local governments, nongovernmental organizations, and Federal partners to raise awareness of the dangers of drugged driving and meet the President's goal.

Results of the latest National Highway Traffic Safety Administration (NHTSA) National Roadside Survey are expected in late 2014 and will provide a benchmark regarding how successful efforts have been to meet the goal stated in the 2010 *National Drug Control Strategy.* However, early results from other sources are promising. In 2012, according to NSDUH, 10.3 million persons (3.9 percent) aged 12 or older reported driving under the influence of illicit drugs during the past year. The 2012 rate was lower than the 2002 rate (4.7 percent), but it was higher than the 2011 rate (3.7 percent).[85]

The Administration has focused on four key areas to reduce drugged driving: increasing public awareness; enhancing legal reforms to get drugged drivers off the road; advancing technology for drug tests and data collection;

and increasing law enforcement's ability to identify drugged drivers. These efforts remain the Administration's focus for the upcoming year.

Collaboration among Federal partners is essential to meeting the President's goal. ONDCP works closely with DOT (specifically with NHTSA), the National Transportation Safety Board, and HHS to partner on key projects and research opportunities. Support of research to improve drug testing and to evaluate the prevalence of drugged driving on the Nation's roads is a priority of the Administration. ONDCP is also working with its international partners in the European Union, Australia, and other countries to exchange best practices and the latest research related to drugged driving. In 2012, the European Union completed the most comprehensive analysis of drugged driving ever conducted, *Driving Under the Influence of Drugs, Alcohol and Medicines in Europe*, known as the DRUID Project.

Ensuring that young drivers drive safely is of particular concern to the Administration. *Monitoring the Future*, an annual survey of high school seniors, provides data from 2001 through 2012 on the driving and substance use habits of high school seniors. Consistent with national trends in marijuana use, the number of teens driving after using marijuana has increased in recent years, and the number of teens driving after using other illicit substances has not changed. Students in 2012 indicated that they were more likely to drive after using marijuana than after drinking (11.0 percent vs. 8.7 percent).[86] ONDCP has developed relationships with youth-serving organizations including RADD: The Entertainment Industry's Voice for Road Safety, Students Against Destructive Decisions, and National Organizations for Youth Safety to ensure that young people are aware of the dangers of driving after using marijuana and other drugs.

Preventing Drugged Driving Must Become a National Priority on Par with Preventing Drunk Driving

Encourage States to Adopt Per Se Drug Impairment Laws

The Administration continues to encourage states to enact drug *per se*—analogous to "zero tolerance"—laws to reduce the prevalence of drug-impaired drivers on the road. This standard, which has been adopted in 17 states and has been applied to commercial drivers for decades, increases the ability to prosecute drivers using drugs other than alcohol without specifying a bodily fluid concentration.[87] The Governors Highway Safety Association has joined ONDCP in supporting the elevation of drugged driving as a national priority and supports *per se* standards in the states. In 2013, NHTSA also sought interest from the states in pursuing pilot test implementation of administrative license revocation in cases of drugged driving, which would require that law enforcement have the ability to screen suspected drug impaired drivers for drug use. To this end, NHTSA initiated a field examination of oral fluid drug screening devices to look at their accuracy and reliability.

ADVOCATE FOR ACTION: STEVE TALPINS

Stephen K. Talpins, an attorney with Rumberger, Kirk & Caldwell, is Vice President of the Institute for Behavior and Health (IBH), a non-profit organization devoted to identifying and promoting new strategies to reduce illegal drug use and its consequences. IBH was founded and is led by Dr. Robert L. DuPont, the first Director of NIDA and the second White House drug policy advisor.

Mr. Talpins is an innovator and recognized authority on the full range of drugged driving issues. For more than 20 years he has worked collaboratively with public, private, and non-profit stakeholders on drugged driving. In 1994, Mr. Talpins argued and won a precedent-setting Frye hearing on the admissibility of Drug Recognition Expert (DRE) testimony and evidence, including the horizontal gaze nystagmus test. Since that time, Stephen has consulted with prosecutors around the country on issues involving the DRE protocol and field sobriety tests. In 2010-2011, Mr. Talpins drafted a model *per se* drugged driving law for IBH. The model law was designed to be adapted to the needs of any state and provided the basis for a bill filed in the Florida legislature. In 2012, following a conversation with NHTSA, Mr. Talpins identified ways to incorporate drugged driving into the established Administrative License Review (ALR) system. Mr. Talpins drafted a model provision that was presented to the Board of Directors of the Governors Highway Safety Administration. The model ALR drug law was well-received and, in August 2013, the Governors Highway Safety Administration adopted a resolution encouraging states to study the efficacy of an ALR system for drugged drivers. Steve's legal work and advocacy have served as important contributions to the national effort to prevent drugged driving and its public health and safety consequences.

Collect Further Data on Drugged Driving

Collecting data on the prevalence and effects of drugged driving is crucial to establishing strong policy. In 2013, NHTSA implemented data collection for the National Roadside Survey, a voluntary and anonymous survey that collected data, including oral fluid and a blood sample, from drivers to determine the prevalence of driving after consuming alcohol or an illicit drug or medication with the ability to impair. Results of this survey are expected in late 2014. The Crash Risk Study, conducted in Virginia Beach, Virginia, assessed the relative risk of becoming involved in a crash after consuming drugs. Results from the study are expected in 2014. ONDCP has partnered with NHTSA and NIDA to support driver simulator research to examine driving impairment as a result of marijuana and combined marijuana and alcohol use and correlate it with the results of oral fluid testing to identify behavioral indicators of impairment. Results from this research are expected by the end of 2014.

Enhance Prevention of Drugged Driving by Educating Communities and Professionals

President Obama declared December 2013 *National Impaired Driving Prevention Month* for the fourth consecutive year, showing a continued dedication to reduce deaths on our Nation's roads. ONDCP has worked with national organizations including RADD: The Entertainment Industry's Voice for Road Safety, the Governors Highway Safety Association, National Organizations for Youth Safety, and Students Against Destructive Decisions to raise awareness of drugged driving. The Drugged Driving Toolkit, created as part of the ATI campaign, was shared with hundreds of parents and community leaders, and more than 300 youth participated in drugged driving prevention workshops conducted by ONDCP. In November 2013, the National Transportation Safety Board declared that impaired driving, to include both drug and alcohol influenced operation of a motor vehicle, would serve as one of their 10 "Most Wanted" policy priorities for the year.

Provide Increased Training to Law Enforcement on Identifying Drugged Drivers

NHTSA, in partnership with ONDCP, developed an online Advanced Roadside Impaired Driving Enforcement program (ARIDE) that launched in August 2013. The online ARIDE training is a vital tool that can help law enforcement officers recognize the signs that a driver may be impaired by drugs, alcohol, or both. Online ARIDE is available for free to all police departments and can be completed at an officer's convenience. There is no travel expense involved in completing this training, and the online ARIDE module provides an officer up to 60 days to complete the course. More than 550 learners enrolled in the Online ARIDE training during the first month of availability.

Develop Standard Screening Methodologies for Drug-Testing Labs to Use in Detecting the Presence of Drugs

SAMHSA is expected to propose oral fluid testing guidelines in 2014. ONDCP began supporting the development of guidelines on toxicology laboratory standards for detecting drugs and their metabolites in oral fluids in 2011 and expects further developments in oral fluid screening technology to make feasible on site drug screening by law enforcement. Once guidelines are adopted, these guidelines may also be adopted for use in the DOT-regulated program. In addition to roadside testing, oral fluids testing will enhance how drug testing is carried out in the workplace.

POLICY FOCUS: PREVENTING AND ADDRESSING PRESCRIPTION DRUG ABUSE

Reducing and preventing the abuse of prescription medications remains a core priority for the Administration. As communities across the Nation know far too well, the diversion and misuse of prescription drugs, particularly opioid analgesics, have taken a significant toll on public health and safety in the United States. Over the past decade, there have been increases in rates of diagnosable abuse or dependence,[88] substance abuse treatment admissions,[89] and emergency department visits[90] involving prescription medications.

In 2010, more than 38,300 Americans died from drug overdose, with prescription drugs involved in the majority of those deaths.[91] Opioid pain relievers like oxycodone, hydrocodone, and methadone were involved in more than 16,600 of these deaths—approximately 45 Americans every day.[92] This startling figure is approximately 4 times greater than the number of deaths just a decade earlier in 2000.[93] The scope and urgency of this problem has reached such a level that the CDC labeled prescription drug overdose an epidemic, bringing the severity of this problem to the forefront.[94]

In April 2011, the Administration released a comprehensive *Prescription Drug Abuse Prevention Plan* that created a national framework for reducing prescription drug diversion and abuse. The *Plan* focuses on improving education for patients and health care providers, supporting the expansion of state-based prescription drug monitoring programs (PDMPs), developing more convenient and environmentally responsible disposal methods to remove unused medications from the home, and reducing the prevalence of pill mills and diversion through targeted enforcement efforts. There are signs that national efforts to address this problem are working. The latest national survey data indicate that while the 2012 rate of past month non-medical use of prescription drugs among young adults (18 to 25 years old) was 5.3 percent, up from 5.0 percent in 2011, these rates are still lower than those from 2003-2007.[95] State efforts also may be having an impact. For example, in 2011, Florida enacted legislation to shutter rogue pain clinics. Overdose deaths in the state involving prescription drugs declined 10 percent from 2011 to 2012.[96] In another example of progress, Tennessee, which requires prescriber usage of PDMPs, has reported declines in the number of patients using multiple prescribers from 2012 through 2013.[97]

The Administration's *Plan* calls for reducing drug-induced deaths by 15 percent from 2010 to 2015 and extending this 15 percent goal to include unintentional overdose deaths related to opioids. Given the urgency of drug overdose in the United States, the Administration is focusing its efforts on not only preventing the diversion and abuse of prescription drugs but also reducing the number of Americans dying every day from overdose nationwide.

While focused on reducing overdose deaths, the Federal Government also continues to address other aspects of this problem, including prescription drug abuse among expectant mothers and the potential consequences to their children (neonatal abstinence syndrome), as well as the potential transition from prescription opioid abuse to heroin and injection drug use, particularly among young adults. These issues, together with ongoing efforts to reduce rates of misuse more broadly, require coordinated action from public health and safety leaders at the Federal, state, local, and tribal levels.

The Administration has made considerable progress in all four areas of the *Plan*, including expanding available continuing education for health care providers, improving the operations and functionality of prescription monitoring across the country, safely removing millions of pounds of expired and unwanted medications from circulation, and targeting Federal law enforcement efforts to meet state and local needs.

Pillar 1: Education

Educate Health Care Providers about Opioid Painkiller Prescribing

As many health care practitioners know, managing a patient's pain is a crucial and often difficult task. Despite the importance of this area of clinical practice, research indicates that students in medical school receive on average only 11 hours of training on pain education, and most schools do not offer specific training on opioids, substance use disorders, or clinical decision making.[98] A 2011 Government Accountability Office report on education related to the abuse of prescription pain relievers found that "most prescribers receive little training on the importance of appropriate prescribing and dispensing of prescription pain relievers, on how to recognize substance abuse in their patients, or on treating pain."[99]

For these reasons, the Administration's Plan includes a core action to require practitioners (such as physicians, dentists, and others authorized to prescribe) who request DEA registration to prescribe controlled substances to be trained on responsible opioid prescribing practices as a precondition of registration. Several states, including Iowa,[100] Kentucky,[101] Massachusetts,[102] Ohio,[103] Tennessee,[104] and Utah,[105] have passed mandatory prescriber education legislation, and the Administration strongly encourages other states to explore this option. At the Federal level, HHS is implementing education requirements for HHS agency health care personnel, including professionals serving tribal communities through the IHS, and those working with underserved populations through HRSA. Similar efforts are underway at BOP, and education efforts are underway at DoD and the VA.

The Administration also supports other education efforts, including free and low-cost options to provide online and field-based training for prescribers and dispensers of these medications. ONDCP worked with NIDA to develop two free online training tools on safe prescribing for pain and managing pain patients who abuse prescription opioids. These courses, eligible for continuing medical education and continuing education (CME/CE) credit, provide health care professionals with critical skills to manage high-risk patients and more safely prescribe in their day-to-day practice. Since their launch in October 2012, thousands of doctors, nurses, and pharmacists have completed these training modules.

Moreover, the FDA now requires manufacturers of extended-release and long-acting opioid pain relievers to make available free or low-cost continuing education to prescribers under the *Risk Evaluation and Mitigation Strategy* for extended-release and long-acting (ER/LA) opioid analgesic drugs. Eligible curricula have been developed by experts from the Boston University School of Medicine, the American Academy of Family Physicians, and the Henry Ford Health System, among many others.[106] Approximately 60 CME/CE-eligible courses were launched in 2013 and early 2014, offering practitioners a broad array of online and in-person education options.[107]

The Administration is also committed to improving medication safety by better informing prescribers and patients about opioid risks and prescribing practices. SAMHSA published a guide for clinicians entitled *Managing Chronic Pain in Adults with or in Recovery from Substance Use Disorders*. The guide provides practitioners with guidelines on assessing chronic pain patients as well as effectively educating and managing the risk of substance use disorders among patients treated with opioids.[108]

In addition, in September 2013, ONDCP joined the FDA to announce significant new measures to enhance the safe and appropriate use of ER/LA opioids.[109] FDA required class-wide labeling changes for these medications, including modifications to the products' indication, limitations of use, and warnings, as well as post-market research requirements. The new language states that ER/LA opioids are indicated only for management of pain severe enough to require daily, around-the-clock, long-term opioid treatment and for which alternative treatment options are inadequate. The changes also include a new boxed warning that chronic maternal use during pregnancy can result in opioid withdrawal symptoms for newborns. FDA also announced that certain ER/LA opioid application holders must conduct postmarketing studies and clinical trials to assess the serious risks of misuse, abuse, addiction, overdose, and death associated with the long-term use of these drugs. And in April 2013, FDA approved updated labeling for reformulated OxyContin that describes the medication's abuse-deterrent properties, which the FDA expects will deter abuse by non-oral routes of administration.[110] Finally, in December 2013, after an extensive review of scientific literature, hundreds of public comments, and several public meetings, FDA completed and HHS transmitted to DEA a recommendation to reschedule hydrocodone combination products into Schedule II of the Controlled Substances Act. Schedule II drugs are subject to more stringent requirements regarding storage, record keeping, and prescribing than Schedule III drugs, and, should DEA reschedule hydrocodone combination products, these requirements may help reduce diversion and abuse. By exercising its legal and regulatory authorities to take these actions, FDA is helping safeguard access to pain relievers while reducing the risks of abuse, misuse, and overdose.

ADVOCATE FOR ACTION: DR. STEPHEN LOYD

Dr. Stephen Loyd is making a difference in the national effort to prevent and address prescription drug abuse through prescriber education. Dr. Loyd is an Internal Medicine physician and medical educator in Tennessee with expertise in proper prescribing of controlled substances and substance use disorders. He is in recovery from his own prescription opioid and benzodiazepine disorder and now regularly lectures and educates health care professionals, law enforcement, policymakers, and others on the potential dangers of prescription narcotics. He is the Associate Chief of Staff of Education at the Mountain Home VA Medical Center, has considerable expertise in neonatal addiction issues/neonatal abstinence syndrome (NAS), and is a vocal advocate for public health and public safety cooperation. In a November 2012 article about him, Dr. Loyd discussed the challenges related to addressing substance use disorders: "Will addiction ever go away? No way. There'll always be something The key is to treat the underlying problems. We're not going to get a handle on this until we get a multi-pronged approach and erase the stigma associated with addictive disease."[113]

The Administration is also working to educate the general public. The DFC Support Program enables approximately 670 community coalitions to work with local youth, parent, business, religious, civic, and other groups to help prevent youth substance use. These coalitions implement an array of prevention strategies and programs in their communities to help reduce prescription drug abuse, including prescription drug take back events to enable communities to safely dispose of unused and unwanted medications.[111] In another example, the United States Attorneys' Offices have joined with community leaders to educate young people on the dangers of prescription drugs through local and national initiatives.[112]

Pillar 2: Monitoring

Expand Prescription Drug Monitoring Programs and Promote Links among State Systems and to Electronic Health Records

The careful monitoring of prescription medications and safe prescribing practices—while also ensuring appropriate privacy protections—can be of great benefit to patients, health care providers, public health professionals, and law enforcement agencies. The second pillar of the Administration's *Plan* focuses on strengthening PDMPs, secure state-administered databases that monitor the prescribing and dispensing of controlled substances. The records contained in PDMPs can assist prescribers and pharmacists in identifying patients who are at risk for substance use disorders, overdose, or other significant health consequences of misusing prescription medications. State regulatory and law enforcement agencies may also use this information to identify and prevent unsafe prescribing, doctor-shopping (seeing multiple doctors to obtain prescriptions), and other methods of illegally diverting controlled substances. In 2006, only 20 states had PDMPs. Today, 49 have laws authorizing PDMPs, and 48 states have operational programs.

Building upon this progress, the Administration is working with state governments and private sector technology experts to make PDMPs more user-friendly so prescribers can access them quickly and easily. As of April 2014, 24 operational PDMPs can share data with other states' systems,[114] and many PDMP administrators are working to better integrate these systems into other health IT programs. To further these efforts, the Office of the National Coordinator for Health Information Technology and SAMHSA funded nine pilot studies, completed in 2012 and 2013, that improved integration of PDMPs into provider workflow and other health records systems. For example, the Indiana Network for Patient Care leveraged its secure hospital network to offer information from the state PDMP along with a "narcotic score" alert (using a formula to determine high risk based on the number of prescriptions) to emergency department doctors as part of their normal view of a patient's record. In Kansas, a secure e-mail protocol sent a PDMP report to a patient's electronic health record when a certain threshold was met, such as when the patient sought to fill five prescriptions from five providers during 1 calendar quarter. These examples, along with the other pilots, are driving innovation that will better enable health care providers to protect the safety of their patients.

To further encourage the development of innovative health IT integration with PDMPs, SAMHSA awarded nine 2-year grants in FY 2011. CDC is conducting an evaluation of this initiative, and in 2013 SAMHSA awarded additional grants.[115] Ongoing support from BJA through the Harold Rogers PDMP Program is facilitating ongoing efforts to enhance interoperability among state systems.

Prescription monitoring systems must continue to mature, and the Administration continues to focus on expanding interstate data sharing, streamlining PDMP operations, ensuring that data from prescribers in Federal agencies are shared with state PDMPs, and working with state leaders to effectively fund these programs over the long term. In February 2013, VA issued an Interim Final Rule authorizing VA physicians to access state PDMPs in accordance with state laws and to develop mechanisms to begin sharing VA prescribing data with state PDMPs. The Interim Final Rule became final on March 14, 2014. IHS clinics are now sharing data with state PDMPs in many states, and IHS is in the process of negotiating data-sharing agreements with more states. With funding from CDC and FDA, the Center for Excellence in PDMPs at Brandeis University has developed the Prescription Behavior Surveillance System, which collects de-identified PMDP data from participating states. The data is being used in a novel way to track trends in the prescribing of controlled substances and indicators of their misuse. This information is used to evaluate the impact of various interventions related to prescribing at the state level.

Pillar 3: Disposal

Increase Prescription Return/Take-Back and Disposal Programs

Nearly 70 percent of people misusing prescription pain relievers report getting them from a friend or relative the last time they misused these drugs.116 This is how many new non-medical users of prescription medication initially obtain these drugs. Medication disposal programs allow individuals to dispose of unneeded or expired medications in a safe, timely, and environmentally responsible manner and can help prevent potential diversion and abuse.

DEA has partnered with thousands of state and local law enforcement agencies and community coalitions, as well as other Federal agencies, to hold eight National Take-Back Days. Through these events, DEA has collected and safely disposed of more than 3.4 million pounds (1,733 tons) of unneeded or expired medications.[117]

As directed under the Secure and Responsible Drug Disposal Act of 2010, DEA issued a Notice of Proposed Rulemaking (NPRM) in December 2012 that would expand the options available for consumers to safely dispose of unused medications. The NPRM outlined options that included allowing authorized manufacturers, distributors, reverse distributors, and retail pharmacies to voluntarily administer mail-back programs and maintain collection receptacles. The DEA is currently reviewing public comments and developing the final rule. In preparation for the completion of the rulemaking process, the Administration is working with state, local, and tribal stakeholders to identify ways to establish long-term, sustainable disposal programs in their communities.

Pillar 4: Enforcement

Assist States to Address Diversion and Pill Mills

Federal law enforcement is partnering with state and local agencies across the country to reduce the number of pill mills and prosecute those responsible for improper or illegal prescribing practices. The Administration is helping improve state and local law enforcement leaders' investigative skills and knowledge around prescription drug cases. The National Methamphetamine and Pharmaceuticals Initiative (NMPI), funded through ONDCP's HIDTA program, is providing critical training on pharmaceutical crime investigations to law enforcement agencies across the country. Since 2009, NMPI has provided training in pharmaceutical crime investigations and prosecutions to over 26,000 law enforcement and criminal justice professionals. These efforts continue to disseminate critical knowledge to enforcement and prosecution professionals.

In addition, the National Institute of Justice awarded three new grants in FY 2012 to promote research on illegal prescription drug market interventions. These research grants are helping Federal, state, and local law enforcement identify high-risk prescribing practices by using PDMP data and identifying best practices and tactics to shut down sources of diversion.

Drive Illegal Internet Pharmacies Out of Business

The Administration has taken steps to reduce the role of illegal Internet pharmacies in diversion of opioid pharmaceuticals. The Ryan Haight Online Pharmacy Consumer Protection Act requires all Internet pharmacies dispensing controlled substances to obtain a special DEA registration and report monthly to DEA. The Act also requires Internet pharmacies to disclose detailed information on their home page and to not provide pharmaceuticals to individuals who have not had at least one face-to-face evaluation by a prescribing medical practitioner, subject to limited exceptions for telemedicine practice. The Act allows the DEA to better monitor unlawful Internet pharmacy operations, and reduces the number of Internet pharmacies distributing controlled substances illegally.

Crack Down on Rogue Pain Clinics that Do Not Follow Appropriate Prescription Practices

Pain clinics operating outside accepted medical practice and legal boundaries continue to contribute to the prescription drug abuse problem. Federal law enforcement is working closely with state and local enforcement and regulatory bodies to address this problem. As of February 2014, DEA had 66 operational Tactical Diversion Squads that investigate suspected violations of Federal and state laws governing the diversion of controlled substances. These unique groups combine the skill sets of Federal agents, diversion investigators, and a variety of state and local law enforcement agencies. These squads investigate, disrupt, and dismantle organizations engaged in the illegal diversion of prescription drugs, including "pill mills," prescription forgery rings, and practitioners or pharmacists who divert pharmaceuticals.

With the expansion of Tactical Diversion Squads across the country, the number of diversion-related criminal and administrative cases has increased significantly. Between FY 2008 and FY 2013, these Tactical Diversion Squads have also increased the number of diversion-related Priority Target Organization investigations by approximately 45 percent (from approximately 294 to 426). Priority Target Organization investigations focus on those criminal organizations or groups that significantly affect particular areas of the country.

Overdose Prevention and Intervention

Overdoses persist as a major cause of preventable death in the United States, and the 2010 *National Drug Control Strategy* established a goal of reducing drug-induced deaths by 15 percent by 2015. The Administration is committed to reducing overdose deaths nationwide and is focusing on several key areas, including educating the public about overdose risks and interventions; increasing access to naloxone, an emergency overdose reversal medication; and working with states to promote Good Samaritan laws and other measures that can help save lives.

With the recent rise in overdose deaths across the country,[118] it is increasingly important to prevent overdoses and make antidotes available. In August 2013, ONDCP and SAMHSA released the *Opioid Overdose Prevention Toolkit,* which provides communities and local governments with information that can help prevent opioid-related overdoses and deaths.[119] This comprehensive document addresses issues for first responders, treatment providers, and those recovering from opioid overdose.

In addition, working closely with ONDCP, the American Society of Anesthesiologists has created an informational card on recognizing and responding to an opioid overdose.[120] The ASA's "Opioid Overdose Resuscitation" card lists symptoms to look for when an opioid overdose is suspected and details step- by-step instructions for assisting a person suspected of an overdose prior to the arrival of emergency medical personnel. The Administration is working with the American Society of Anesthesiologists and other key stakeholders to provide this card to those who may encounter and can intervene with victims of opioid overdoses.

The Administration continues to promote the use of naloxone, the emergency opioid overdose reversal medication, among those likely to encounter overdose victims.[121] Profiled in the 2013 *National Drug Control Strategy,* the Police Department in Quincy, Massachusetts, has partnered with the Commonwealth's health department to train and equip police officers to resuscitate overdose victims using naloxone. Since October 2010, officers in Quincy have administered naloxone in more than 170 overdose events, almost all of them resulting in successful overdose reversals.[122] The Lorain Police

Department in Ohio, working with county public health and substance abuse leaders, started a similar pilot program in October 2013. Lorain officers, equipped with and trained in the use of naloxone, have already reversed overdoses in their community. ONDCP is working with health officials in these states and other experts to provide technical assistance and best practices information to health and law enforcement officials in other states

SAMHSA's Opioid Overdose Toolkit

The Administration is committed to reducing overdose deaths by 15 percent by 2015. In support of this goal, SAMHSA released the *Opioid Overdose Toolkit* in August 2013. This toolkit provides communities and local governments with material to develop policies and practices to help prevent opioid-related overdoses and deaths. It contains sections dedicated to addressing issues for first responders, treatment providers, and those recovering from opioid overdose. This kit will enable state and community leaders to implement effective overdose prevention initiatives, saving lives and connecting people to the treatment they need.

.In addition, the Administration is working with health care leaders to identify and promote other promising naloxone distribution models. For example, a joint program with the University of Rhode Island's College of Pharmacy, the Rhode Island Pharmacy Foundation, the state Board of Pharmacy, and Walgreens, has created a continuing education program and collaborative practice agreement that allows pharmacists to initiate naloxone therapy for patients who may be at risk for an opioid overdose.[123] A Department of Defense-led program, Operation Opioid Safe at Fort Bragg,

North Carolina, educates patients about the risks and abuse issues surrounding long-term use of prescription opioids and distributes naloxone to high-risk patients.[124] These programs represent leading community-driven efforts that the Administration is exploring as models for the Nation.

NEONATAL ABSTINENCE SYNDROME

The Administration continues to focus on vulnerable populations affected by prescription drug abuse, including pregnant women and their newborns. Research suggests that over the last decade the prevalence of pregnant women using prescription drugs may have increased.[126,127] Over the same period of time the number of infants displaying symptoms of drug withdrawal after birth, known as neonatal abstinence syndrome (NAS), increased approximately threefold nationwide.[128] Newborns with NAS have more complicated and longer initial hospitalizations than other newborns. In 2012, the Administration held a symposium of key stakeholders and researchers aimed at improving outcomes for opioid dependent women and their newborns.

From this symposium, partnerships developed around the country focused on this emerging issue, including partnerships with the National Governor's Association and the Association of State and Territorial Health Officials. In 2013, ONDCP worked with the Vermont Oxford Network to improve care for mothers and infants affected by opioid dependence. The network's multidisciplinary effort involves teams from 205 hospitals from 42 states, Canada, Ireland, and the United Kingdom. This ambitious project aims to improve every aspect of care delivered to families, from standardizing newborn treatment to engaging community partners at the local level. The Administration will continue to engage key stakeholders to improve public health systems and outcomes for pregnant women and infants affected by prescription drug abuse.

Naloxone is an extremely valuable tool, but it is only one element in the broad range of overdose prevention efforts. The Administration is committed to removing legal impediments that can mean the difference between life and death. The odds of surviving an overdose, much like the odds of surviving a heart attack, depend on how quickly the victim receives treatment. At least 14 states have passed Good Samaritan laws, which protect victims and witnesses who seek medical aid for an individual who is overdosing.[125] As these laws are implemented, the Administration will carefully monitor their effect on public health and safety.

CONCLUSION

The year 2013 was an important time for drug policy reform in America—a year that saw significant changes that promise to make our public health and safety policies more effective and more equitable. Important progress was made in providing support to those in need, particularly individuals with substance use disorders who are involved with the criminal justice system—as well as their families. Increased focus was placed on overdose prevention and intervention, with local governments taking important steps to save lives and the Federal Government providing resources such as the Opioid Overdose Toolkit to support their efforts. The implementation of the Affordable Care Act provided millions of Americans with the opportunity to obtain health insurance, and the implementation of the Mental Health Parity and Addiction Equity Act helped to ensure those individuals could obtain mental health and substance use disorder treatment services "at parity" with treatment for other kinds of health disorders.

This progress significantly advances the long-term plan to reduce drug use and its consequences originally set forth in the 2010 *National Drug Control Strategy*. The Administration has sustained its commitment to an evidence-based continuum of prevention, early intervention, treatment, and recovery support services. We have worked to promote substance use disorder services within correctional facilities, through alternative sentencing programs, and in community corrections and reentry systems. We have maintained our support for effective multi-agency law enforcement initiatives to protect our communities from drugs and associated violence. And working with our global partners, we have promoted evidence-based public health approaches, cooperated to reduce drug production and trafficking, and brought some of the most dangerous transnational organized crime leaders to justice.

Yet we must continue to challenge ourselves to do better. We must be mindful of how we discuss issues related to substance use disorders, making sure that we do not stigmatize those with the disease of addiction, yet also ensuring that our young people get the right information about the risks of drug use. And we must seek to avoid over-simplified debates between the idea of a "war on drugs" and the notion of legalization as a panacea. In reality, drug use and its consequences are complex phenomena requiring an array of evidence-based policy responses. The Administration remains committed to charting this "third way" toward a healthier, safer, and more prosperous America.

LIST OF ABBREVIATIONS

ACF	Administration for Children and Families (U.S. Department of Health and Human Services)
ADAM	Arrestee Drug Abuse Monitoring
AIDS	Acquired Immunodeficiency Syndrome
ALR	Administrative License Review
ARIDE	Advanced Roadside Impaired Driving Enforcement
ATF	Bureau of Alcohol, Tobacco, Firearms, and Explosives
ATI	Above the Influence
ATR	Access to Recovery
ATTC	Addiction Technology Transfer Center
BCTF	Border Corruption Task Force
BEST	Border Enforcement Security Task Force
BJA	Bureau of Justice Assistance
BOP	Federal Bureau of Prisons
CADCA	Community Anti-Drug Coalitions of America
CAMP	California Campaign Against Marijuana Planting
CARSI	Central America Regional Security Initiative
CBP	U.S. Customs and Border Protection
CBSI	Caribbean Basin Security Initiative
CCDB	Consolidated Counterdrug Data Base
CCSF	Caribbean Corridor Strike Force
CDC	Centers for Disease Control and Prevention
CDCR	California Department of Corrections and Rehabilitation
CDEWS	Community Drug Early Warning System
CGII	California Gang Intelligence Initiative
CME	Continuing Medical Education
CMS	Centers for Medicare & Medicaid Services
CNWG	Counternarcotics Working Group
CPOT	Consolidated Priority Organizational Target
CSAP	Center for Substance Abuse Prevention
CTF	Counter Threat Finance
DAWN	Drug Abuse Warning Network

DEA	Drug Enforcement Administration
DEC	Drug Endangered Children
DFC	Drug Free Communities
DFE	Demonstration Field Experiment
DHS	U.S. Department of Homeland Security
DICE	DEA Internet Connectivity Endeavor
DMI	Drug Market Intervention
DoD	U.S. Department of Defense
DOJ	U.S. Department of Justice
DOT	U.S. Department of Transportation
DPAI	Drug Prevention and Awareness Initiative (Houston HIDTA)
DRE	Drug Recognition Expert
EPIC	El Paso Intelligence Center
ER	Emergency Room
ER/LA	Extended-Release/Long-Acting
ESP	EPIC System Portal
FBI	Federal Bureau of Investigation
FDA	Food and Drug Administration
FinCEN	Financial Crimes Enforcement Network (U.S. Department of the Treasury)
HHS	U.S. Department of Health and Human Services
HIDTA	High Intensity Drug Trafficking Area
HIV	Human Immunodeficiency Virus
HOPE	Hawaii's Opportunity Probation with Enforcement or Honest Opportunity Probation with Enforcement
HRSA	Health Resources and Services Administration (U.S. Department of Health and Human Services)
HSI	Homeland Security Investigations
HSIN	Homeland Security Information Network
HUD	U.S. Department of Housing and Urban Development
IBH	Institute for Behavior and Health
ICE	U.S. Immigration and Customs Enforcement
IHS	Indian Health Service
INL	Bureau of International Narcotics and Law Enforcement Affairs
ISC	Investigative Support Center
JIATF	Joint Interagency Task Force
JJ-TRIALS	Juvenile Justice Translational Research on Interventions

	for Adolescents in the Legal System
LEO	Law Enforcement Online
LSS	Laboratories and Scientific Services
MSB	Money Services Business
NADCP	National Association of Drug Court Professionals
NAGIA	National Alliance of Gang Investigators Associations
NAS	Neonatal Abstinence Syndrome
NATIVE	Native American Targeted Investigation of Violent Enterprises
NFLIS	National Forensic Laboratory Information System
NGIC	National Gang Intelligence Center
NHTSA	National Highway Traffic Safety Administration
NIC	National Institute of Corrections
NIDA	National Institute on Drug Abuse
NIFA	National Institute of Food and Agriculture (U.S. Department of Agriculture)
NIJ	National Institute of Justice
NMPI	National Methamphetamine and Pharmaceuticals Initiative
NPRM	Notice of Proposed Rulemaking
NREPP	National Registry of Effective Prevention Programs and Practices
NSDUH	National Survey on Drug Use and Health
NSS	National Seizure System
NVSS	National Vital Statistics System
OAS/CICAD	Organization of American States/Inter-American Drug Abuse Control Commission
OASAS	Office of Alcoholism and Substance Abuse Services (New York State)
OCDETF	Organized Crime Drug Enforcement Task Forces
OFC	OCDETF Fusion Center
ONDCP	Office of National Drug Control Policy
PDMP	Prescription Drug Monitoring Program
PEPFAR	President's Emergency Plan for AIDS Relief
PSA	Public Service Announcement
RCO	Recovery Community Organization
RSAT	Residential Substance Abuse Treatment
SADD	Students Against Destructive Decisions

SAMHSA	Substance Abuse and Mental Health Services Administration
SBIRT	Screening, Brief Intervention, and Referral to Treatment
SEDSS	SAMHSA Emergency Department Surveillance System
STAR	Success Through Addiction Recovery
TAFT	Technical Assistance Field Team
TASC	Treatment Alternatives for Safe Communities
TEDS	Treatment Episode Data Set
TOC	Transnational Organized Crime
TSA	Transportation Security Administration
UN	United Nations
UNAIDS	Joint United Nations Programme on HIV/AIDS
UNODC	United Nations Office on Drugs and Crime
USA	U.S. Attorney
USAID	United States Agency for International Development
USCG	U.S. Coast Guard
USDA	U.S. Department of Agriculture
USVI	United States Virgin Islands
VA	U.S. Department of Veterans Affairs
VRSS	Veteran Reentry Search Service
Y4Y	You for Youth

End Notes

[1] Substance Abuse and Mental Health Services Administration. (2013). *Results from the 2012 national survey on drug use and health: Summary of national findings* (NSDUH Series H-46, HHS Publication No. (SMA) 13-4795). Rockville, MD: Substance Abuse and Mental Health Services Administration.

[2] Kelly, J.F. & Westerhoff, C.M. (2010.) Does it matter how we refer to individuals with substance-related conditions? A randomized study of two commonly used terms. *International Journal of Drug Policy, 21(3),* 202-207.

[3] Kelly, J. F. (2004). Toward an addiction-ary: A proposal for more precise terminology. *Alcoholism Treatment Quarterly, 22,* 79–87.

[4] Miller, T.R., & Hendrie, D. (2009). Substance abuse prevention dollars and cents: A cost-benefit analysis. Substance Abuse and Mental Health Services Administration, Center for Substance Abuse Prevention. Rockville, MD: DHHS Pub.No (SMA) 07-4298.

[5] Chou, C.; Montgomery, S.; Pentz, M.; Rohrbach, L.; Johnson, C.; Flay, B.; & Mackinnon, D. (1998). Effects of a community-based prevention program in decreasing drug use in high-risk adolescents. *American Journal of Public Health, 88,* 944–948.

[6] Oetting, E., Edwards, R., Kelly, K., & Beauvais, F. (1997). Risk and protective factors for drug use among rural American youth. In: Robertson, E.B., Sloboda, Z., Boyd, G.M., Beatty, L., & Kozel, N.J., eds. Rural substance abuse: State of knowledge and issues. NIDA Research Monograph No.168. Washington, D.C.: U.S. Government Printing Office, pp.90-130.

[7] Hawkins, J.D.; Catalano, R.F.; & Arthur, M. (2002). Promoting science-based prevention in communities. *Addictive Behaviors, 90(5),* 1–26.

[8] Kosterman, R.; Hawkins, J.D.; Haggerty, K.P.; Spoth, R.; & Redmond, C. (2001). Preparing for the drug free years: Session-specific effects of a universal parent-training intervention with rural families. *Journal of Drug Education, 31(1)*, 47–68.

[9] Scheier, L.; Botvin, G.; Diaz, T.; & Griffin, K. (1999). Social skills, competence, and drug refusal efficacy as predictors of adolescent alcohol use. *Journal of Drug Education, 29(3),* 251–278.

[10] Bauman, K.E.; Foshee, V.A.; Ennett, S.T.; Pemberton, M.; Hicks, K.A.; King, T.S.; & Koch, G.G. (2001). The influence of a family program on adolescent tobacco and alcohol. *American Journal of Public Health, 91(4)*, 604–610.

[11] Chou, C.; Montgomery, S.; Pentz, M.; Rohrbach, L.; Johnson, C.; Flay, B.; & Mackinnon, D. (1998). Effects of a community-based prevention program in decreasing drug use in high-risk adolescents. *American Journal of Public Health, 88*, 944–948.

[12] Miller, T.R., & Hendrie, D. (2009). Substance abuse prevention dollars and cents: A cost-benefit analysis. Substance Abuse and Mental Health Services Administration, Center for Substance Abuse Prevention. Rockville, MD: DHHS Pub.No (SMA) 07-4298.

[13] Johnston, L. D., O'Malley, P. M., Miech, R. A., Bachman, J. G., & Schulenberg, J. E. (2014). Monitoring the Future national results on drug use: 1975-2013: Overview, Key Findings on Adolescent Drug Use. Ann Arbor: Institute for Social Research, The University of Michigan. Retrieved from http://www.monitoringthefuture.org//pubs/ monographs/mtf-overview2013.pdf.

[14] Ibid.

[15] Centers for Disease Control and Prevention. (2009). *Health risk behaviors and academic achievement.* Retrieved from http://www.cdc.gov/healthyyouth/health_and_academics/pdf/health_risk_behaviors.pdf.

[16] Meier, M.H., Caspi, A., Ambler, A., Harrington, H., Houts, R., Keefe, R.S., McDonald, K., Ward, A., Poulton, R., & Moffitt, T.E. (2012). Persistent cannabis users show neuropsychological decline from childhood to midlife. *Proceedings of the National Academy of the Sciences of the United States, 109(40)*, E2657-64.

[17] Outreach was conducted to the following professional educational organizations: National Association of School Social Workers, the National Education Association, the National Association of School Nurses, the National Superintendents Association, and the National Association of School Administrators.

[18] The 2012 school survey reported that 12th graders at Yukon High School have seen a decrease in past 30 day alcohol use from 41.7 percent in 2010 to 40.1 percent in 2012, and have a lower rate compared to the state (43.7 percent). For lifetime alcohol use, 8th graders saw a decrease from 50.1 percent in 2010 to 41.8 percent in 2012, and 12th graders saw a decrease of 71.7 percent in 2010 to 64.0 percent in 2012. The FY 2013 report for tobacco compliance checks indicated there were no sales to minors in Yukon.

[19] Slater, M.D., Kelly, K.J., Stanley, L.R., Lawrence, F.R., & Comello, M.L.G. (2011). Assessing media campaigns linking marijuana non-use with autonomy and aspirations: 'Be under your own influence' and ONDCP's 'Above the influence'. *Prevention Science, 12 (1)*, 12-22

[20] Carpenter, C.S. & Pechmann, C. (2011). Exposure to the above the influence antidrug advertisements and adolescent marijuana use in the United States, 2006-2008. *American Journal of Public Health, 101(5)*, 948-54.

[21] Scheier, L.M., Grenard, J.L., & Holtz, K.D. (2011). An empirical assessment of the Above the Influence advertising campaign. *Journal of Drug Education, 41(4)*, 431-461.

[22] Centers for Disease Control and Prevention. (2012). Integrated prevention services for HIV infection, viral hepatitis, sexually transmitted diseases, and tuberculosis for persons who use drugs illicitly: Summary guidance from CDC and the U.S. Department of Health and Human Services. Mortality and Morbidity Weekly Report, Recommendations and Reports,

61(5): 1-47. Retrieved from http://www.cdc.gov/mmwr/preview/mmwrhtml/ rr6105a1.htm?s_cid=rr6105a1_w.

[23] Estee, S., He, L., Mancuso, D., & Felver, B. (2006). *Medicaid cost outcomes.* Department of Social and Health Services, Research and Data Analysis Division: Olympia, Washington.

[24.] B erino, K., Rosa, P., Skopec, L. & Glied, S. (2013). Affordable care act will expand mental health and substance use disorder benefits and parity protections for 62 million Americans. *Research Brief.* Washington, D.C.: Department of Health and Human Services, Assistant Secretary for Planning and Evaluation (ASPE).

[25] Grant, B.F. & Dawson, D.A. (1997). Age at onset of alcohol use and its association with DSM-IV alcohol abuse and dependence: results from the national longitudinal alcohol epidemiologic survey. *Journal of Substance Abuse, 9,* 103-110. Retrieved from http://www.sciencedirect.com/science/article/pii/S0899328997900092.

[26] Gfroerer, J. C., Wu, L.T., & Penne, M. A. (2002). *Initiation of marijuana use: Trends, patterns, and implications.* (Analytic Series: A-17, DHHS Publication No. SMA 02-3711). Rockville, MD: Substance Abuse and Mental Health Services Administration, Office of Applied Studies. Retrieved from www.samhsa.gov/data/mjinitiation/mjinitiation.pdf.

[27] Johnston, L. D., O'Malley, P. M., Miech, R. A., Bachman, J. G., & Schulenberg, J. E. (2014). *Monitoring the Future national results on adolescent drug use: Overview of key findings, 2013.* Ann Arbor, Mich.: Institute for Social Research, the University of Michigan. Retrieved from http://www.monitoringthefuture.org/data/13data/13drtbl1. pdf.

[28] Winters, K.C., Fahnhorst, T., Botzet, A., Lee, S., & Lalone, B. (2012). Brief intervention for drug-abusing adolescents in a school setting: outcomes mediating factors. *Journal of Substance Abuse Treatment, 42(3),* 279-88.

[29] Substance Abuse and Mental Health Services Administration. (2013). *Results from the 2012 national survey on drug use and health: Summary of national findings* (NSDUH Series H-46, HHS Publication No. (SMA) 13-4795). Rockville, MD: Substance Abuse and Mental Health Services Administration.

[30] National Institute on Drug Abuse. (2012). *Medication assisted treatment for opioid addiction.* Retrieved from http://www.drugabuse.gov/publications/topics-in-brief/medication-assisted-treatment-opioid-addiction.

[31] Substance Abuse and Mental Health Services Administration. (2011). Medication-assisted treatment for opioid addiction: Facts for families and friends. Rockville, MD: Substance Abuse and Mental Health Services Administration. Retrieved from http://store.samhsa.gov/ shin/content/SMA09-4443/SMA09-4443.pdf.

[32] Centers for Disease Control and Prevention. (2012). Integrated prevention services for HIV infection, viral hepatitis, sexually transmitted diseases, and tuberculosis for persons who use drugs illicitly: Summary guidance from CDC and the U.S. Department of Health and Human Services. Mortality and Morbidity Weekly Report, Recommendations and Reports, 61(5): 1-47. Retrieved from http://www.cdc.gov/mmwr/preview/mmwrhtml/ rr6105a1.htm?s_cid=rr6105a1_w.

[33] U.S. Department of Veterans Affairs. (2014). *Veterans Health Administration.* http://www.va.gov/health/. Retrieved from http://www.va.gov/health/.

[34] amfAR, The Foundation for AIDS Research. (2013). Syringe exchange program coverage in the United States–July 2013. Retrieved from http://www.amfar.org/uploadedFiles/ _amfarorg/Articles/In_The_Community/2013/ July%202013%20SEP%20Map%20.pdf.

[35] Teplin, L.A., Abram K.M., McClelland, G.M, Dulcan, M.K, & Mericle, A.A. (2002). Psychiatric disorders in youth in juvenile detention. *Archives of General Psychiatry, 59(12),* 1133–1143.

[36] Centers for Disease Control and Prevention. (2012). Integrated prevention services for HIV infection, viral hepatitis, sexually transmitted diseases, and tuberculosis for persons who use drugs illicitly: Summary guidance from CDC and the U.S. Department of Health and Human Services. Mortality and Morbidity Weekly Report, Recommendations and Reports,

61(5): 1-47. Retrieved from http://www.cdc.gov/mmwr/preview/mmwrhtml/rr6105a1.htm?s_cid=rr6105a1_w.

37 Glaze, L. E. & Herberman, E.J. (2013). Correctional populations in the United States, 2012. Bureau of Justice Statistics, NCJ 243936. Retrieved from http://www.bjs.gov/content/pub/pdf/cpus12.pdf.

38 Walmsley, R. (2013) World Prison Population List (10th edition). International Centre for Prison Studies. Retrieved from http://www.prisonstudies.org/sites/prisonstudies.org/files/resources/downloads/wppl_10.pdf.

39 California Department of Corrections and Rehabilitation. (2012). *Outcome evaluation report.* Sacramento: CDCR Office of Research. Retrieved from http://www.cdcr.ca.gov/adult_research_branch/Research_Documents/ARB_FY_0708_Recidivism_Report_10.23.12.pdf.

40 The Federal Interagency Reentry Council includes the Departments of Justice, Health and Human Services, Education, Labor, Veterans Affairs, Interior, Agriculture, Housing and Urban Development, Office of National Drug Control Policy, U.S. Social Security Administration, Domestic Policy Council, U.S. Equal Employment Opportunity Commission, White House Office of Faith-Based and Neighborhood Partnerships, Office of Personnel Management, Office of Management and Budget, Internal Revenue Service, Federal Trade Commission, U.S. Interagency Council on Homelessness, U.S. Small Business Administration, and Court Services and Offender Supervision Agency.

41 Camden, NJ; New Orleans, LA; Philadelphia, PA; Memphis, TN; Minneapolis, MN; San José, CA; Salinas, CA; Detroit, MI; Chicago, IL; and Boston, MA.

42 Clackamas County, OR; Essex County, MA; Saline County, AR; and Tarrant County, TX.

43 The other two regional mentor community courts are in Hartford, CT and Seattle, WA.

44 Holder, E. (2013). *Department policy on charging mandatory minimum sentences and recidivist enhancements in certain drug cases.* Washington: U.S. Department of Justice. Retrieved from www.justice.gov/oip/docs/ag-memo-department-policypon-charging-mandatory-minimum-sentences-recidivist- enhancements-in-certain-drugcases.pdf.

45 Parsons, J., Drucker, E., & Clear, T. (2014). A natural experiment in reform: Analyzing drug law policy change in New York. New York, NY: The Vera Institute of Justice. Retrieved from http://www.vera.org/project/analyzing-drug-policy-change-new-york.

46 Federal Interagency Reentry Council. (2013). Justice-involved veterans: Accomplishments to date. Retrieved from http://csgjusticecenter.org/wp-content/uploads/2013/06/SnapShot_Veterans.pdf.

47 The White House. (2013). *Establishing the White House Council on Native American Affairs* (Executive Order 13647). Retrieved from http://www.whitehouse.gov/the-press-office/2013/06/26/executive-order-establishing- white-house-council-native-american-affairs.

48 National Institute of Justice. (2011). *Evaluating Delaware's decide your time program for drug-using offenders under community supervision.* Washington: U.S. Department of Justice. Retrieved from http://www.nij.gov/topics/corrections/community/drug-offenders/pages/decide-your-time.aspx.

49 Substance Abuse and Mental Health Services Administration. (2013). *Results from the 2012 national survey on drug use and health: Mental health findings* (NSDUH Series H-47, HHS Publication No. (SMA) 13-4805). Rockville, MD: Substance Abuse and Mental Health Services Administration. Retrieved from http://www.samhsa.gov/data/NSDUH/2k12MH_FindingsandDetTables/2K12MHF/NSDUHmhfr2012.htm#ch5.

50 Homeless grants: 110 grants, 5,369 clients served; HIV grants: 112 grants, 7,987 clients served; criminal justice grants: 197 grants, 9,022 clients served.

51 U.S. Department of Justice. (2014). *In new step to fight recidivism, Attorney General Holder announces Justice Department to require federal halfway houses to boost treatment services for inmates prior to release.* Washington: U.S. Department of Justice. Retrieved from http://www.justice.gov/opa/pr/2014/March/14-ag-301.html.

[52] U.S. Equal Employment Opportunity Commission. (2012). *Consideration of arrest and conviction records in employment decisions under Title VII of the Civil Rights Act of 1964.* Retrieved from http://www.eeoc.gov/laws/guidance/arrest_conviction.cfm.

[53] U.S. Department of Labor, Office of Federal Contract Compliance Programs. *Complying with nondiscrimination provisions: Criminal record restrictions and discrimination based on race and national origin.* Retrieved from http://www.dol.gov/ofccp/regs/compliance/directives/Dir306.htm.

[54] U.S. Office of Personnel Management. *Contractor fitness adjudication – Best practices.* Retrieved from http://chcoc.gov/transmittals/TransmittalDetails.aspx?TransmittalID=5585.

[55] Administrative data reported to the Office of National Drug Control Policy by the U.S. Department of Labor, November 2013.

[56] Bureau of Justice Statistics. *Recidivism of Prisoners Released in 30 States in 2005: Patterns from 2005 to 2010.* Retrieved from www.bjs.gov/content/pub/pdf/rprts05p0510.pdf.

[57] The White House. *Continuing to Strengthen Border Security.* Retrieved from http://www.whitehouse.gov/issues/immigration/border-security.

[58] Written responses of the Attorney General to Questions for the Record from the U.S. House of Representatives Committee on the Judiciary; May 15, 2013. Retrieved from http://judiciary.house.gov/_cache/files/33900c77-cbb6-4e1e-9b65-c9c5908af8a4/113-43-doj-response-to-qfrs.pdf.

[59] Office of National Drug Control Policy. (2013). High intensity drug trafficking areas program report to Congress. Washington. D.C.: Office of National Drug Control Policy.

[60] Email communication from OCDETF, November 15, 2013.

[61] U.S. Immigration and Customs Enforcement. (2013). Border Enforcement Security Task Force (BEST). Retrieved from http://www.ice.gov/best/.

[62] These assessments include in-depth analysis of each trafficking corridor's criminal infrastructure—its strengths, weaknesses, and abilities to effectively transport drugs across the border.

[63] Funds are intended to enhance cooperation and coordination among local, tribal, territorial, state, and Federal law enforcement agencies in a joint mission to secure the U.S. borders along routes of ingress from international borders, to include travel corridors in states bordering Mexico and Canada, as well as states and territories with international water borders.

[64] Cole, J.M. (2013). Guidance regarding marijuana enforcement. Washington: Department of Justice. Retrieved from http://www.justice.gov/iso/opa/resources/3052013829132756857467.pdf.

[65] Unpublished data from the DEA Domestic Cannabis Eradication/Suppression Program (DCE/SP).

[66] Unpublished data from the Campaign Against Marijuana Planting (CAMP).

[67] Gabriel, M., Higley, J.M., Wengert, G., Woods, L., & Poppenga, R. (2013). *Intentional poisoning of a fisher (martes pennant) with a carbamate insecticide laced bait at an illegal marijuana trespass cultivation site.* Retrieved from http://www.iercecology.org/wp-content/uploads/2013/08/Fisher_Poisoning_July_2013.pdf.

[68] Drug Enforcement Administration. (2014). DEA programs: Cannabis eradication. Retrieved from http://www.justice.gov/dea/ops/cannabis.shtml.

[69] According to the American Association of Poison Control Centers, "the term 'exposure' means someone has had contact with the substance in some way; for example, ingested, inhaled, absorbed by the skin or eyes, etc. Not all exposures are poisonings or overdoses."

[70] American Association of Poison Control Centers. (2013). *Synthetic marijuana.* Retrieved October 30, 2013 from http://www.aapcc.org/alerts/synthetic-marijuana/.

[71] Montana All Threat Intelligence Center & North Dakota State and Local Intelligence Center. (2012). Impact of population growth on law enforcement in the Williston Basin Region. Retrieved from http://www.ag.nd.gov/reports/JOINTPRODUCTFINAL.pdf.

[72] Drug Enforcement Administration. Data from the National Seizure System.

[73] The Consolidated Counterdrug Database serves as the approved mechanism and national repository for recording international movement, seizures, and disruption of illicit narcotics, to include cocaine, Amphetamine Type Stimulants/Precursors (ATS/P), and heroin.

[74] Johnston, L. D., O'Malley, P. M., Miech, R. A., Bachman, J. G., & Schulenberg, J. E. (2014). Monitoring the Future national results on drug use: 1975-2013: Overview, Key Findings on Adolescent Drug Use. Ann Arbor: Institute for Social Research, the University of Michigan.

[75] American Association of Poison Control Centers. Synthetic Marijuana Data, February 28, 2014. Retrieved from https://aapcc.s3.amazonaws.com/files/library/Syn_Marijuana_Web_Data_through_2.2014.pdf.

[76] American Association of Poison Control Centers. Bath Salts Data, February 28, 2014. Retrieved from https://aapcc.s3.amazonaws.com/files/library/Bath_Salts_Web_Data_through_2.2014.pdf.

[77] Substance Abuse and Mental Health Services Administration. *Drug Abuse Warning Network, 2011: National Estimates of Drug-Related Emergency Department Visits*. HHS Publication No. (SMA) 13-4760, DAWN Series D-39. Rockville, MD: Substance Abuse and Mental Health Services Administration, 2013.

[78] Drug Enforcement Administration. Microgram Bulletin. Volume 44, number 3, March 2011.

[79] Drug Enforcement Administration. Schedules of controlled substances: Extension of temporary placement of five synthetic cannabinoids into Schedule I of the Controlled Substances Act. February 24, 2012. Retrieved from http://www.justice.gov/dea/docs/extension_of_temporary_placement_of_5_synthetic_cannabinoids.pdf.

[80] National Conference of State Legislatures (as of November 28, 2012). Retrieved from http://www.ncsl.org/research/civil-and-criminal-justice/synthetic-cannabinoids-enactments.aspx.

[81] National Conference of State Legislatures (as of November 28, 2012). Retrieved from http://www.ncsl.org/research/civil-and-criminal-justice/substituted-cathinones-enactments.aspx.

[82] Office of National Drug Control Policy. (2013). *Arrestee drug abuse monitoring (ADAM) II 2012 annual report.*Washington: Office of National Drug Control Policy. Retrieved from http://www.whitehouse.gov/sites/default/files/ondcp/policy-and-research/adam_ii_2012_annual_rpt_final_final.pdf.

[83] Office of National Drug Control Policy. (2013). *Community drug early warning system: The CDEWS pilot project.* Washington: Office of National Drug Control Policy. Retrieved from http://www.whitehouse.gov/sites/default/files/finalreport_with_cover_09172013.pdf.

[84] O'Malley, P. & Johnston, L. (2013). Driving after drug or alcohol use by US high school seniors, 2001 2011. *American Journal of Public Health*, 103(11), 2027-2034.

[85] Substance Abuse and Mental Health Services Administration. (2013). *Results from the 2012 national survey on drug use and health: Summary of national findings* (NSDUH Series H-46, HHS Publication No. (SMA) 13-4795). Rockville, MD: Substance Abuse and Mental Health Services Administration.

[86] Ibid.

[87] National Traffic Highway Safety Administration. (2010). *Drug per se laws: A review of their use in the states* (Traffic Tech: Technology Transfer Series, 393). Washington: National Traffic Highway Safety Administration.

[88] Substance Abuse and Mental Health Services Administration. (2013). *Results from the 2012 national survey on drug use and health: Detailed tables* (NSDUH Series H-46, HHS Publication No. (SMA) 13-4795). Rockville, MD: Substance Abuse and Mental Health Services Administration. Retrieved from http://www.samhsa.gov/data/ NSDUH/2012SummNatFindDetTables/NationalFindings/NSDUHresults2012.htm#fig7.3.

[89] Substance Abuse and Mental Health Services Administration. (2011). *Treatment Episode Data Set (TEDS) 1999-2010, National Admissions to Substance Abuse Treatment Services.* Rockville, MD: Substance Abuse and Mental Health Services Administration. Retrieved

from http://wwwdasis.samhsa.gov/webt/tedsweb/tab_year.choose_year_web_table?t_state =US.

[90] Substance Abuse and Mental Health Services Administration. (2013) Drug Abuse Warning Network, 2011: National estimates of drug-related emergency department visits. HHS Publication Number (SMA) 13-4760, DAWN Series D-39. Rockville, MD: Substance Abuse and Mental Health Administration.

[91] Centers for Disease Control and Prevention, National Center for Health Statistics. Underlying Cause of Death 2000-2010 on CDC WONDER Online Database. Extracted February 2013.

[92] Jones, C.M., Mack, K.A., & Paulozzi, L.J. (2013). Pharmaceutical overdose deaths, United States, 2010. *Journal of theAmerican Medical Association, 309(7)*, 657-9.

[93] Centers for Disease Control and Prevention, National Center for Health Statistics. Underlying Cause of Death 2000-2010 on CDC WONDER Online Database. Extracted February 2013.

[94] Paulozzi, L.; Baldwin, G.; Franklin, G.; Kerlikowske, R.G.; Jones, C.H.; Ghiya, N.; and Popovic, T. CDC grand rounds: prescription drug overdoses—a U.S. epidemic. MMWR 61(01); 10-13, January 13, 2012.

[95] Substance Abuse and Mental Health Services Administration. (2013). *Results from the 2012 national survey on drug use and health: Summary of national findings* (NSDUH Series H-46, HHS Publication No. (SMA) 13-4795). Rockville, MD: Substance Abuse and Mental Health Services Administration. http://www.samhsa.gov/data/ NSDUH/2012SummNat FindDetTables/NationalFindings/NSDUHresults2012.htm#ch2.3.

[96] Florida Department of Law Enforcement. (2013). Drugs identified in deceased persons by Florida medical examiners: 2012 report [PowerPoint slides]. Retrieved from http://www. fdle.state.fl.us/Content/getdoc/79241c67-253b-45eb-a238-1a07cf4a2a0c/2012-Drug-Report_Final.aspx.

[97] Tennessee Department of Health. (2014). Controlled substance monitoring database: 2014 report to the 108th Tennessee General Assembly. Retrieved from http://health.tn.gov/statistics/Legislative_Reports_PDF/CSMD_AnnualReport_2014.pdf.

[98] Mezei, L. & Murinson, B.B. (2011). Pain education in North American medical schools. *The Journal of Pain, 12(12)*, 1199-1208.

[99] U.S. Government Accountability Office. (2011). *Prescription pain reliever abuse*. Washington: Government Accountability Office. Retrieved from http://www.gao.gov/assets/ 590/587301.pdf.

[100] Iowa Board of Medicine. (2011). *New rules require physicians to complete training on chronic pain, end-of-life care.* Retrieved from http://medicalboard.iowa.gov/ Board%20News/2011/New%20rules%20physicians%20to%20 complete%20training%20chronic%20pain_08182011.pdf.

[101] Kentucky Board of Medical Licensure. (2012). *House bill 1.* Retrieved from http://kbml.ky.gov/hb1/Pages/default.aspx.

[102] Massachusetts Executive Office of Health and Human Services. (2011). *PMP and mandatory educational requirements for prescribers*. Retrieved from http://www.mass.gov/eohhs/ provider/licensing/occupational/dentist/ pmp-and-mandatory-educational-requirements-for-pre.html.

[103] General Assembly of the State of Ohio. (2012). *129th General Assembly – Amended Substitute Senate Bill Number 83.* Retrieved from http://www.legislature.state.oh.us/ bills.cfm?ID=129_SB_83.

[104] State of Tennessee. (2013). *Public Chapter No. 430 – Senate Bill 676.* Retrieved from http://www.tn.gov/sos/acts/108/pub/pc0430.pdf.

[105] Utah Division of Occupational and Professional Licensing. (2012). *Utah Controlled Substances Act, 58-37-6.5.* Retrieved from http://www.dopl.utah.gov/laws/58-37.pdf#page=24.

[106] ER/LA Opioid Analgesics REMS Program Web Site. (2014). *Listing of Accredited CME/CE REMS-Compliant Activities Supported by RPC.* Retrieved from https://search.er-[1]a-opioidrems.com/Guest/GuestPageExternal.aspx.

[107] Ibid.

[108] Substance Abuse and Mental Health Services Administration. (2013). *Managing chronic pain in adults with or in recovery from substance use disorders.* Rockville, MD: Substance Abuse and Mental Health Services Administration. Retrieved from http://store.samhsa.gov/shin/content/SMA12-4671/TIP54_LitRev_Jan2012.pdf.

[109] U.S. Food and Drug Administration. (2013). *ER/LA opioid analgesic class labeling changes and postmarket requirements – Letter to ER/LA opioid application holders.* Retrieved from http://www.fda.gov/downloads/Drugs/DrugSafety/InformationbyDrugClass/UCM367697.pdf.

[110] U.S. Food and Drug Administration. (2013). FDA approves abuse-deterrent labeling for reformulated OxyContin.Retrieved from http://www.fda.gov/newsevents/newsroom/pressannouncements/ucm348252.htm.

[111] Drug-free communities support program: 2012 national evaluation report. (2013). Fairfax, VA: ICF International.

[112] Offices of the United States Attorneys. USAOs involved in prevention. Retrieved from http://www.justice.gov/usao/briefing_room/dp/usaoprevention.html.

[113] Lakin, M. (2012). Doctor: Drug war in East Tennessee needs 'multi-pronged approach'. Knoxnews.com. Retrieved from http://www.knoxnews.com/news/2012/nov/28/doctor-drug-war-in-east-tennessee-needs-multi/?print=1.

[114] National Association of Boards of Pharmacy. (2014). *NABP PMP InterConnect.* http://www.nabp.net/programs/pmp-interconnect/nabp-pmp-interconnect.

[115] Substance Abuse and Mental Health Services Administration. (2013). FY 2013 SAMHSA Grant Awards, CSAT / TI-13-013, EHR and PDMP Integration. Retrieved from http://www.samhsa.gov/grants/2013/awards/ti_13_013.aspx.

[116] Substance Abuse and Mental Health Services Administration. (2013). *Results from the 2012 national survey on drug use and health: Summary of national findings* (NSDUH Series H-46, HHS Publication No. (SMA) 13-4795). Rockville, MD: Substance Abuse and Mental Health Services Administration. Retrieved from http://www.samhsa.gov/data/ NSDUH/2012SummNatFindDetTables/NationalFindings/NSDUHresults2012.htm#ch2.16.

[117] Drug Enforcement Administration. (2014). *DEA holds its eighth prescription drug take back day on Saturday April 26.* Retrieved from http://www.justice.gov/dea/divisions/hq/2014/hq042114.shtml.

[118] Centers for Disease Control and Prevention, National Center for Health Statistics. Underlying Cause of Death 2000-2010 on CDC WONDER Online Database. Extracted January, 2013.

[119] Substance Abuse and Mental Health Services Administration. (2013). *Opioid Overdose Prevention Toolkit.* Rockville, MD: Substance Abuse and Mental Health Services Administration. Retrieved fromhttp://store.samhsa.gov/product/Opioid-Overdose-Prevention-Toolkit/SMA13-4742.

[120] American Society of Anesthesiologists. (2013). *Opioid overdose resuscitation card.* Retrieved fromhttp://www.asahq.org/WhenSecondsCount/~/media/For%20the%20Public%20Media/Patient%20Education/ Opioid%20Overdose%20Card.pdf.

[121] U.S. Department of Justice. (2014). Attorney General Holder, calling rise in heroin overdoses 'urgent public health crisis,' vows mix of enforcement, treatment. Retrieved from http://www.justice.gov/opa/pr/2014/March/14-ag-246.html.

[122] Unpublished data from the Quincy Police Department.

[123] University of Rhode Island College of Pharmacy. (2011). *Opioids: Addiction, overdose prevention (naloxone) and patient education.* Retrieved from http://prescribetoprevent.org/wp-content/uploads/2012/11/naloxoneCEU_vURI_CE.pdf.

[124] Bennet, A.S., Elliott, L., & Golub, A. (2013). Opioid and other substance misuse, overdose risk, and the potential for prevention among a sample of OEF/OIF veterans in New York City. *Substance Use and Misuse, 48(10):* 894–907. Retrieved from http://www.ncbi.nlm.nih.gov/pmc/articles/PMC3789237/.

[125] The Network for Public Health Law. (2013). *Legal interventions to reduce overdose mortality: Naloxone access and overdose good samaritan laws*. Retrieved from http://www.networkforphl.org/_asset/qz5pvn/network-naloxone-10-4.pdf.

[126] Creanga, A.A., Sabel, J.C., Ko, J.Y., Wasserman, C.R., Shapiro-Mendoza, C.K., Taylor, P., Barfield, W., Cawthon, L., & Paulozzi, L.J. (2012). Maternal drug use and its effect on neonates: A population-based study in Washington State. *Obstetric Gynecology, 119(5):* 924-33. Retrieved from http://www.ncbi.nlm.nih.gov/pubmed/22525903.

[127] Epstein, R.A., Bobo, W.V., Martin, P.R., Morrow, J.A., Wang, W., Chandrasekhar, R., & Cooper, W.O. (2013). Increasing pregnancy-related use of prescribed opioid analgesics. *Annals of Epidemiology, 23(8)*: 498-503. Retrieved from http://www.ncbi.nlm.nih.gov/pubmed/23889859.

[128] Patrick, S., Schumacher, R.E., Benneyworth, B.D., Krans, E.E., McAllister, J.M., & Davis, M.M. (2012). Neonatal abstinence syndrome and associated health care expenditures: United States, 2000-2009. *Journal of the American Medical Association, 307(18)*: 1934-40. Retrieved from http://www.ncbi.nlm.nih.gov/pubmed/22546608.

In: Drug Control in the United States
Editor: Ivan T. Rains
ISBN: 978-1-63321-969-4

Chapter 2

INSANITY: FOUR DECADES OF U.S. COUNTERDRUG STRATEGY*

Michael F. Walther

ABSTRACT

In the four decades since President Richard Nixon first declared war on drugs, the U.S. counterdrug strategy has remained virtually unchanged—favoring supply-reduction, law enforcement, and criminal sanctions over demand reduction, treatment, and education. While the annual counterdrug budget has ballooned from $100 million to $25 billion, the availability of most illicit drugs remains at an all-time high. The human cost is staggering—nearly 40,000 drug-related deaths in the United States annually. The societal impact, in purely economic terms, is now estimated to be approximately $200 billion per year. The global illicit drug industry now accounts for 1 percent of all commerce on the planet—approximately $320 billion annually. Legalization is almost certainly not the answer; however, an objective analysis of available data confirms that: 1) the United States has pursued essentially the same flawed supply-reduction strategy for 40 years; and, 2) simply increasing the amount of money invested each year in this strategy will not make it successful. Faced with impending budget cuts and a future of budget austerity, policymakers must replace the longstanding U.S. counterdrug strategy with a pragmatic, science-based, demand-reduction strategy that

* This is an edited, reformatted and augmented version of a Carlisle Paper, issued by the Strategic Studies Institute, December 2012.

offers some prospect of reducing the economic and societal impacts of illicit drugs on American society.

> The definition of insanity is doing the same thing over and over again and expecting different results.
>
> Albert Einstein[1]

For nearly 2 centuries, North America was "a dope fiend's paradise."[2] American colonists and their native predecessors came to rely upon derivatives of natural substances to cure ailments, increase sexual potency, relieve pain, and provide pleasure.[3] By the early-1800s, a burgeoning patent medicine industry advertised preparations containing large quantities of opium;[4] in 1844, cocaine was first isolated in pure form from coca leaves;[5] in 1874, heroin was synthesized and recommended as more effective, and less dangerous and addicting, than morphine;[6] and amphetamines were first synthesized in 1887.[7] Most Americans know little of their nation's antebellum drug history, i.e., the 200 years that preceded the war on drugs, and nearly all are unaware that drugs were legal for most of that period.

However, late in the 19th century, a nascent drug prohibition movement began to develop.[8] Before long, a combination of evangelical prohibitionists and Progressive Era reformers mounted a successful campaign for the first federal anti-narcotics legislation.[9] The Harrison Act,[10] passed in 1914, became the basis for narcotics regulation over the next half-century.[11] In 1918, 3 years after the Act went into effect, a congressional study found that the use of drugs—narcotics as well as cocaine—had actually increased.[12]

On January 1, 1932, the Treasury Department's newly formed Federal Bureau of Narcotics (FBN) assumed responsibility for the enforcement of federal drug laws. The FBN's first director, Harry Anslinger, has been described as "the personification of the antinarcotic regime."[13] Over the course of 30 years and five administrations, he championed a punitive drug policy that today, more than a half-century later, still serves as the foundation of our prohibitionist drug strategy.[14]

Our national drug strategy has essentially always been two-dimensional: supply-reduction (controlling the supply of drugs through legislation, law enforcement, interdiction, prosecution, and incarceration); and demand-reduction (reducing the demand for drugs through education, prevention, and treatment).[15] Although perhaps oversimplified, the distinction between supply and demand programs has framed much of the drug policy debate in America over the past 40 years.[16] Every administration has advocated a "balanced" approach incorporating both supply-reduction and demand-reduction programs. However, the distribution of resources, i.e., the supply/demand split, has become "the metric for the debate."[17] Thus, accurate analysis of any administration's drug strategy requires that we ignore the rhetoric and "follow the money."[18]

Soon after his inauguration, President Nixon unveiled the first comprehensive national strategy aimed at reducing drug abuse and ameliorating its harmful effects. The early emphasis was on treatment and rehabilitation, and budget expenditures between 1970 and 1974 included dramatic increases, with a spending distribution that disproportionately favored demand-reduction over enforcement.[19] The 1973 drug budget was the high-water mark for demand-reduction funding—at approximately 70 percent of the total counterdrug budget.[20]

Was the Nixon approach favoring demand-reduction an effective strategy? If one measures results by falling crime rates in major cities, the large-scale successful treatment of addicts, and a reduction in the availability of illicit drugs, the answer is almost certainly "yes."[21] However, the 1972 reelection campaign and the Watergate scandal marked a turning point in the Nixon strategy.[22] Despite evidence that a balance between law enforcement and demand-reduction could be effective, the need to be seen as "tough-on-crime" allowed politics to trump a well-reasoned public policy and a strategy based on science-driven methodologies.[23] Future drug budgets would reflect this shift in strategy.

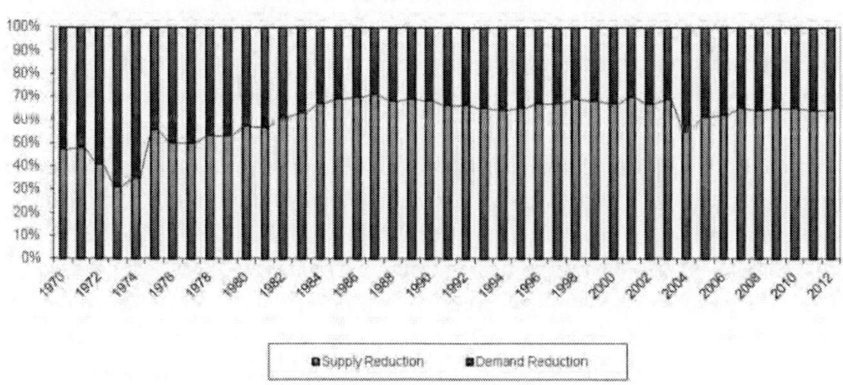

Figure 1. Spending Ratio as a Percentage of the Total Counterdrug Budget.

The percentage of resources allocated to demand-reduction declined steadily after 1973.[24] By the end of the Gerald Ford administration, federal drug spending was nearly evenly divided between supply-reduction and demand-reduction, and remained that way through the Jimmy Carter administration.[25] The Ronald Reagan administration and the drug strategies of the 1980s shifted the emphasis even further toward supply-reduction and "took a far more punitive approach toward drug use."[26] The allocation of the federal drug budget reflected this change in policy. The spending balance ultimately became two-thirds for supply-reduction and one-third for demand-reduction and, as detailed herein, that ratio has essentially remained unchanged. See Figure 1.

Over the past 40 years, the federal counterdrug budget has ballooned from $100 million to $25 billion.[27] Yet, the availability of most illicit drugs remains at an all-time high, and the United States has an estimated 10 times as many hardcore users as it did in 1969.[28] The global illicit drug industry now accounts for 1 percent of all commerce on the planet—about $320 billion annually.[29] An estimated 40,000 Americans die each year from drug-related causes; another 500,000 Americans are incarcerated for nonviolent, drug-related crimes;[30] and, in purely economic terms, the cost of illicit drug use is nearly $200 billion per year.[31] Yet, we continue to pursue the same failing strategy—favoring supply-reduction over demand-reduction—while expecting different results.

The U.S. counterdrug strategy—its focus on supply-reduction largely unchanged over the last 4 decades—has been an abject failure. The current Drug Czar, Gil Kerlikowske, has conceded as much: "In the grand scheme, it has not been successful. . . . Forty years later, the concern about drugs and drug problems is, if anything, magnified, intensified."[32] Meanwhile, research (and history[33]) has shown that demand-reduction programs are "very effective in reducing drug demand, saving lives, and lessening health and crime consequences."[34] Moreover, demand-reduction programs make economic sense. Eradication of drugs in source countries and interdiction on the high seas is expensive and has had little effect on drug availability.[35] In general, law enforcement efforts cost 15 times as much as treatment to achieve the same reduction in societal costs,[36] whereas, every dollar spent on treatment saves taxpayers between $7.46 and $11.54.[37]

Clearly, law enforcement and the criminal justice system must remain among the pillars of any new strategy. They are powerful tools of "coercion" to help users stop abusing drugs and committing drug-related crimes. Therefore, we must focus our efforts on those drugs that inherently pose greater risk to the individuals and to society lest we squander valuable law enforcement resources and escalate the economic and societal cost of imprisoning hundreds of thousands of Americans.

At the turn of the last century, Americans could generally buy cocaine, morphine, and heroin over the counter at any pharmacy.[38] Addiction rates ranged from 0.4 percent to 1.2 percent of the adult population.[39] Today, after 100 years of drug prohibition policies, an estimated 7 million Americans—approximately 2.3 percent of the adult population—depend on or abuse illicit drugs.[40]

A brief review of the counterdrug policies pursued by each administration over the last 40 years demonstrates that a new, more pragmatic, strategic approach is clearly required—one that begins with an armistice in the war on drugs and a reallocation of spending toward demand-reduction programs that have proven more effective in reducing drug use and its damaging consequences.[41]

The Nixon and Ford Administrations: 1969-77

> This Administration has declared all-out, global war on the drug menace.
>
> Richard M. Nixon[42]

The 1968 Presidential election occurred against a backdrop that included the assassinations of civil rights leader Martin Luther King, Jr., and presidential candidate Robert F. Kennedy; race riots in major cities across the country; widespread violent demonstrations against the Vietnam War; and a growing epidemic of drug use among America's youth.[43] Troubling accounts of drug abuse by servicemen in Southeast Asia filled the media,[44] along with reports of escalating drug-related crime in major urban centers.[45]

Former Vice President Nixon won the election, following a campaign that promised to restore law and order to the nation's cities. In a special message to Congress on July 14, 1969, Nixon declared the abuse of drugs "a serious national threat to the personal health and safety of millions of Americans."[46] Citing narcotics as "a primary cause of the enormous increase in street crimes over the last decade," Nixon's counterdrug strategy combined enhanced criminal penalties, interdiction, education, research, and rehabilitation.[47]

Nixon remained "viscerally opposed to drugs"[48] and refused any suggestion of legalization.[49] However, the center of gravity of his strategy was clearly demand-reduction.[50] The best evidence of this is the drug program budget, which increased from $81.3 million in FY 1969 to $783.6 million in FY 1973, with two-thirds of the new resources allocated to treatment and only one-third to law enforcement.[51] His appointment of an addiction-treatment specialist, Dr. Jerome Jaffe, as Director of the White House Special Action Office of Drug Abuse Prevention (SAODAP), and his legislative agenda further demonstrated his administration's commitment to a demand-reduction strategy.[52]

On June 17, 1971, Nixon officially declared the "War on Drugs."[53] Yet, despite the "get-tough" rhetoric, demand-reduction remained the strategic focus throughout his first term. Ever the pragmatist, Nixon recognized that "the laws of supply and demand function in the illegal drug business as in any other," and that the best prospect for success lay in demand-reduction and treatment programs.[54] For the first—and only—time in the history of the war on drugs, Nixon designated more federal funding for prevention and treatment than for law enforcement.[55] See Figure 2.

During Nixon's first term, new prevention strategies and data collection tools were introduced and innovative substance abuse treatment, rehabilitation, and research were supported. More funds were allocated for drug abuse prevention and treatment than for law enforcement. However, Nixon's abbreviated second term, which ended with his resignation on August 9, 1974, witnessed a clear shift in emphasis toward supply-reduction and enforcement.[57]

The national drug strategy saw little change during the Ford administration. Like Nixon, Ford appointed a task force to assess the extent of drug abuse in America. And, like Nixon, he ignored its recommendation that "priority in federal counterdrug efforts be directed to those drugs which inherently pose greater risk to the individuals and to society."[58] Smarting from criticism of the Nixon pardon and, hoping to gain support for his own election, it was politically inexpedient for Ford to appear "soft" on marijuana.[59]

The Ford administration's rhetoric called for a "balance [of] the law enforcement effort with the provision of humane and effective treatment for drug users."[60] However, overall growth of the drug budget slowed, and the spending balance between supply reduction and demand-reduction reached parity in 1976.[61] See Figure 3.

FY	$ Supply Reduction (Millions)	Percent	$ Demand Reduction (Millions)	Percent
1970	53	47	59	53
1971	82	48	89	52
1972	164	41	239	59
1973	214	31	466	69
1974	278	35	510	65

- FY 1970 represented a 50 percent increase in the overall drug budget from FY 1969.
- Spending on demand-reduction consistently exceeded spending on supply-reduction.
- 1973 was the high-water mark for demand-reduction spending (as a percentage of the total counterdrug budget).

Figure 2. The Nixon Drug Spending Record.[56]

FY	$ Supply Reduction (Millions)	Percent	$ Demand Reduction (Millions)	Percent
1975	300	40	447	60
1976	362	50	367	50
1977	368	50	369	50

- Overall growth of counterdrug budget slowed from Nixon era.
- FY 1976 brought a 10 percent decline in demand-reduction spending.
- Spending between demand-reduction and supply-reduction reached parity

Figure 3. The Ford Drug Spending Record.[62]

Unfortunately, parity in spending did not translate into a balanced counterdrug strategy—any more than an equal division of the Department of Defense (DoD) budget between the uniformed services would guarantee a balanced national defense strategy. Nevertheless, every politician wanted to be viewed as pro-law enforcement, and the "drug-abuse industrial complex"[63] soon became a powerful lobbying force, causing policy, strategy, and funding to tilt even further toward a supply-reduction orientation.

The Carter Administration: 1976-80

> Penalties against possession of a drug should not be more damaging to an individual than the use of the drug itself; and where they are, they should be changed.
>
> Jimmy Carter[64]

Jimmy Carter was inaugurated President on January 20, 1977, following a campaign that included calls to decriminalize the possession of small amounts of marijuana. Drug abuse was no longer "public enemy number one." It was merely "a serious social problem."[65]

Carter appointed Dr. Peter Bourne to serve as Director of the newly created Office on Drug Abuse Policy[66] and, soon thereafter, consistent with his campaign pledge, proposed legislation to decriminalize federal penalties for possession of up to one ounce of marijuana.[67] Carter made a very clear distinction between marijuana and "hard drugs."[68] Consistent with that view, he called for federal resources to be allocated "intelligently," urging Congress to "revise our penalty structure where necessary to concentrate on the actions (and the drugs) that are the most dangerous."[69]

Whatever hopes Carter may have had for effecting meaningful changes in drug policy were shattered on July 19, 1978, by a *Washington Post* headline: "Carter Aide Signed Fake Quaalude Prescription."[70] The story revealed that Dr. Bourne had written a prescription sedative for a fellow White House aide, using a pseudonym to mask her identity.[71] The incident erupted into a major scandal when the *Washington Times* reported that Bourne had used cocaine and marijuana at a DC party 7 months earlier.[72] Bourne quickly resigned in disgrace, and Carter retreated from drug-law reform for the rest of his embattled term.[73]

In the area of demand-reduction, Carter called on the National Institute on Drug Abuse (NIDA) to develop more programs for abusers of barbiturates and amphetamines, and supported rehabilitation and job-training programs for former heroin addicts. Like his predecessors, he frequently acknowledged the need for better coordination of federally sponsored research efforts on a variety of drugs, including opiates, alcohol, and tobacco, and expressed hope that this would save money and "lead to greater scientific understanding of addiction problems." However, in retrospect, it appears the Carter administration misjudged public and political support for any "softening" of the prohibitionist drug strategy.

Like his predecessors (and successors), Carter publicly supported international law-enforcement efforts to eradicate drugs and dismantle international trafficking networks.[74] He promoted law enforcement programs calling for "swift and severe punishment" of drug traffickers, including easing restrictions on law enforcement access to tax records of suspected traffickers, the freezing of trafficker assets, and bail restrictions for major offenders. See Figure 4.

FY	$ Supply Reduction (Millions)	$ Demand Reduction (Millions)	Percent
1978	417	376	47
1979	470	415	47
1980	553	410	43
1981	860	672	43

- Decline in demand-reduction spending that began in 1974 continued.
- Decline in demand-reduction spending would eventually stabilize at + 33 percent during the Reagan administration.

Figure 4. The Carter Drug Spending Record.[75]

Carter's drug strategy ultimately proved indistinguishable from that of Nixon and Ford. The decline in demand-reduction spending that began in 1973 continued and, in Carter's last drug budget, the demand share stood at only 43 percent. The results of the strategy were also indistinguishable. By the end of Carter's term, illegal drugs were less expensive, more available, and more widely used than on the day of his inauguration.

The Reagan Administration: 1981-89

> We've taken down the surrender flag and run up the battle flag. And we're going to win the war on drugs.
>
> Ronald Reagan[76]

"Government *is* the problem" was a slogan often repeated during the election campaign of Ronald Reagan. However, the underlying philosophy was not always practiced by his presidential administration, particularly in the area of drug policy.[77] Oversight of drug policy became concentrated in the White House, and the national drug strategy took a decidedly more supply-reduction approach, with an increased emphasis on law enforcement and increased military involvement in the war on drugs.[78]

Although the White House announced another "new, more-balanced, and better-coordinated strategy" of supply-reduction and demand-reduction programs,[79] the 1980s saw the passage of four major antidrug bills increasing criminal sanctions for drug-related offenses.[80] As evidenced by budget distribution, demand-reduction programs were a low priority. Funding for law enforcement rose to three times that for abuse-prevention and treatment programs.[81]

FY	$ Supply Reduction (Millions)	Percent	$ Demand Reduction (Millions)	%
1982	1,052	61	667	39
1983	1,259	63	738	37
1984	1,579	67	784	33
1985	1,896	69	855	31
1986	2,013	70	868	30
1987	3,379	71	1,413	29
1988	3,225	68	1,483	32
1989	4,584	69	2,080	31

- FY 1982 included a 25 percent increase for supply-reduction over FY 1981 levels, but a 1 percent decrease in demand-reduction spending.
- Demand-reduction spending steadily grew, reaching a maximum of 71 percent in FY 1987.
- FY 1982-FY 1989 witnessed the largest increases in the counterdrug budget over the last 4 decades.
- In just 13 years (FY 1973 - FY 1986), the ratio of spending—demand-reduction versus supply-reduction—shifted from 70/30 to 30/70.

Figure 5. The Reagan Drug Spending Record.[87]

It was the age of "zero tolerance."[82] Reagan shifted responsibility for the anti-drug effort from Health and Human Services to the Department of Justice.[83] Oversight and funding of demand-reduction and treatment programs were largely left to the states and the private sector.[84] In 1984, First Lady Nancy Reagan's "Just Say No" anti-drug campaign became a centerpiece of the Reagan administration's demand-reduction effort.[85] In addition to "Just Say No," the Partnership for a Drug-Free America launched a similarly memorable television ad campaign in 1987 featuring a hot skillet, a raw egg, and the phrase, "This is your brain on drugs."[86] See Figure 5.

Reagan gave Vice President George Bush the drug portfolio and free rein to expand military and intelligence community involvement in the counterdrug effort.[88] In January 1982, in response to increasing drug violence in Miami—the primary locus of cocaine smuggling at the time—Reagan created the "Vice President's Task Force on South Florida," which combined agents from Drug Enforcement Administration (DEA); Customs; Federal Bureau of Investigation (FBI); Alcohol, Tobacco and Firearms (ATF); Internal Revenue Service (IRS); Army; and Navy to mobilize against drug traffickers.[89] To whatever extent the administration's supply-reduction efforts were successful, they also had unintended consequences.[90] The South Florida Drug Task Force's successes led Colombian traffickers into partnerships with Mexican marijuana smugglers to move cocaine across the 2,000-mile U.S.-Mexican border. As more and more cocaine entered the smuggling pipeline, prices fell. Between 1980 and 1988, the wholesale price of cocaine in the United States dropped from $60,000 to $10-15,000 per kilo.[91] The per-ounce price declined from over $120 in early 1981 to just $50 in late 1988.[92]

By August 1986, Reagan had to admit that: "Despite our best efforts, illegal cocaine is coming into our country at alarming levels, and 4 to 5 million people regularly use it."[93] In October 1986, Reagan signed the Anti-Drug Abuse Act of 1986, appropriating $1.7 billion to fight the drug crisis; however, only about 25 percent of that amount was dedicated to education and treatment.[94] The bill's most consequential action was the creation of mandatory minimum penalties for drug offenses.[95]

By the mid-80s, cocaine use had spread to middle-class and poor Americans, in part because it could be purchased in smaller and less expensive units. It was the beginning of the "crack epidemic."[96] Cocaine powder retailed for $50-75 per gram, but crack sold in small vials for $5 or less.[97] It was powerfully addictive and began to devastate inner city neighborhoods.[98]

While reasonable men and women can argue how best to measure success and failure in the war on drugs, it is clear that the supply-reduction strategy of the Reagan administration failed. The magnitude of the drug problem was at least as great when Reagan left office as when he entered it.[99] In the words of one drug policy writer:

> When Reagan came into office, marijuana was cheap and plentiful, cocaine was scarce and expensive, and AIDS was unknown. When Reagan left office, pot was expensive and hard to find, cocaine was cheap and plentiful, and AIDS had become a full-blown epidemic.[100]

The George H. W. Bush Administration: 1989-93

> Take my word for it: This scourge will stop
>
> George H. W. Bush[101]

During his presidential campaign, Vice President Bush promoted an expansion of the supply-reduction strategy, declaring: "The logic is simple. The cheapest way to eradicate narcotics is to destroy them at their source. . . . We need to wipe out crops wherever they are grown and take out labs wherever they exist."[102] However, the strategy he outlined in the first prime-time address of his presidency differed significantly from his campaign rhetoric.[103] The primary focus, he announced, would be ending illicit drug use by Americans.[104] Although not abandoning foreign eradication and interdiction efforts, Bush embraced a prohibitionist strategy employing measures designed to deter drug use by enhancing the punitive consequences of such use.

FY	$ Supply Reduction (Millions)	Percent	$ Demand Reduction (Millions)	Percent
1990	6,594	68	3,165	32
1991	7,263	66	3,695	34
1992	7,815	66	4,095	34
1993	7,957	65	4,214	35

- Steady growth in overall counterdrug budget.
- Decline in demand-reduction spending stabilized at + 33 percent.

Figure 6. The George H. W. Bush Drug Spending Record.[110]

Bush's Drug Czar, William Bennett, renewed the call for an all-out war on drugs— with more resources for police, more prosecutors, and more convictions.[105] He also campaigned to make drug abuse socially unacceptable—an approach he called "denormalization."[106] This would be accomplished, Bennett argued, through a media campaign aimed at "deglamorizing" drug use and a legislative strategy aimed at denying drug abusers welfare and social services.[107] The workplace also became a new front in the war on drugs.[108] Despite a 20 percent increase in the overall federal drug budget between 1990 and 1993, the emphasis remained supply-reduction, maintaining a two-thirds to one-third ratio between supply-reduction and demand-reduction.[109] See Figure 6.

As Vice President, Bush had orchestrated an expansion of the military's role in the drug war.[111] As President, he gave the DoD increased responsibility for monitoring, detecting, and intercepting illicit drug trafficking;[112] for quadrupling funding for military drug interdiction missions; military assets; and counterdrug personnel.[113] Nevertheless, despite the $2.4 billion budgeted for it in Bush's initial proposal, the interdiction effort failed to have a meaningful impact on the drug supply.[114] In 1989, 181,000 pounds of cocaine were seized, compared with only 12,000 pounds in 1982.[115] However, this significant increase in seizures produced only a modest rise in wholesale prices and no affect at all on street prices.[116] Between 1980 and 1989, the United States spent $10 billion on interdiction, and successfully confiscated perhaps 10 percent of all cocaine entering the country.[117]

In his public rhetoric, Bush urged support for demand-reduction programs; however, research to identify and develop more effective treatment regimens remained underfunded.[118] The "treatment gap" continued to grow.[119] In contrast to Nixon's commitment that "no addict should have to commit a crime because he can't get treatment,"[120] Drug Czar Bennett argued that facilities to treat only one-quarter of America's four million addicts were enough, because two million could help themselves (without the help of a treatment facility) and the other million were lost causes.[121] The reality—ignored by Bennett and his successors—is that treatment is substantially less expensive than incarceration.[122] Providing inpatient services to four million addicts would cost a maximum of $60 billion annually, whereas holding them in jail would cost $100 billion annually.[123] Incarceration is neither a cost efficient nor an effective strategy for America's drug problems.[124]

As the Bush administration neared an end, more people were using drugs than when the war on drugs began, and the crime rate was higher than ever.[125] America's jails were bursting at the seams, as drug arrests rose from 56,013 in 1985 to 94,490 in 1989, an increase of almost 69 percent.[126] Overcrowding meant shorter sentences,[127] and shorter sentences meant drug dealers and untreated drug abusers were soon back on the street, fueling demand.[128]

The Clinton Administration: 1993-2001

> When I was in England, I experimented with marijuana a time or two, and I didn't like it. I didn't inhale and never tried it again.
>
> William J. Clinton[129]

During his presidential campaign, Governor Clinton raised the hopes of many advocates for a change in the national drug strategy by calling for treatment on demand, regardless of the cost.[130] When President Clinton took office in January 1992, specialists in academia, health care, and law enforcement around the country expected immediate and significant changes in the way the federal government addressed the national drug problem.[131] Many were disappointed when, in the early days of the Clinton administration, illicit drug use was not given the prominence and visibility that it had during the Reagan-Bush eras.[132] More would be disappointed when electoral politics and the need to appear "tough" on drugs led Clinton to adopt the same strategy and budget policies as his predecessors.[133]

It took 15 months before Clinton finally nominated a drug advisor.[134] However, the choice he ultimately made seemed to presage a new and more balanced drug strategy. Lee Brown had impeccable law enforcement credentials,[135] but was also viewed as an intellectual, with a Ph.D. in Criminology from the University of California, Berkeley. Although Clinton raised the status of the drug czar to cabinet level, he did little to enhance the prestige and nothing to enhance the authority of that office.[136]

FY	$ Supply Reduction (Millions)	Percent	$ Demand Reduction (Millions)	Percent
1994	7,760	64	4,425	36
1995	8,560	65	4,692	35
1996	9,013	67	4,441	33
1997	10,182	67	4,977	33
1998	11,106	69	4,991	31
1999	11,578	68	5,464	32
2000	12,387	67	6,067	33
2001	12,656	70	5,397	30

- Despite a steady growth in the overall counterdrug budget, the ratio of spending—supply-reduction/demand-reduction—remained + 66/33 percent.
- Despite calls for treatment on demand, demand-reduction spending failed to match the rhetoric.

Figure 7. The Clinton Drug Spending Record.[140]

In 1993, Clinton presented a $13.04 billion anti-drug budget that offered little change from the widely criticized approach followed by Presidents Reagan and Bush.[137] The budget designated $8.30 billion for law enforcement and $4.74 billion for rehabilitation and education—a proportional split of 63.66 percent to 36.34 percent—about 1 percent more for demand-reduction than Bush included in his last drug budget.[138] Overall, the Clinton budget proposal increased the funding of drug enforcement efforts to four times what they had been under Reagan.[139] See Figure 7.

Clinton's FY 1995 budget included increases of $355 million for treatment of "chronic hard-core drug users" and $191 million for "safe and drug-free school programs."[141] The budget provided additional funding to increase the availability of treatment services by 9 percent.[142] However, despite Clinton's campaign promises of "treatment on demand, regardless of the cost,"[143] it would still leave approximately one million hard-core users without access to rehabilitation.[144]

The Clinton administration introduced several initiatives designed to deter illicit drug use, including: Operation SAFE HOME,[145] the National Violent Crime Initiative,[146] and a program calling for drug testing of high school athletes.[147] However, when juvenile drug use continued to climb, and the rate of drug-related crimes increased throughout the country, administration critics demanded a more aggressive approach. Drug Czar Brown's tenure soon ended with his resignation on December 12, 1995.[148]

Giving the war on drugs a more literal spin, Clinton named General Barry McCaffrey as Drug Czar during his State of the Union address in February 1996.[149] The Senate confirmed McCaffrey's appointment 2 days later without debate.[150] McCaffrey introduced the 1996 Drug Control Strategy, a 10-year strategy that again promised a balanced approach. Rather than "zero tolerance," it established a goal of returning America to "a 1960s level, pre-Vietnam era level of drug use."[151] However, despite a substantial increase to $15.1 billion, the FY 1997 drug budget continued the two-third/one-third ratios between supply-and demand-reduction program funding.[152]

The Clinton administration continued the international supply-reduction efforts begun under Bush. In July 2000, Congress approved an emergency supplemental assistance request for fiscal years 2000-01 of $1.32 billion, as part of "Plan Colombia."[153] In addition to funding the Colombian counternarcotic effort, the aid would also be used to combat leftist guerrilla groups such as the Revolutionary Armed Forces of Colombia (FARC), which were also involved in narcotrafficking.[154]

The Clinton administration record on demand-reduction programs was, at best, mixed. The Behavioral Therapies Development Program, begun in 1994, broadened the scope of NIDA-supported behavioral research beyond clinical studies of established treatments for drug abuse.[155] The 2000 Drug Addiction Treatment Act (DATA) permitted physicians, for the first time in more than 80 years, to legally prescribe opioid medications for the nonregulated, outpatient treatment of opioid dependence.[156] However, Clinton prevented the Department of Health and Human Services from implementing its plans for a politically volatile needle-exchange program.[157]

In the end, despite the campaign rhetoric, there was no fundamental change in drug control policy during the Clinton administration. The drug budget grew from $12.1 billion in 1993 to $19.2 billion in FY 2000.[158] However, expenditures for the criminal justice system and supply-reduction programs continued to outstrip investment in prevention, treatment, and research. Incarceration for drug-law violations increased 1,100 percent between 1980 and 2002. By 1997, one million Americans were being arrested each year for violating drug laws.[159] Meanwhile, cocaine and heroin prices fell by 80 percent, and 14,000 Americans were dying annually from drug-related causes.[160]

The George W. Bush Administration: 2001-09

> When I was young and irresponsible, I was young and irresponsible.
>
> George W. Bush[161]

During the presidential election campaign, Governor George W. Bush called teen drug statistics “one of the worst public policy failures of the ‘90s.” Under the Clinton administration, Bush claimed, fighting drug abuse had ceased to be a national priority; drug policy was underfunded and lacked consistency.[162] Despite candidate Bush’s tough talk, some elements of the drug-reform community hoped that President Bush— a man who confessed his own struggle with alcohol addiction—might favor a more demand-reduction-oriented strategy. Those reformists were soon disappointed when Bush formed a counterdrug team consisting of Congressman Asa Hutchinson,[163] John Walters,[164] and former-Senator John Ashcroft.[165]

Bush’s initial drug strategy included three short-term initiatives designed to “reinvigorate” the drug war: 1) establishment of a faith-based initiative office to fund religious groups engaged in anti-drug efforts; 2) a survey of drug treatment needs and capacity along with proposals to close the treatment gap; and, 3) expanded drug testing of federal prisoners, probationers and parolees.[166] The administration also renewed its commitment to the National Youth Anti-Drug Media Campaign, calling it “the most visible symbol of the federal government’s commitment to drug prevention.”[167]

The administration’s FY 2003 drug budget requested $19.2 billion, an increase of about 2 percent over FY 2002.[168] Still smarting from the September 11, 2001 (9/11), terror attacks, the government accompanied the budget request with a campaign designed to highlight the link between drugs and terrorism.[169] See Figure 8.

FY	$ Supply Reduction (Millions)	Percent	$ Demand Reduction (Millions)	Percent
2002	12,686	67	6,136	33
2003	13,315	69	5,847	31
2004	6,705	55	5,377	45
2005	7,639	61	5,005	39
2006	7,765	62	4,810	38
2007	8,164	65	4,492	35
2008	8,344	64	4,618	36
2009	9,862	65	5,417	35

- Beginning in FY 2004, ONDCP made significant changes in the methodology used to compute the cross-cutting national drug budget. The impact of the new accounting methodology (indicated by shaded area in chart) “reduced” overall totals beginning in FY 2004 by excluding at least $7.5 billion in costs associated with the prosecution and incarceration of federal prisoners. Yet, even with these changes in methodology, the spending ratio remained virtually unchanged.

Figure 8. The George W. Bush Drug Spending Record.[170]

In announcing his strategy, Bush promised an increased emphasis on treatment and prevention and major new funding for demand-reduction initiatives.[171] Drug Czar Walters echoed the President's rhetoric, insisting that the administration was "putting a larger emphasis on treatment than the last budget and strategy did."[172] However, despite continued annual increases in the counterdrug budget, a simple review of the math demonstrates that the Bush "strategy" was the same as the Clinton strategy—"talking treatment and funding law enforcement."[173] The single largest increase in funding (10 percent) was for foreign eradication and interdiction, one of the most expensive and least effective drug fighting techniques,[174] while spending for treatment increased by only 6 percent.[175]

Like his predecessors, George W. Bush tried to spend his way to victory, allocating nearly $200 billion to the war on drugs over 8 years. Yet, a poll in October 2008, found that three in four Americans believed that the war on drugs was failing.[176] In 2009, an estimated 20 million Americans aged 12 or older used illicit drugs on a current, i.e., past month, basis—statistically unchanged since 2002.[177] Moreover, nearly half of all drug addicts who needed treatment, approximately 3.5 million, did not have access to suitable programs.

Despite the clear record of failure, the drug budget remained overwhelmingly weighted toward supply-reduction. Less than one-third of the total was designated for treatment or prevention, and much of that was appropriated for anti-drug commercials and school programs of questionable efficacy. Although overall funding grew by 39 percent between 2002 and 2009 (approximately $4.2 billion), 90 percent of the increase went to supply-reduction, while only 10 percent went to demand-reduction programs.[178] According to John Carnevale, former director of planning and budget at the ONDCP: "The strategy totally failed to achieve any progress in this key goal area. . . . Eight years were wasted."[179]

The Obama Administration: 2009-

I inhaled frequently. That was the point.

Barack Obama[180]

Barack Obama was not the first candidate to admit drug use; however, he was the first to be so completely open about it. To some, Obama's honesty about drugs reflected a generational change in politics. Voters cared more about having an honest person in the White House and less about youthful drug use.[181] Supporters and drug policy reformers were impatient for the "change" Obama promised.

Although candidate Obama called the war on drugs "an utter failure," President Obama's drug strategy has not differed significantly from that of previous administrations.[182] His Drug Czar, Gil Kerlikowske, pledged to "change the conversation on our drug problem" and abandon the "drug war" metaphor. However, the change in that rhetorical convention has meant little in the face of spending patterns, which still disproportionately favor supply-reduction over demand-reduction.

President Obama and his Drug Czar publicly express support for expanding demand-reduction initiatives, but the budget dollars have failed to match the rhetoric. The FY 2010 drug budget of $15.1 billion ($1 billion more than the Bush administration's final budget request) included the usual two-to-one spending ratio in favor of supply-reduction, as in previous administrations.[183] The Obama spending plan called for an increase in every aspect of drug-war funding except drug-use prevention (which decreased by 11 percent).[184] See Figure 9.

ONDCP promised at the time that future budgets would "reflect the President's balanced and evidence-based approach to reducing illicit drug use and will encompass . . . prevention, enforcement, and treatment." However, the 2011 drug budget still maintained the roughly two-to-one imbalance between supply-reduction and demand-reduction.[186]

On February 13, 2012, the Obama administration released its FY 2013 National Drug Control Budget, requesting nearly $26 billion for anti-drug programs. What appears to be a dramatic increase in the overall budget, however, is merely the result of another change in accounting methodology.[187] The FY 2013 proposal would increase total funding by only 1.6 percent over FY 2012, and is remarkable only in the way it closely tracks previous budgets regarding allocation of resources.[188]

As a result of this accounting "sleight of hand," the spending ratio also appears to have incrementally shifted toward demand-reduction, allocating 41.2 percent for treatment and prevention and 58.2 percent for law enforcement.[189] However, as in the previous Obama budgets, the accuracy of these percentages is questionable, since changes in the accounting methodology actually undercount the real cost of the drug war "by failing to include some significant drug policy-driven costs."[190]

FY	$ Supply Reduction (Millions)	Percent	$ Demand Reduction (Millions)	Percent
2010	9,772	65	5,260	35
2011	9,952	64	5,600	36
2012	9,690	64	5,618	36
2013	15,062	59	10,538	41

• Further changes in accounting methodology make precise comparison to earlier drug budgets difficult. However, there is no significant change in the supply-reduction/demand-reduction spending ratio.

Figure 9. The Barack Obama Drug Spending Record.[185]

In adopting talking points about treating drug abuse as a health problem, the administration has scored political points with those Americans who see the war on drugs as a failure; however, the budget has not matched the rhetoric.[191] Nowhere is the contrast clearer than in a comparison between spending for punishment and interdiction and spending for prevention, treatment, and other health approaches. In the view of many, little or nothing has changed. Despite Obama's politically popular statement that "we have to think more about drugs as a public-health problem," only appearances, not realities, have changed. While declaring that "we cannot arrest our way out of the drug problem,"[192] prevention and treatment remain severely underfunded, while law enforcement and incarceration continue to dominate our national drug strategy and consume the lion's share of the counterdrug budget.[193]

President Obama now presides over a war on drugs that employs a strategy virtually indistinguishable from that of his predecessors.[194] "The Obama drug budget is the Bush drug budget, which was the Clinton drug budget."[195] The rhetoric has remained largely unchanged for 4 decades. Successive administrations have promised new, balanced approaches while delivering the same failed strategy favoring supply-reduction (which actually did little to reduce supply[196]) over more effective and less expensive demand-reduction strategies.[197]

Proposal for an Armistice: Ending the Insanity

By nearly every measure, America's 40-year war on drugs has been an expensive failure.[198]

- $1 trillion—estimated total federal, state, and local expenditures in support of the national drug strategy since 1969.[199]
- 150 million—estimated number of Americans who will use illicit drugs at some time in their lives (nearly 50 percent of the population).[200]
- 38 million—estimated number of Americans who use illicit drugs each year (roughly 12 percent of the population).[201]
- 20 million—estimated number of Americans aged 12 and older who use illicit
- drugs on a current, i.e., past month, basis (about 6% of the population).[202]
- 7.5 million—estimated number of Americans (about 2.3 percent of the adult population) categorized as abusers or dependent on illicit drugs.[203]
- 6.3 million—estimated number of Americans needing drug treatment, but not receiving it.[204]
- 400,000—estimated number of state prisoners (approximately 25 percent of all state prisoners) serving time today for drug convictions.[205]
- 100,000—estimated number of federal prisoners (approximately half of all federal prisoners) serving time today for drug convictions.[206]
- 40,000—estimated number of Americans who die each year from drug-related causes.[207]
- 1—estimated number of drug addicted babies born every hour.[208]

Our supply-reduction efforts have had some impact on production and trafficking patterns. However, as the center of gravity of our national strategy, supply-reduction is "doomed to failure . . . by the structure and size of the drug industry."[209] Research indicates that even if the U.S. supply-reduction strategy pursued for the last 40 years had been relatively "successful" in its goals of eradication and interdiction, it would not have substantially reduced U.S. illicit drug supply.[210] Nevertheless, we have continued to invest more each year in the same, failed strategy while expecting different results.

Reasonable minds may differ regarding the exact details of a new strategy, but not about the need for one.[211] **We must make demand-reduction the focal point of our new strategy.**[212] The 2011 Report of the Global Commission on Drug Policy[213] incorporated important recommendations regarding drug abuse and trafficking, including treatment for nonviolent drug offenders and a concentrated international effort to combat violent criminal organizations rather than nonviolent, low-level offenders.[214] These recommendations are supported by ample research showing that most people who enter and remain in treatment stop using drugs; decrease their criminal activity; and improve their occupational, social, and psychological functioning.[215]

Moreover, there is abundant evidence of treatment's cost-effectiveness.[216] Accordingly, **treatment on demand must finally become a reality**, because the societal cost of untreated addiction is simply too high.[217] To be effective, treatment must be tailored to the individual and, in many cases, will require a combination of drug and behavioral therapy.[218] Research has shown such approaches effective, with 40-70 percent of patients remaining drug free.[219] Moreover, the potential for failure or relapse should not deter our efforts. Successful treatment for addiction typically requires continual evaluation and modification, just as treatments for other chronic diseases. In fact, relapse rates for addiction resemble those of other chronic diseases such as diabetes, hypertension, and asthma.[220]

Statistics show that most people who need treatment are not seeking it.[221] Therefore, **our new strategy must create incentives and opportunities for addicts to choose treatment voluntarily**.[222] Drug courts have proven to be an extremely effective incentive for many.[223] While our primary strategy should not be criminalization, studies have shown that treatment does not need to be voluntary to be effective.[224] Thus, any new strategy must include criminal sanctions to serve as "an instrument for exercising therapeutic leverage."[225] This can be accomplished in a variety of ways, including diverting nonviolent offenders to treatment and mandating treatment as a condition of probation or pretrial release.[226]

In the past, funding has never been sufficient to provide treatment on demand. Now, faced with record budget deficits and a future of austere budgets, it will be extremely difficult to find "new money" to support demand-reduction initiatives. Therefore, **we should begin by cutting wasteful spending—especially in unproductive supply-reduction programs.**[227] Reducing or eliminating expensive crop eradication programs and aid programs for foreign police and military counterdrug units that do little to directly reduce drug availability in the United States is a good place to start.[228] In addition, we should reduce DoD counterdrug dollars and reprogram the savings to fund additional drug courts along with the necessary support network.

A prerequisite to any reorientation of the national drug strategy will be **a major reorganization of ONDCP.**[229] In order to become a more effective policy leadership organization and eliminate the unhealthy interagency rivalries that have hampered productivity and led to duplication of effort and wasteful spending, ONDCP must be given more control of the counterdrug budget. Until then, no administration's rhetoric will ever become a reality.[230]

America's drug problem is extraordinarily complex. However, described in the simplest terms, it is a matter of supply and demand—the demand for drugs makes trade in illicit drugs profitable, and the resulting profits drive supply.[231] An objective review of our experience over the past 40 years confirms that our supply-reduction-focused strategy has failed. Even with unlimited resources, we could not hermetically seal America's borders to prevent illicit drugs from entering.[232]

While it would be folly to suggest that we abandon all supply-reduction efforts,[233] it is clear that prohibition "is no match for the obstinacy and ingenuity of many human beings,"[234] and, therefore, **more punitive drug policies are not the answer**.[235] Instead, we must adopt a pragmatic, science-based, demand-reduction strategy that offers some hope of reducing the economic and societal impacts of illicit drugs on America.

End Notes

[1] Although most frequently attributed to Albert Einstein, this definition of insanity has also been variously attributed to either Benjamin Franklin or Mark Twain. Another quote (indisputably Einstein's) is perhaps just as relevant to the discussion that follows:

> The prestige of government has undoubtedly been lowered considerably by the prohibition law. For nothing is more destructive of respect for the government and the law of the land than passing laws which cannot be enforced. It is an open secret that the dangerous increase of crime in this country is closely connected with this.

Albert Einstein, "My First Impression of the U.S.A.," 1921.

[2] Edward M. Brecher and the Editors of Consumer Reports, *Licit and Illicit Drugs*, Mount Vernon, NY: Consumers Union, 1972, p. 3.

[3] *Ibid.*

[4] These elixirs claimed to cure everything from nerves to marital problems, and were available at a modest price. *Ibid.*

[5] In Atlanta, Confederate veteran and pharmacist John Pemberton developed his own cocktail—a combination of wine and an extract from coca leaves—which he called Pemberton's French Wine Coca. In 1885, when Atlanta and Fulton County, Georgia, enacted temperance legislation, Pemberton replaced the wine in his recipe with a non-alcoholic syrup, and the "tonic" assumed the now-more-well-known name "Coca-Cola." Mark Pendergrast, *For God, Country, and Coca-Cola: The Definitive History of the Great American Soft Drink and the Company that Makes It*, New York: Basic Books, enlarged 2nd Ed., 2000, p. 24. Federal pure food and drug laws, enacted in 1906, forced Pemberton's successors to switch from using unadulterated coca leaves to decocainized leaves. Brecher, *Licit and Illicit Drugs*, p. 6.

[6] Samuel M. Levine, *Narcotics and Drug Abuse,* Cincinnati, OH: The W.H. Anderson Company, 1974.

[7] Elaine Casey, *History of Drug Use and Drug Users in the United States*, from "Facts About Drug Abuse— Participant Manual," The National Drug Abuse Center for Training Resource and Development, 1978, available from www.druglibrary.org/schaffer/history/casey1.htm.

[8] This prohibition movement targeted the immigrant Chinese laborers building the transcontinental railroad, who brought their opium-smoking habit with them to America. Dale Gieringer, *Anniversary of the Opium Exclusion Act*, Free Internet Press, February 15, 2006, available from drugnewsvault.blogspot.com/2006/02/anniversary-of-opium-exclusion-act.html.

[9] In mid-1906, Congress passed the Pure Food and Drug Act, which effectively eliminated cocaine and opium from all patent medicines and soft drinks by requiring accurate labeling. However, the legislation did not prohibit or outlaw the use of cocaine and opiate drugs. Lana D. Harrison, Michael Backenheimer, and James A. Inciardi, "History of Drug Legislation," available from www.cedro-uva.org/lib/harrison.cannabis.05.html .

[10] P.L. 63-223. For a full discussion of the Act, its historic underpinnings and repercussions, see *ibid*.

[11] The Act was an effort to simplify record keeping for the dispensing of narcotic drugs and regulate the production and distribution of opium and coca derivatives through licensing and taxation. Edward Jay Epstein, *Agency of Fear: Opiates and Political Power in America, 1977*, New York: G. P. Putnam's Sons, p. 26. There was little or no debate over the policy and health consequences of the Act. It was a result of the administrative fiat of the Department of the Treasury—the same agency later charged with enforcing alcohol prohibition—and gave no consideration to the views of the mainstream medical community. David Court-wright, *Dark Paradise: Opiate Addiction in America Before 1940,* Cambridge, MA: Harvard University, 1992.

[12] Brecher, "Licit and Illicit Drugs." The Congressional Committee, which included Dr. A. G. Du Mez, Secretary of the United States Public Health Service, released these findings:

> Opium and other narcotic drugs [including cocaine] . . . were being used by about a million people. The underground traffic in narcotic drugs was about equal to the legitimate medical traffic. The dope peddlers appeared to have established a national organization, smuggling the drugs in through seaports or across the Canadian or Mexican borders. . . .

The wrongful use of narcotic drugs had increased since the passage of the Harrison Act. Twenty cities, including New York and San Francisco, had reported such increases.

[13] Courtwright, *Dark Paradise: Opiate Addiction in America Before 1940.*

[14] Anslinger had previously served as Assistant Commissioner for Prohibition. He served as Commissioner of the Federal Bureau of Narcotics from 1930 until 1962.

[15] Incarceration can be both a method of demand-reduction and supply-reduction. Supply is arguably reduced, at least temporarily, whenever a drug producer or dealer goes to prison. Similarly, when a drug user goes to prison there is, albeit temporarily, a reduction in demand. In addition, many would argue that the possibility of incarceration itself has a deterrent effect on both the supply and demand elements. However, history has shown that the mere threat of incarceration—even the relative certainty of eventual incarceration—is insufficient to overcome the desire for profit and the power of addiction. Moreover, as the present Drug Czar has said on more than one occasion: "We cannot arrest our way out of the problem." R. Gil Kerlikowske, "Study: More Than Half of Adult Male Arrestees Test Positive for at Least One Drug," The Huffington Post, May 17, 2012, available from www.huffingtonpost.com/news/arrestee-drug-use. As discussed here, the issue is not whether we should do one or the other, i.e., either demand-reduction or supply-reduction; the question is whether supply-reduction should remain the center of gravity of our strategy when, after 40 years, it has failed to produce the desired results.

[16] John Carnevale and Patrick Murphy, "Matching Rhetoric to Dollars: Twenty-Five Years of Federal Drug Strategies and Budgets," *Journal of Drug issues*, Vol. 29, No. 2, Spring 1999.

[17] Patrick Murphy, "Keeping Score: The Frailties of the Federal Drug Budget," Santa Monica, CA: Rand Corporation, 1994, available from www.rand.org/pubs/issue_papers/IP138/index2.html.

[18] "Follow the money," may be the most famous "made-up" line about the Watergate reporting of *The Washington Post.* The comment, attributed to the stealthy "Deep Throat" source cultivated by Bob Wood-ward of *The Washington Post,* was a quote from the screenplay of *All the President's Men,* the movie about the work of Woodward and his *Post* colleague, Carl Bernstein. However, the phrase, "Follow the money" does not appear in Woodward and Bernstein's book about Watergate, nor was it uttered it real life by "Deep Throat." W. Joseph Campbell, "Those delicious but phony quotes 'that refuse to die'," *Media Myth Alert*, June 25, 2011, available from mediamythalert.wordpress.com/ 2011/06/25/those-delicious-but-phony-quotes-that-refuse-to-die/.

[19] Overall, the federal drug budget increased nearly tenfold, from $81.3 million in FY 1969 to $783.6 million in FY 1973. Only $228.3 million, approximately 30 percent of the total, went to law enforcement and supply-reduction efforts. The remaining 70 percent was committed to treatment, rehabilitation, research, and education. Only $58.2 million was allocated to drug treatment programs in 1971; however, by 1973, this budget had increased to $256.7 million. Strategy Council on Drug Abuse, Executive Office of the President, *Federal Strategy for Drug Abuse and Drug Traffic Prevention*, Washington, DC, U.S. Government Printing Office,1973; Carnevale and Murphy, "Matching Rhetoric to Dollars," p. 6.

[20] Demand-reduction funding, as a percentage of the total budget, began to decline during Nixon's abbreviated second term, eventually leveling off at approximately one-third of the total budget. *Ibid.*

[21] The impact was almost immediate. In New York City, the crime rate in 1972 dropped 18 percent, and, in Washington, 26.9 percent. Nationally, the crime rate fell by 3 percent, the first decline in 17 years. The rate of heroin overdose deaths, hepatitis transmission, and drug-related hospital visits also declined. Michael Massing, "Winning the Drug War Isn't So Hard After All," *The New York Times*, September 7, 1998.

[22] *Ibid.*

[23] In a speech on November 17, 1973, Nixon assured the American public: "I am not a crook." Richard Nixon's Question-and-Answer Session at the Annual Convention of the Associated Press Managing Editors Association, held at the Contemporary Hotel at Walt Disney World in Orlando, Florida, on November 17, 1973, Emerson Kent.Com, available from www.emersonkent.com/speeches/ i_am_not_a_crook.htm.

[24] Carnevale and Murphy, "Matching Rhetoric to Dollars," p. 15.

[25] *Ibid.*

[26] *Ibid.*, p. 7.

[27] An increase of approximately 40,000 percent over 40 years, adjusted for inflation. Although regular estimates of expenditures by state and local governments are not available, a 1991 federally sponsored study estimated that such expenditures nearly equaled those of the federal government. Peter Reuter, "An Assessment of ONDCP's Budget Concept," Testimony presented to the House of Representatives Committee on Government, February 10, 2005.

[28] Michael Massing, "The Fix," Berkeley, CA: University of California Press, 2000, p. 271. The same period saw only about a one-third increase in the total U.S. population, from 203 million in 1969 to 313 million in 2012.

[29] Martha Mendoza, "U.S. Drug War Has Met None of its Goals," *Associated Press*, May 13, 2010, available from www.msnbc.msn.com/id/37134751 /ns/us_news-security/t/us-drug-war-has-met-none-its-goals/.

[30] Between 1980 and 2005, the total number of inmates incarcerated for drug possession in state prisons or local jails grew by more than 1,000 percent. Paige M. Harrison and Allen J. Beck, *Prisoners in 2005*, Washington, DC: Bureau of Justice Statistics, 2005. By 2004, 419,000 drug possessors were incarcerated in state prisons or local jails at a cost of nearly $8.3 billion annually. The estimated number of inmates is based on an analysis of data collected through the *Survey of Inmates in Local Jails* and the *Survey of Inmates in State Correctional Facilities* conducted by the Bureau of Justice Statistics. The costs of incarceration are based on the conservative estimated cost of $20,000 per inmate per year. Don Stemen, "Reconsidering Incarceration: New Directions for Reducing Crime," *Crime and Incarceration*, January 2007.

[31] U.S. Department of Justice, National Drug Intelligence Center, "The Economic Impact of Illicit Drug Use on American Society," April 2011.

[32] Mendoza, "U.S. Drug War Has Met None of its Goals."

[33] Evidence that treatment works can be found by examining the one time it was actually tried—during the Nixon administration. Massing, "Winning the Drug War Isn't So Hard After All."

[34] John Carnevale, "FY02-09 Budget Emphasizes Least Effective Ingredients of Drug Policy," PRNewswire, February 20, 2009, available from www.prnewswire.com/news-releases/fy02-09-budget-emphasizes-least-effective-ingredients-of-drug-policy-57040872.html.

[35] *Ibid.*

[36] Study by the National Association of State Alcohol and Drug Abuse Directors, Johnathan Harris, *Drugged America*, New York: Four Winds Press, 1991, p. 154; C. P. Rydell and S. S. Everingham, "Controlling Cocaine," Prepared for the Office of National Drug Control Policy and the United States Army, Santa Monica, CA: Drug Policy Research Center, RAND Corporation, 1994, p. xvi.

[37] *Ibid.*

[38] Dale Gieringer, "America's Hundred Years War on Drugs: Centennial of the 1st Congressional Anti-Drug Law Prohibiting Opium in the Philippines—March 3, 1905-2005," 2005, available from www. drugsense.org/dpfca/DrugWarCentennial1.htm.

[39] Brecher, *Licit and Illicit Drugs,* p. 3.

[40] Carnevale Associates, "Policy Brief: The Continued Standstill in Reducing Illicit Drug Use," Gaithersburg, MD: September 2009. While one can hardly say that drug prohibition caused the addiction rate to double in America, it can be said with certainty that our prohibitionist approach has not prevented the increased addiction rate. A survey of 17 countries published in 2008 found that despite its punitive drug policies, the United States has the highest levels of illegal cocaine and cannabis use. The study, by Louisa Degenhardt, University of New South Wales, Sydney, Australia, and colleagues, is based on the World Health Organization's Composite International Diagnostic Interview (CIDI). A summary of the report and its findings can be found in "United States Has Highest Level Of Illegal Cocaine And Cannabis Use," *Science Daily*, June 30, 2008, available from www.sciencedaily.com/releases/2008/06/080630201007.htm. The authors found that 16.2 percent of people in the United States had used cocaine in their lifetime, a level much higher than any other country surveyed; the second-highest level of cocaine use was in New Zealand, where 4.3 percent of people reported having used cocaine. Cannabis use was also highest in the United States, at 42.4 percent, followed by New Zealand at 41.9 percent. The authors also concluded that drug use "does not appear to be simply related to drug policy, since countries with more stringent policies towards illegal drug use did not have lower levels of such drug use than countries with more liberal policies." For example, in the Netherlands, which has more liberal policies than the United States, 1.9 percent of people reported cocaine use, and 19.8 percent reported cannabis use.

[41] The scope of this paper, limited to 6,000 words, is necessarily narrow. It is a brief examination of the two-dimensional national drug strategy pursued by eight administrations over 4

decades. Any change in the strategy, or the absence of change, is measured not by the overall growth of the drug budget, but by changes in the ratio of spending between demand-reduction and supply-reduction programs. It is safe to assume that with unlimited resources, the United States would eventually spend enough on the "right" programs, or combination of programs, to ensure success regardless of our spending strategy. However, as this paper suggests, faced with the reality of finite budget resources, one must adopt a new strategy that uses limited resources for programs that promise the greatest likelihood of success.

[42] Richard Nixon: "Message to the Congress Transmitting Reorganization Plan 2 of 1973 Establishing the Drug Enforcement Administration," March 28, 1973. Online by Gerhard Peters and John T. Woolley, *The American Presidency Project*, available from www. presidency.ucsb.edu/ ws/?pid=4159.

[43] "Mixing of Mind-Altering Drugs Rises as Spread of Heroin Addiction Slows," *The New York Times*, March 25, 1973.

[44] Peter Brush, "Higher and Higher: American Drug Use in Vietnam," *Vietnam*, Vol. 15, No. 4, December 2002. Shortly after the United States began military support to South Vietnam, a high incidence of drug abuse, particularly of marijuana and more-dangerous drugs such as amphetamines and barbiturates occurred among the military stationed there. The DoD appointed several Task Forces, which reported there was a relatively low rate of drug abuse in the services. However, based on independent research, it is now generally accepted that there were anywhere from 25,000 to 50,000 American troops in Vietnam were heroin users by mid-1971, and this estimate does not include addicted servicemen who had previously served in Vietnam and returned to civilian life. Levine, *Narcotics and Drug Abuse.* In 1971, U.S. Army medical officers estimated that 10 to 15 percent of the lower-ranking enlisted personnel in Vietnam were heroin users. Alfred W. McCoy, *The Politics of Heroin*, Chicago, IL: Lawrence Hill, 1991, pp. 222-223; George S. Prugh, *Law at War: Vietnam 1964-1973*, Washington, DC: Department of the Army, 1975, p. 107.

[45] The number of heroin users has always been difficult to estimate. One author estimates the number of heroin users rose from about 50,000 in 1960 to roughly a half-million in 1970. David F. Musto, *The American Disease: Origins of Narcotic Control,* 3rd Ed., New York: Oxford University Press, 1999, p. 248. Musto cites the rapid rise of narcotic-related hepatitis cases, from about 4,000 in 1966 to about 36,000 in 1971, as an indicator of the increase in intravenous heroin use. *Ibid.*, citing Domestic Council Drug Abuse Task Force, *White Paper on Drug Abuse*, Washington, DC: Government Printing Office, 1975, p 15. An editorial on the election in *Time Magazine* stated that "law and order is a rallying cry that evokes quieter days. To some, it is also a shorthand message promising repression of the Black community," *Time Magazine*, "The Fear Campaign," October 4, 1968, available from www.time.com/ time/magazine/article/0,9171,838794,00.html#ixzz0k9Zo4DEX.

[46] Richard Nixon: "Special Message to the Congress on Control of Narcotics and Dangerous Drugs.," July 14, 1969; Gerhard Peters and John T. Woolley, *The American Presidency Project*, available from www. presidency.ucsb.edu/ws/?pid=2126. See also, www.williammhynes.com/uploads/6/3/6/7/6367404/nixon_drug_ policy_paper.pdf.

[47] *Ibid.*

[48] David F. Musto and Pamela Korsmeyer, *The Quest for Drug Control*, New Haven, CT: Yale University Press, 2002. Nixon also strongly opposed heroin-maintenance programs as an approach to reducing drug-related crime, calling heroin maintenance "a concession to weakness and defeat in the drug abuse struggle, a concession which would surely lead to the erosion of our most cherished values for the dignity of man." Richard Nixon, "Letter to Representative Peter A. Peyser Supporting Legislation To Prevent Heroin Maintenance Program," August 20, 1972, online by Gerhard Peters and John T. Woolley, *The American Presidency Project*, available from www.presidency.ucsb.edu/ws/?pid=3533. Nixon once told his drug-policy adviser, "You're the drug expert, not me, on every issue but one, and that's decriminalization of marijuana. If you make any hint of supporting [it], you are history." Richard Cortes, "Sketches of the Drug Czars," *Vanity Fair*, July 29, 2009,

available from www.vanityfair.com/politics/features/2009/07/drug-czarsslideshow200907#slide=1.

49 In March 1972, Nixon created the National Commission on Marihuana and Drug Abuse to examine the nature and extent of drug abuse demand-reduction activities and issue recommendations for future action by the administration. The Shafer Commission, named for its Chairman, Ray Shafer, conducted the first surveys of the drug use of the noninstitutionalized civilian population over 12 years of age. The Shafer Committee's report, *Marihuana: A Signal of Misunderstanding,* offered the following unanimous conclusion: "We believe that experimental or intermittent use of this drug carries minimal risk to the public health, and should not be given overzealous attention in terms of a public health response." The Shafer Committee recommended the decriminalization of marijuana, which Nixon rejected out of hand.

50 In March 1970, Nixon created the National Clearinghouse on Drug Abuse Information. Richard Nixon: "Statement Announcing an Expanded Federal Program To Combat Drug Abuse," March 11, 1970, online by Peters and Woolley, *The American Presidency Project,* available from www.presidency.ucsb.edu/ ws/?pid=2906. In July 1970, he established the Domestic Council to formulate and coordinate domestic policy recommendations. Executive Order 11151, July 1, 1970.

51 On the day he announced the War on Drugs, Nixon proposed additional FY 1972 budget appropriations of $105 million for treatment and $10 million for education and training. Richard Nixon: "Statement on Establishing the Office for Drug Abuse Law Enforcement," January 28, 1972, online by Peters and Woolley, *The American Presidency Project*, available from www.presidency.ucsb.edu/ws/?pid=3552.

52 Executive Order 11599. Richard Nixon: "Remarks About an Intensified Program for Drug Abuse Prevention and Control," June 17, 1971, online by Peters and Woolley, *The American Presidency Project*, available from www.presidency.ucsb.edu/ws/?pid=3048. The mission of the SAODAP was to provide "overall planning and policy and establish objectives for all Federal demand-reduction programs." The 2-year period between 1971 and 1973 saw the development of more treatment capacity than in the preceding 50 years. Methadone maintenance doubled in size, while nonmaintenance programs expanded by a factor of five. The Narcotics Treatment Administration (NTA) was established in 1970 to implement a bold public health strategy of providing addiction treatment on a massive scale in an effort to deal with the escalating heroin epidemic and related crime wave in Washington, DC. After only 1 year, burglaries in DC had decreased by 41 percent. DuPont worked with heroin addicts and methadone treatment in Washington, DC, during the early 1970s. Interview of Dr. Robert DuPont, PBS *Frontline*, available from www.pbs.org/wgbh/pages/frontline/shows/drugs/interviews/dupont.html. The National Institute on Drug Abuse (NIDA) was created in 1972 to serve as the centerpiece for a major Federal effort in demand-reduction. Richard Nixon: "Statement About the Drug Abuse Office and Treatment Act of 1972," March 21, 1972, Peters and Woolley *The American Presidency Project*, available from www.presidency.ucsb.edu/ws/?pid=3782.

53 In one of his most frequently quoted speeches, Nixon said, "America's public enemy number one in the United States is drug abuse. In order to fight and defeat this enemy, it is necessary to wage a new, all-out offensive." See Richard Nixon: "Remarks About an Intensified Program for Drug Abuse Prevention and Control," June 17, 1971, Peters and Woolley, *The American Presidency Project*, available from www. presidency.ucsb.edu/ws/?pid=3047. Nixon would return to the "war" metaphor throughout his administration, often in Pattonesque terms:

I consider keeping dangerous drugs out of the United States just as important as keeping armed enemy forces from landing in the United States. Dangerous drugs which come into the United States can endanger the lives of young Americans just as much as would an invading army landing in the United States. Every government which wants to move against narcotics should know that it can count on this country for our wholehearted support and assistance in doing so.

[W]e launched our crusade to save our children and now we can see that crusade moving off the defensive and on to the offensive, and beginning to roll up some victories in country after country around the world and in the United States as well.

And what is our goal now? We are living in an age, as we all know, in the era of diplomacy, when there are times that a great nation must engage in what is called a limited war. I have rejected that principle in declaring total war against dangerous drugs.

Our goal is the unconditional surrender of the merchants of death who traffic in heroin, our goal is the total banishment of drug abuse from American life, our children's lives are what we are fighting for, our children's future is the reason we must succeed.

We are going to fight this evil with every weapon at our command, and, with your help and the support of millions of concerned Americans, we are going to win.

Richard Nixon: "Remarks to the Washington Conference on International Narcotics Control," September 18, 1972, Peters and Woolley, *The American Presidency Project*, available from www.presidency.ucsb.edu/ ws/?pid=3578.

[54] Richard Nixon: "Special Message to the Congress on Drug Abuse Prevention and Control," June 17, 1971, Peters and Woolley, *The American Presidency Project*, available from www.presidency.ucsb.edu/ ws/?pid=3048.

[55] Richard Nixon: "Remarks About an Intensified Program for Drug Abuse Prevention and Control," June 17, 1971, Peters and Woolley, *The American Presidency Project*, available from www.presidency.ucsb.edu/ ws/?pid=3408.

[56] John Carnevale and Patrick Murphy, "Matching Rhetoric to Dollars: Twenty-Five Years of Federal Drug Strategies and Drug Budgets," *Journal of Drug Issues*, Vol. 29, No. 2, Spring 1999.

[57] The reasons for the shift toward a strategy of supply-reduction and law enforcement are not entirely clear. In January 1972, 6 months before the Watergate scandal erupted, Nixon established the Office of Drug Abuse Law Enforcement (ODALE) to provide advice on the effective enforcement of drug laws and to establish joint federal/local task forces to fight the drug trade at the street level. Richard Nixon: "Statement on Establishing the Office for Drug Abuse Law Enforcement," January 28, 1972, Peters and Woolley, *The American Presidency Project*, available from www.presidency.ucsb.edu/ws/?pid=3552. ODALE was intended to be an 18-month experimental project involving a dozen different departments and agencies designed to enhance cooperation between federal and local forces in the war on drug in the streets. The Executive Order that created ODALE also established the Office of National Narcotics Intelligence. A year later, both agencies would be merged into the new Drug Enforcement Agency (DEA) in the Justice Department. As time went on, and perhaps as an unintended consequence of the Watergate scandal, Nixon appears to have concluded that being tough on crime in general and drugs in particular would help him get re-elected.

[58] In September 1975, Ford's Domestic Council Drug Abuse Task Force released a report recommending that "priority in Federal efforts in both supply and demand-reduction be directed toward those drugs which inherently pose a greater risk to the individual and to society." The White Paper called marijuana a "low priority drug" in contrast to heroin, amphetamines and mixed barbiturates. Public Broadcasting System, "Thirty Years of America's Drug War—A Chronology," PBS Frontline, available from www.pbs.org/ wgbh/pages/frontline/shows/drugs/cron/.

[59] Smarting over criticism of his decision to pardon Nixon, Ford may have realized that being tough on drugs would help him get re-elected. J. Y. Smith and Lou Cannon, "Gerald R. Ford, 93, Dies; Led in Watergate's Wake," *The Washington Post,* December 27, 2006, available from www.washingtonpost.com/wp-dyn/content/article/2006/12/26/ AR2006122601257. html.

[60] Gerald R. Ford: "Remarks Upon Signing the Drug Abuse Message," April 27, 1976, Peters and Woolley, *The American Presidency Project*, available from www.presidency.ucsb.edu/ws/?pid=5874.

[61] In addition, the Ford administration proposed a revival of mandatory minimum sentencing for drug trafficking, The Narcotics Sentencing and Seizure Act of 1976. Ford's proposal was ultimately rejected by Congress. Gerald R. Ford: "Statement on Actions To Combat Drug Abuse," December 26, 1975, Peters and Woolley, *The American Presidency Project*, available from www.presidency.ucsb.edu/ws/?pid=5458; Gerald R. Ford: "Statement on Drug Abuse," February 23, 1976, Peters and Woolley, *The American Presidency Project*, available from www.presidency.ucsb.edu/ws/?pid=5609; Gerald R. Ford: "Special Message to the Congress on Drug Abuse," April 27, 1976, Peters and Woolley, *The American Presidency Project,* available from www.presidency.ucsb.edu/ws/?pid=5875; Gerald R. Ford: "Letter to the Speaker of the House and the President of the Senate Transmitting Proposed Narcotic Sentencing and Seizure Legislation," April 30, 1976, Peters and Woolley, *The American Presidency*, available from www.presidency.ucsb.edu/ws/?pid=5926.

[62] Carnevale and Murphy, "Matching Rhetoric to Dollars."

[63] David Musto, "Historical Perspectives," J. Lowinson, P. Ruiz, R. Millman, and J. Langrod, eds., *Substance Abuse: A Comprehensive Textbook*, 4th Ed., Philadelphia, PA: Lippincott, Williams & Wilkins, 2005.

[64] Jimmy Carter: "Drug Abuse Message to the Congress," August 2, 1977, Peters and Woolley, *The American Presidency Project*, available from www.presidency.ucsb.edu/ ws?pid=7908.

[65] *Ibid*. Some popular media outlets even glamorized cocaine use. A May 30, 1977, *Newsweek* story reported:

> Among hostesses in the smart sets of Los Angeles and New York, a little cocaine, like Dom Perignon and Beluga caviar, is now de rigueur at dinners. Some partygivers pass it around along with the canapes on silver trays . . . the user experiences a feeling of potency, of confidence, of energy.

"The Cocaine Scene," *Newsweek*, May 30, 1977, pp. 20-25.

[66] Jimmy Carter: "Office of Drug Abuse Policy Memorandum for the Heads of Certain Departments and Agencies," March 14, 1977, Peters and Woolley, *The American Presidency Project*, available from www. presidency.ucsb.edu/ws/?pid=7174; Jimmy Carter: "Office of Drug Abuse Policy Nomination of Peter G. Bourne to Be Director and Lee I. Dogoloff To Be Deputy Director.," February 7, 1977, Peters and John T. Woolley, *The American Presidency Project*, available from www.presidency.ucsb.edu/ws/?pid=7655.

[67] Jimmy Carter: "Drug Abuse Remarks on Transmitting a Message to the Congress," August 2, 1977, Peters and Woolley, *The American Presidency Project*, available from www.presidency.ucsb.edu/ws/?pid=7907. Carter's proposal to Congress left "the States free to adopt whatever laws they wish concerning marijuana." *Ibid*. Interestingly, Carter cited the recommendations of the National Commission on Marijuana and Drug Abuse—recommendations that were rejected out of hand by President Nixon—in support of his call for decriminalization. Jimmy Carter: "Drug Abuse Message to the Congress," August 2, 1977, Peters and Woolley, *The American Presidency Project*, available from www.presidency.ucsb.edu/ws?pid=7908; *Time Magazine*, "Carter's Grass-Roots Appeal: Can 35 million Americans be wrong about pot?" August 15, 1977.

[68] Since "heroin, barbiturates and other sedative/hypnotic drugs account for 90 percent of the deaths from drug abuse," Carter argued, "they should receive our principal emphasis." *Ibid*.

[69] Testifying before the Select Committee on Narcotics Abuse and Control in July 1978, the Associate Director of the Domestic Policy Staff went even further, arguing that the administration's position regarding small amounts of marijuana for personal use would, in effect, "merely codify what is already occurring, since Federal law enforcement efforts should not be directed at people who possess small amounts of *any drug*, particularly marijuana." Harrison, Backenheimer, and Inciardi, *History of Drug Legislation*; "Cannabis

Use in the United States: Implications for Policy," *Cannabisbeleid in Duitsland, Frankrijk en deVerenigde Staten* (*Cannabis Policy in Germany, France, and the United States*), Peter Cohen and Arjan Sas, eds., Amsterdam, The Netherlands: Centrum voor Drugsonderzoek, Universiteit van Amsterdam, 1996, pp. 179-276, available from www.cedro-uva.org/lib/harrison.cannabis.pdf.

[70] Lawrence Meyer and Alfred E. Lewis, "Carter Aide Signed Fake Quaalude Prescription," *The Washington Post*, July 19, 1978, p. A-1.

[71] "Flak over fake prescription puts Carter's drug fighter on paid leave," *Miami Times*, July 20, 1978.

[72] Reporter Gary Cohn published the story regarding a party hosted by the National Organization for the Reform of Marijuana Laws (NORML). The guests at the December 1977 party included author Hunter Thompson; Christie Hefner, daughter of Hugh Hefner; Tom Forcade, founder of *High Times* magazine; White House drug chief Bourne; and *Post* reporter Cohn. The July 21st *Washington Post* story reported that Bourne had used cocaine and marijuana at the NORML party. Bourne resigned from his position at the Office on Drug Abuse Policy within 24 hours. Cortes, *Sketches of the Drug Czars*.

[73] The "Bourne Affair" was not the only drug-related embarrassment suffered by the Carter administration; other Carter associates, including White House Chief of Staff Hamilton Jordan and White House Appointments Secretary, and later National Campaign Manager, Tim Kraft, also faced allegations of drug use. In Jordan's case, a special prosecutor ultimately found insufficient evidence to support an allegation that Jordan had used cocaine at Studio 54, a Manhattan discotheque, in 1978. Kraft resigned from his post as National Campaign Director in September 1980, following allegations he had used cocaine in 1977. Bourne's successor, his deputy Lee Dogoloff, helped shift policy away from the hard drugs/soft drugs distinction, away from the concern for treatment solutions for heroin addicts, and toward concerns about marijuana. He and DEA Administrator Peter Bensinger advocated for increasing, rather than eliminating, federal penalties for marijuana possession. Andrew B. Whitford and Jeff Yates, "Presidential Rhetoric and the Public Agenda: Constructing the War on Drugs," p. 54. Carter, through Dogoloff, distanced himself from decriminalization. Baum, 1996, p. 129. As Dogoloff would later write, "Decriminalizing marijuana flies in the face of public opinion and, more importantly, scientific evidence of the physical damage this drug causes." Lee I. Dogoloff, "On Health—Don't Legalize Marijuana," *The New York Times Op-Ed.*, December 1, available from www.nytimes.com/1987/12/01/opinion/l-on-health-don-t-legalize-marijuana-979187.html. In the view of some critics, Dogoloff helped effect the biggest change in drug policy since Nixon launched the war on drugs. Baum, 1996, p. 135.

[74] Jimmy Carter: "Illegal Drug Traffic on the High Seas Statement on Signing H. R. 2538 into Law," September 15, 1980, Peters and Woolley, *The American Presidency Project*, available from www.presidency. ucsb.edu/ws/?pid=45047.

[75] Carnevale and Murphy, "Matching Rhetoric to Dollars"; The White House, Drug Abuse Policy Office, "Federal Strategy For Prevention of Drug Abuse and Drug Trafficking 1982," Washington, DC: 1982.

[76] Ronald Reagan: "Radio Address to the Nation on Federal Drug Policy," October 2, 1982, Peters and Woolley, *The American Presidency Project*, available from www.presidency.ucsb.edu/ws/?pid=43085.

[77] Bill Piper, Director of National Affairs for the Drug Policy Alliance, www.drugpolicy.org, quoted in: DRC Net, "The Reagan-Era Drug War Legacy," June 11, 2004, available from stopthedrugwar.org/chronicle-old/341/reagan.shtml.

[78] Reagan vetoed the bill creating a "Drug Czar" within the Executive Branch with the power to coordinate and direct all domestic and international Federal drug efforts. Ronald Reagan: "Memorandum Returning Without Approval a Bill Concerning Contract Services for Drug Dependent Federal Offenders," January 14, 1983, Peters and Woolley, *The American Presidency Project*, available from www.presidency.ucsb.edu/ws/?pid=41310. The

administration found substantial support in the Democratically controlled Congress. In the 1980s, the drug war was a bipartisan issue. Congress was controlled by Democrats, "who not only did not need to have their arms twisted, but in many cases were trying to get to Reagan's right on these issues." DRC Net, "The Reagan-Era Drug War Legacy." Reagan later compared his administration's determination to discourage the flow and use of banned substances to the obstinacy of the French army at the Battle of Verdun in World War I, quoting a French soldier who said: "There are no impossible situations. There are only people who think they're impossible." Ronald Reagan, "Remarks on Signing Executive Order 12368, Concerning Federal Drug Abuse Policy Functions," June 24, 1982, Peters and Woolley, *The American Presidency Project*, available from www.presidency.ucsb.edu/ws/?pid=42671.

79 The President frequently acknowledged the importance of demand-reduction in his public statements:

All the confiscation and law enforcement in the world will not cure this plague as long as it is kept alive by public acquiescence. So, we must now go beyond efforts aimed only at affecting the supply of drugs; we must affect not only supply but demand.

Ronald Reagan: "Remarks Announcing the Campaign Against Drug Abuse and a Question-and-Answer Session With Reporters," August 4, 1986, Peters and Woolley, *The American Presidency Project*, available from *www.presidency.ucsb.edu/ws/?pid=37701*. Reagan expressed the same view in more succinct terms in 1988, "The real answer must come from taking the customer away from the drugs, not the other way around." See Ronald Reagan: "Remarks at a Seminar on Substance Abuse in the Workplace in Durham, NC," February 8, 1988, Peters and Woolley, *The American Presidency Project*, available from www.presidency. ucsb.edu/ws/?pid=35188.

80 The Comprehensive Crime Control Act of 1984 broadened criminal and civil asset forfeiture laws and increased federal criminal sanctions for drug offenses. The 1986 Anti-Drug Abuse Act, while providing money for prevention and treatment, also restored mandatory prison sentences for large-scale distribution of marijuana, imposed new sanctions on money laundering, and other demand-reduction components. 18 U.S.C. Section 1, Repealed Pub. L. 98-473, title II, Sec. 218(a(1, Oct. 12, 1984, 98 Stat. 2027. The 1988 Anti-Drug Abuse Amendment Act primarily increased the sanctions for crimes related to drug trafficking and established several new federal offenses. Eric Schlosser, "Reefer Madness," *The Atlantic Monthly*, 1994, p. 52. The fourth bill, the Crime Control Act of 1990, was focused on supply-reduction and law enforcement, doubling the appropriations for drug law-enforcement grants to states and localities, and strengthening forfeiture and seizure statutes. Bureau of Justice Statistics, 1992, *Crime and the Justice System*, Washington, DC: U.S. Department of Justice, Office of Justice Programs, p. 86.

81 Between 1981 and 1987, federal spending on drug abuse tripled, reaching nearly $4 billion. Ronald Reagan: "Radio Address on Drug Abuse and Trafficking," May 30, 1987, Peters and Woolley, *The American Presidency Project*, available from www.presidency. ucsb.edu/ws/?pid=34347. However, the two-thirds/one-third, supply/demand ratio that took shape in the second Nixon term and continued through the Ford and Carter presidencies would become three-fourths/one fourth under Reagan. Cortes, *Sketches of the Drug Czars*.

82 Ronald Reagan: "Remarks at the National Conference on Corporate Initiatives for a Drug Free Workplace," June 9, 1988, Peters and Woolley, *The American Presidency Project*, available from www. presidency.ucsb.edu/ws/?pid=35950.

83 As Assistant Attorney General of DOJ's Criminal Division, Rudolph Giuliani helped orchestrate the expansion of the FBI into the drug fight; he added 500 DEA agents, established 13 regional anti-drug task forces, and chalked up record numbers of drug seizures and convictions. Lou Cannon, *President Reagan: The Role of a Lifetime*, New York: Touchstone, 1991, p. 813.

84 President Reagan's signature of the Omnibus Budget Reconciliation Act of 1981 repealed the Mental Health Systems Act of 1980 signed by President Carter. Under the new Alcohol,

Drug Abuse and Mental Health Services Block Grant, the percentage of federal funding was reduced and the burden of financing shifted to state and local agencies. Services were cut back, and the development of partnerships and alternative funding strategies became a vital necessity. Minnesota Psychiatric Society, *The Minnesota Mental Health System: Demand, Capacity, and Cost*, St. Paul, MN: MPS Report, 2004. Much of the effort was left to philanthropic foundations, professional organizations, nongovernment organizations, and community groups. Ronald Reagan, "Remarks at a White House Briefing for Service Organization Representatives on Drug Abuse," July 30, 1986, Peters and Woolley, *The American Presidency Project*, available from www. presidency.ucsb.edu/ws/?pid=37676.

[85] As drug use among children became more of a national issue, Nancy Reagan toured elementary schools warning students about the danger of illegal drug use. When one fourth-grader at Longfellow Elementary School in Oakland, CA, asked Mrs. Reagan what she should do if approached by someone offering drugs, Reagan responded: "Just say no." The slogan, and Nancy Reagan's activism on the issue, became central to the administration's antidrug message. Within a year, 5,000 "Just Say No" clubs had formed around the country, with Soleil Moon Frye (Punky Brewster) as honorary chairperson. See www.time.com/ time/world/article/0,8599,1887488,00.html#ixzz17k2sruhh.

[86] *Ibid.*

[87] Carnevale and Murphy, "Matching Rhetoric to Dollars."

[88] The *Posse Comitatus* Act of 1876, which essentially banned military involvement in domestic law-enforcement activities, was amended in 1981 to permit the military to provide training, intelligence, and investigative assistance in cases involving violations of federal drug laws. Harrison, Backenheimer, and Inciardi, *History of Drug Legislation*. As early as 1982, Vice President Bush and his aides began pushing for the involvement of the CIA and U.S. military in drug interdiction efforts. Peter Dale Scott and Jonathan Marshall, *Cocaine Politics*, Berkeley, CA: University of California Press, 1991, p. 2.

[89] Ronald Reagan, "Statement Announcing the Establishment of a Federal Anticrime Task Force for Southern Florida," January 28, 1982, Peters and Woolley, *The American Presidency Project*, available from www.presidency.ucsb.edu/ws/?pid=42775. Reagan later created other regional task forces throughout the United States based on the South Florida Drug Task Force model. These eventually became known as the Organized Crime Drug Enforcement Task Forces (OCDETF, pronounced "Osa Def"), which currently falls under the authority and supervision of the Deputy Attorney General.

[90] In what experts have come to call the "balloon effect," destroying drug crops in one region causes cultivation to move to another. Similarly, disruption of a supply route in one place simply forces traffickers to adopt a new route. In the 1970s and early-1980s, almost all the cocaine consumed in the United States was grown in Colombia and shipped to South Florida along a variety of sea and air routes. Colombian traffickers fighting for market share turned Miami into a city where shootouts, contract killings, and kidnappings became part of daily life. Bernd Debusmann, "Drug wars and the balloon effect," *Reuters Online*, March 26, 2009, available from blogs.reuters.com/great-debate/2009/03/26/drug-wars-and-the-balloon-effect/. Within weeks of its formation, the South Florida Task Force scored several spectacular successes, including a number of major seizures of cocaine and marijuana. In response, Colombian trafficking organizations simply shifted their smuggling routes to Mexico, where they partnered with Mexican criminal networks. "By 1988, the balloon effect had become obvious: The Mexican Defence Ministry reported it had discovered 4.8 tons of cocaine in a cave in Chihuahua near the U.S. border. It was then the world's biggest seizure of the drug. Its Colombian origin was not in doubt—Mexico produced no cocaine of its own." *Ibid.* Today, the U.S. State Department and DOJ's National Drug Intelligence Center estimate that as much as 90 percent of the cocaine consumed in the United States comes through Mexico.

[91] Rensselaer W. Lee III, *The White Labyrinth: Cocaine and Political Power*, New Brunswick, NJ, Transaction Publishers, 1989, p. 100. See also Musto, *Illicit price of cocaine*, p. 323.

[92] U.S. Office of National Drug Control Policy, Executive Office of the President, *Price and Purity of Cocaine: The Relationship to Emergency Room Visits and Deaths, and to Drug Use Among Arrestees*, Washington, DC: Office of National Drug Control Policy, 1992, pp. 5-6.

[93] Some have referred to this as the "Len Bias effect." In June 1986, the nation was shocked when University of Maryland basketball star Len Bias died from a cocaine overdose shortly after being drafted by the Boston Celtics. Ensuing media reports highlighted the health risks of cocaine, and drugs become a significant political issue. After Bias's death, in another display of the bipartisan nature of the drug war, House Speaker Tip O'Neill, D-MA, was determined to "get the Republicans on drugs." O'Neill tasked the Democrats and their staffers to come up with harsh measures, and "they did." DRC Net, "The Reagan-Era Drug War Legacy," June 11, 2004, available from stopthedrugwar.org/chronicle-old/341/ reagan.shtml. In August, President Reagan ordered that all federal employees refrain from using illegal drugs or risk losing their jobs. The Executive Order further required every federal agency to develop a comprehensive drug-free workplace program. Executive Order No. 12564.

[94] The Anti-Drug Abuse Act of 1986, Pub.L. 99-570, 100 Stat. 3207, enacted October 27, 1986, H.R. 5484. The $1.7 billion included $97 million to build new prisons, $200 million for drug education, and $241 million for treatment. *Ibid.*

[95] Possession of at least one kilogram of heroin or five kilograms of cocaine was made punishable by at least 10 years in prison. In response to the crack epidemic, the sale of just five grams of the drug carried a mandatory 5-year sentence. *Ibid.*

[96] David T. Courtwright, "Cocaine in the United States," Jordan Goodman, Paul E. Lovejoy, and Andrew Sherratt, eds., *Consuming Habits: Drugs in History and Anthropology*, London, UK: Routledge Publishers, 1995, p. 217. Heating cocaine powder in a solution of baking-soda-and-water produced a residue of cocaine that could be smoked in a pipe. "Because these chunks made a crackling sound when smoked, they came to be called 'crack'." *Ibid.*, p. 218.

[97] Because crack was so inexpensive and did not have to be injected, an unusually high percentage of its smokers were women. *Ibid.*, p. 219. "Like their turn-of-the-century counterparts, they frequently resorted to prostitution or its equivalent, trading sex for drugs. . . . Thus crack contributed to the other great American epidemic of the 1980s, the spread of HIV infection." *Ibid.*

[98] DRC Net, "The Reagan-Era Drug War Legacy," *6/11/04*, available from stopthedrugwar.org/ chronicle-old/341/reagan.shtml.

[99] Cannon, *The Role of a Lifetime*, p. 813. It is estimated that there was 10 times more cocaine in the United States in 1988 than in 1982.

[100] Drug abuse and addiction have been inextricably linked with HIV/AIDS since the beginning of the epidemic. The link has to do with heightened risk—both of contracting and transmitting HIV, often through intravenous drug use or prostitution to support a drug addiction, and of worsening its consequences. National Institute on Drug Abuse, "Drug Facts: HIV/AIDS and Drug Abuse: Intertwined Epidemics," May 2012, available from www.drugabuse.gov/publications/drugfacts/hivaids-drug-abuse-intertwined-epidemics. Eric Sterling, President of the Criminal Justice Policy Foundation and former Counsel to the U.S. House of Representatives Committee on the Judiciary from 1979 until 1989, quoted in DRC Net, "The Reagan-Era Drug War Legacy," *6/11/04*, available from stopthedrugwar. org/chronicle-old/341/reagan.shtml. Sterling also served on the staff of the Subcommittee on Crime, Representative William J. Hughes, D-NJ, Chairman, and was responsible for drug enforcement, gun control, money laundering, organized crime, pornography, terrorism, corrections, and military assistance to law enforcement, among many issues. He was a principal aide in developing the Comprehensive Crime Control Act of 1984, the Anti-Drug Abuse Acts of 1986 and 1988, and other laws. See flexyourrights.org/about/ board_of_advisor/ sterling.

[101] George W. Bush: "Inauguaral Address," January 20, 1989, Peters and Woolley, *The American Presidency Project*, available from www.presidency.ucsb.edu/ws/?pid=16610. In a 1988 poll, 48 percent of Americans reported that drugs were the most important foreign policy challenge, and 63 percent believed that drugs should take precedence over America's anti-Communist efforts. R. Crandall, *Driven by Drugs: US Policy toward Colombia*, London, UK: Phillips, 2002, p. 32.

[102] P. Andreas *et al.*, "Dead-End Drug Wars," *Foreign Policy*, No. 85, Winter 1991-92, p. 108.

[103] Jonathan Harris, *Drugged America*, New York: Four Winds Press, 1991, p. 146.

[104] Bernard Weintraub, "President Offers Strategy for United States on Drug Control," *The New York Times*, September 6, 1989, p. B7. Although Bush committed himself to ending all drug abuse, his administration actually set more modest goals: a 10 percent decrease in casual drug use over 2 years, and a 50 percent reduction over 10 years. Richard L. Berke, "No Change in Basics," *The New York Times*, September 6, 1989; Harris, *Drugged America*, p. 149.

[105] In 1990, 1 year into his term, Bennett proposed extending capital punishment to "drug kingpins." Bennett was the first U.S. drug chief in 20 years with no professional expertise in health or science. He was also a heavy smoker—he went through two packs a day, or about one ounce of tobacco—and promised to kick his addiction upon taking office. Dan Check, "The Success and Failure of George Bush's War on Drugs," available from tfy.drugsense.org/bushwar.htm, overall Federal spending on treatment and law enforcement increased during Bennett's tenure, but treatment consistently remained less than one-third of the total budget.

[106] Public Broadcasting System, "Thirty years of America's drug war—a chronology," PBS Frontline, available from www.pbs.org/wgbh/pages/frontline/shows/drugs/cron/.

[107] The Personal Responsibility and Work Opportunity Act, P.L. 104-193, otherwise known as the Welfare Reform Act, subjected individuals convicted of drug offenses to a lifetime ban on cash assistance and food stamps, and gave states the authority to institute drug-testing requirements for welfare recipients.

[108] In March 1989, the Supreme Court approved the requirement of drug testing as part of the security clearance process. In *National Treasury Employees Union v. Von Raab*, 489 US 656, 109 S. Ct. 1384, 103 L. Ed. 2d 685, 1989, the Court validated the requirements for drug testing of U.S. Customs Service employees applying for jobs involving interdiction of illegal drugs or possession of a gun. The safety and security risks associated with those jobs, the court reasoned, make such searches "reasonable," and thus permissible under the Fourth Amendment even without a suspicion of wrongdoing. In another case involving drug tests in the workplace, the Court upheld mandatory testing of railroad employees following rail accidents. *Skinner v. Railway Labor Executives Association,* 489 U.S. 602, 109 S. Ct. 1402, 103 L. Ed. 2d 639, 1989. The court cited public safety concerns as its reason for concluding that such testing is a "reasonable" search under the Fourth Amendment.

[109] Bernard Weintraub, "President Offers Strategy for United States on Drug Control," *The New York Times*, September 6, 1989. It is somewhat ironic that in 1989, the National Institute on Drug Abuse (NIDA) released a report stating that there had been a 37 percent drop in casual, nonaddicted use from 1979 to 1989. Harris, *Drugged America*, p. 156. In FY 1990, 40 percent of the drug-control budget was specified for law enforcement, 20 percent for the construction of correctional facilities, and less than 12 percent for improvement of drug-abuse treatment. Sidney H. Schnoll, Lori D. Karan, "Substance Abuse," *Journal of the American Medical Association*, May 1990, Vol. 263, pp. 2682-2683. Estimated 1990 antidrug expenditures illustrate the growing burden on the states: Expenditures for law enforcement at the federal level were $7 billion and $17 billion at the state/local level.

[110] Carnevale and Murphy, "Matching Rhetoric to Dollars."

[111] In January 1990, Bush proposed a further increase of $1.2 billion for the war on drugs, including a 50 percent increase in military spending for DoD's part in the drug war.

Amendments to the National Defense Authorization Acts, Public Laws 101-189, 101-510, and 102-190.

[112] *Ibid*. The Pentagon was designated as the lead federal agency for anti-drug intelligence. It integrated U.S. command, control, communications, and intelligence (C3I) systems; provided an improved interdiction role for the National Guard; directed the armed forces to conduct training exercises in known drug-trafficking areas in the United States; and expanded military authority to assist foreign police and military in anti-drug operations. David Isenberg, "Militarizing the Drug War," *Covert Action*, Fall 1992, p. 42. In November 1989, under the direction of then-Defense Secretary Cheney, Joint Task Force-6 (JTF-6) was established at Fort Bliss in El Paso, TX, to coordinate military and law enforcement anti-drug operations along the U.S.-Mexico border. Chad Thevenot, "The 'Militarization' of the Anti-Drug Effort," July 1997, available from www.ndsn.org/july97/military.html. See also Martin Jelsma, "The Development of International Drug Control: Lessons Learned and Strategic Challenges for the Future," Working Paper Prepared for the First Meeting of the Global Commission on Drug Policy, January 24, 2011.

[113] M. Falco, "Foreign Drugs, Foreign Wars," *Daedalus*, No.121, Summer 1992, p. 65. Major Kimberly J. Corcoran, "DOD Involvement in the Counterdrug Effort—Contributions and Limitations," Montgomery, AL: Air Command and Staff College, AU/ACSC/0077/97-03, March 1997. Few were surprised when, on December 20, 1989, the U.S. military executed Operation JUST CAUSE, an invasion of Panama to arrest Panamanian President Manuel Noriega and return him to the United States for trial on drug trafficking-related charges. The operation employed 25,000 troops. Kevin Buckley, *Panama: The Whole Story,* New York: Simon and Schuster, 1991. On July 10, 1992, Noriega was convicted in the Southern District of Florida of drug trafficking, money laundering, and racketeering, and sentenced to 40 years imprisonment. *Ibid.*

[114] Louis Krane, "How to Win the War on Drugs," *Fortune*, March 12, 1990, p. 75. Congress wanted to know what percentage of all cocaine coming into the country was seized, and how much it would cost to seize half of it. Paul A. Yost, Commandant of the Coast Guard, responded by saying that the Coast Guard had seized only 3 percent of all cocaine entering the country, and that there wasn't enough money in the entire federal budget to seize half the cocaine entering the United States. Harris, *Drugged America,* p. 152.

[115] *Ibid.*, p. 157.

[116] Treaster, "Four Years of Bush's Drug War: New Funds but an Old Strategy," p. A12. This meant reduced profits for those involved in the production, traffic, and sale of drugs. However, since the ultimate goal of the war on drugs was to decrease drug use in the United States, and since interdiction did nothing toward that end, it can be safely said that interdiction was a failure.

[117] Harris, *Drugged America*, p. 157.

[118] *Ibid.*

[119] Public facilities were overcrowded, and those who wanted treatment were often put on long waiting lists. Richard L. Berke, "No Change in Basics," *The New York Times*, September 6, 1989, p. B7.

[120] David E. Smith, "San Francisco Roots: The Evolution of Addiction Medicine," *California Society of Addiction Medicine History*, June 2010, available from www.csam-asam.org/csam-history.

[121] Krane, "How to Win the War on Drugs," p. 72.

[122] Imprisoning an addict costs between $25,000 and $50,000 annually; inpatient treatment for addiction costs only $15,000. According to Dr. Peter Pinto of the Samaritan Village, Inc. Harris, *Drugged America*, p. 155.

[123] Krane, "How to Win the War on Drugs," p. 71.

[124] In 1989, soon after becoming Drug Czar, Bennett had suggested that the nation's capital should stand as a test case for the administration's strategy. After a year of fighting drugs in Washington, DC, Bennett admitted failure. Drug use did not decline, and the homicide rate

remained steady. Joseph B. Treaster, "Echoes of Prohibition; 20 Years of War on Drugs, and No Victory Yet," *The New York Times,* June 14, 1992.

[125] *Ibid.*

[126] Treaster, "Police in New York Shift Drug Battle Away From Streets," p. A1. By 1992, there were more people in federal jails on drug charges than there were for all crimes in 1980. Chief Justice of the Supreme Court William Rehnquist publicly remarked that there were just too many arrests. Twice as many people were arrested for possession of drugs as for selling them. Dan Baum, "The Drug War on Civil Liberties," *The Nation*, June 29, 1992, p. 886.

[127] Despite spending $1.6 billion to build new federal prisons, there were still not enough cells. Treaster, "Police in New York Shift Drug Battle Away From Streets."

[128] *Ibid.* Another impact of the shorter sentences was that many prisoners preferred to serve out their prison term rather than go into treatment because the prison sentences were so much shorter than any treatment program. Ian Fisher, "Selling Addicts on Treatment Rather Than Prison," *The New York Times*, December 1, 1992. Drug dealers did an average of 8 months at Riker's Island in New York City. *Ibid.* Drug traffickers did an average of 22 months. Krane, "How to Win the War on Drugs," p. 75. Drug-addicted dealers who showed a good chance of recovery were offered an alternative to serving out their sentences: rehabilitation at Phoenix House. The treatment was rejected by many, simply because it can take up to 2 years. Ian Fisher, "Selling Addicts on Treatment Rather Than Prison," *The New York Times*, December 1, 1992, p. B3.

[129] Gwen Ifill, "The 1992 Campaign: New York; Clinton Admits Experiment with Marijuana in 1960s," *The New York Times*, March 30, 1992.

[130] Joseph B. Treaster, "Clinton Continues Old Drug Policies," April 12, 1993, available from www. cato.org/pubs/fpbriefs/fpb026.pdf. Clinton's campaign position was that rehabilitation should be made available to anyone who asked for it, despite the fact that it would cost hundreds of millions of dollars. *Ibid.* It appears that no one in the news media noticed that the last President to call for treatment on demand was Richard M. Nixon.

[131] *Ibid.*

[132] William S. Smith, a senior official in the White House anti-drug office under President Bush, said national drug policy appeared to be "on cruise control." *Ibid.* One of Clinton's first decisions was to reduce the size and budget of the Office of National Drug Control Policy by 80 percent. Ted Galen Carpenter, "Declaring an Armistice in the International Drug War," *Cato Institute Foreign Policy Briefing*, No. 26, July 26, 1993.

[133] He had also left most other drug-related federal positions in the hands of acting directors or holdovers from the Bush administration. Treaster, "Clinton Continues Old Drug Policies." Many in law enforcement were disappointed by Clinton's decision to sign the North American Free Trade Agreement, which resulted in an enormous increase in legitimate trade across the U.S.-Mexican border. The increased volume of trade also made it more difficult for U.S. Customs officials to find narcotics hidden within legitimate goods.

[134] William J. Clinton, "Remarks Announcing the Appointment of the Director of the Office of National Drug Control Policy and an Exchange with Reporters," April 28, 1993, Peters and Woolley, *The American Presidency Project*, available from www.presidency.ucsb.edu/ws/?pid=46491. Brown was not sworn into office until July 1, 1993. William J. Clinton, "Remarks on the Swearing-In of National Drug Control Policy Director Lee Brown," July 1, 1993, Peters and Woolley, *The American Presidency Project*, available from www. presidency.ucsb.edu/ws/?pid-46783.

[135] Brown previously headed the police departments of Atlanta, Houston, and New York City. *Ibid.*

[136] ONDCP's mission was continually criticized by members of Congress, who called for a stiffer anti-drug message from the White House. Pierre Thomas and Jim McGee, "Brown Ends Two-Year Tenure as Drug Policy Chief," *The Washington Post*, December 13, 1995, p. A27, available from www.ndsn.org/jan96/ drugczar.html.

137 Treaster, "Clinton Continues Old Drug Policies." "What we have here is a budget that says 'business as usual,'" said Dr. LaMond Tullis, a professor of political science at Brigham Young University in Provo, Utah, and a drug policy consultant to the United Nations. "It seems we're going to go on doing things we know don't work." *Ibid.* Carpenter, Cato Institute Foreign Policy Briefing No. 26.

138. Treaster, "Clinton Continues Old Drug Policies."

139. *Ibid.* In his last year in office, President Bush cut $336 million from international operations and anti-smuggling efforts. He increased spending for drug treatment by $168 million while President Clinton proposed a $170 million increase. *Ibid.* Administration officials apologetically explained that the budget had been prepared before a detailed drug strategy could be worked out, and suggested that "the healthcare overhaul being developed under the leadership of Hillary Rodham Clinton was likely to include increased spending for drug treatment."

140. Carnevale and Murphy, "Matching Rhetoric to Dollars"; 1998 figures are available from the White House: Office of National Drug Control Policy website, available from https://www.ncjrs.gov/ondcppubs/publications/policy/00ndcs/v.html. Federal drug-control agencies received an emergency supplemental appropriation of $844 billion in FY 1999 that is not reflected in these totals. The supplemental appropriation was divided as follows: Defense, $42 million; Justice, $11.7 million; ONDCP, $3.2 million; State, $232.6 million; Transportation, $264.7 million; Treasury, 266.7 million; All others, $23.0 million. For FY 2000, see White House Office of National Drug Control Policy; and for FY 2001 figures, see Executive Summary, White House Office of National Drug Control Policy.

141. William J. Clinton: "Press Briefing by Director of National Drug Control Policy, Dr. Lee Brown," February 9, 1994; Peters and Woolley, *The American Presidency Project*, available from www.presidency.ucsb. edu/ws/?pid=59752. In announcing the new budget, Brown emphasized that there would be no reduction in the funding for supply-reduction, law enforcement, and interdiction. The enhanced funding requested for treatment and prevention was "new money." *Ibid.*

142 *Ibid.*

143. Joseph B. Treaster, "Clinton Continues Old Drug Policies," April 12, 1993, available from www. cato.org/pubs/fpbriefs/fpb026.pdf. Clinton's campaign position was that rehabilitation should be made available to anyone who asked for it, despite the fact that it would cost hundreds of millions of dollars. *Ibid.*

144 *Ibid.* ONDCP then estimated the hard-core drug population was then about 2.7 million, approximately 600,000 heroin addicts, and the rest, crack cocaine and cocaine addicts.

145 William J. Clinton, "Press Briefing by Attorney General Janet Reno, Secretary of H.U.D. Henry Cisneros, Director of the Office of National Drug Control Policy Lee Brown, and Assistant Secretary of Treasury Ron Noble," March 29, 1994, Peters and Woolley, *The American Preisdency Project*, available from www.presidency.ucsb.edu/ws/?pid=59891.

146 Among other things, the initiative funded a designated prosecutor in every U.S. Attorney's Office to coordinate the investigation and prosecution of federal violent crimes. William J. Clinton, "Press Briefing by Attorney General Janet Reno, Secretary of H.U.D. Henry Cisneros, Director of the Office of National Drug Control Policy Lee Brown, and Assistant Secretary of Treasury Ron Noble," March 29, 1994, Peters and Woolley, *The American Preisdency Project*, available from www.presidency.ucsb.edu/ws/?pid=59891. William J. Clinton, "Press Briefing by Attorney General Janet Reno, Secretary of H.U.D. Henry Cisneros, Director of the Office of National Drug Control Policy Lee Brown, and Assistant Secretary of Treasury Ron Noble," March 29, 1994, Peters and Woolley, *The American Preisdency Project*, available from www. presidency.ucsb.edu/ws/?pid=59891.

147 William J. Clinton, "Statement on the Resignation of Lee Brown as Director of the Office of National Drug Control policy," December 12, 1995, Peters and Woolley, *The American Presidency Project*, available from www.presidency.ucsb.edu/ws/?pid=50889. Most significant was the passage of the Violent Crime Control and Law Enforcement Act of

1994. "Three strikes and you're out" became the law of the land, and the federal government provided funding for 100,000 new police officers and 30,000 additional prison cells. William J. Clinton, "Remarks on Signing the Violent Crime Control and Law Enforcement Act of 1994," September 13, 1994, Peters and Woolley, *The American Presidency Project*, available from www.presidency. ucsb.edu/ws/?pid=49072. Whatever their long-term potential might have been, Clinton's demand-reduction initiatives produced little in the way of positive, short-term results. As in other administrations, political expediency demanded a pro-law enforcement, "tough-on-crime" approach, with little regard for the cost or outcome.

148 Pierre Thomas and Jim McGee, "Brown Ends Two-Year Tenure as Drug Policy Chief," *The Washington Post*, December 13, 1995, p. A27. Announcing his resignation in Houston, Brown expressed frustration at the current climate in Washington. "At a time when we see a rise in the use of illegal drugs by our adolescents, the proposed budget cuts in drug-fighting are wrong-headed and must be reversed," he said. *Ibid.*

149 Clinton's selection of McCaffrey was "widely seen as a direct response to Republican election–year criticisms that the president was soft on drugs." Major Barrett K. Peavie, U.S. Army, "United States War on Drugs: Addicted to a Political Strategy of No End," Fort Leavenworth, KS: School of Advanced Military Studies, U.S. Command and General Staff, College, January 2001 28, available from www.dtic.mil/cgi-bin/GetTRDoc?AD=ADA 391171&Location=U2&doc=GetTRD.

150 *Ibid.*

151 William J. Clinton, "Press Briefing by General Barry McCaffrey," April 29, 1996, Peters and Woolley, *The American Presidency Project*, available from www.presidency.ucsb.edu/ws/ ?pid=48807. The "Five Pillar Strategy," called for motivating American youth to reject illegal drugs and substance abuse but did not include "treatment on demand." Other pillars of the strategy included: reducing drug-related crime and violence; eliminating the social consequences of illegal drug use; shielding our frontiers against drug trafficking; and reducing drug cultivation, production, and trafficking abroad and at home. The get-tough approach included get-tough legislation, such as the Comprehensive Methamphetamine Control Act of 1996, which was designed to "stop meth before it becomes the crack of the 1990s." The Act followed the doubling of methamphetamine-related deaths between 1994 and 1996. William J. Clinton, "Remarks on Signing the Comprehensive Methamphetamine Control Act of 1996," October 3, 1996, Peters and Woolley, *The American Presidency Project*, available from www.presidency. ucsb.edu/ws/?pid=52038. William J. Clinton, "Press Briefing by General Barry McCaffrey," April 29, 1996, Peters and Woolley, *The American Presidency Project*, available from www.presidency.ucsb.edu/ws/?pid=48807. William J. Clinton, "Remarks Announcing the 1997 National Drug Control Strategy and an Exchange with Reporters," February 25, 1997, Peters and Woolley, *The American Presidency Project*, available from www.presidency.ucsb.edu/ws/?pid=53779.

152 *Ibid.* Peavie, "United States War on Drugs," p. 46. The FY 1998 budget climbed to $17.4 billion, with virtually no change in the funding ratio. William J. Clinton, "Press Briefing by General Barry McCaffrey," December 11, 1997, Peters and Woolley, *The American Presidency Project*, available from www. presidency.ucsb.edu/ws/?pid=48650. In 1998, President Clinton and Director McCaffrey launched a 5-year, $2 billion National Youth Anti-Drug Media Campaign, the largest targeted effort ever to teach youth about the dangers of drugs. William J. Clinton, "Remarks Announcing the 1997 National Drug Control Strategy and an Exchange with Reporters," February 25, 1997, Peters and Woolley, *The American Presidency Project*, available from www.presidency.ucsb.edu/ws/ ?pid=53779. The media campaign created a public furor when it was revealed that ONDCP had violated domestic propaganda and publicity prohibitions by preparing prepackaged news stories that did not disclose to television viewers that the government had produced them and had illegally spent appropriations to develop, produce, and distribute the covert propaganda. "Office of National Drug Control Policy—Video News Release," Washington,

DC: U.S. Government Accountability Office. 2005-01-04, available from www.gao.gov/ decisions/appro/ 303495.htm. Retrieved 2008-09-06.

[153] Most of that amount, $862.3 million, was allocated to Colombia and the balance to neighboring countries, primarily Peru, Bolivia, and Ecuador, and to U.S. agencies' Andean region antidrug operations. Of the $862.3 million allocated to Colombia, $521.2 million was new assistance to the Colombian armed forces, and $123.1 million was assistance to the police, with the rest, $218 million, going to alternative economic development, aid to displaced persons, judicial reform, law enforcement, and promotion of human rights. Angel Rabasa and Peter Chalk, *Colombian Labyrinth: The Synergy of Drugs and Insurgency and Its Implications for Regional Instability*, Santa Monica, CA: RAND Corporation, 2001, pp. 62-63, available from www. rand.org/pubs/monograph_reports/MR1339/MR1339.ch6.pdf. The bulk of the military assistance was intended to support the Colombian armed forces' three counternarcotics battalions, which received 16 UG-60 Black Hawk and 30 UH-1H transport helicopters. In addition, the cap on U.S. military personnel assisting in the Colombian drug/insurgent conflict was doubled to 500. *Ibid.*

[154] *Ibid.* In 2010, the Washington Office on Latin America concluded that both Plan Colombia and the Colombian government's security strategy "came at a high cost in lives and resources, only did part of the job, are yielding diminishing returns and have left important institutions weaker." "Colombia: Don't Call it a Model," *The Washington Office on Latin America*, July 13, 2010, available from www.wola.org/index.php?option=com_ content& task=viewp&id=1134&Itemid=2.

[155] The development of treatment for co-occurring mental and substance abuse disorders was one of the program's goals. H. Harwood, D. Fountain, and G. Livermore, *The Economic Costs of Alcohol and Drug Abuse in the United States 1992*, NIH Pub. No. 98-4327, Rockville, MD: National Institutes of Health, 1998.

[156] This change in the law permits Schedule III, IV, or V narcotic medications that are FDA-approved for treatment of narcotic-use disorders to be used for medically supervised detoxification or maintenance, facilitates patients' access to treatment by addiction-medicine specialists, and makes office-based care possible. *Ibid.*

[157] Between 1999 and 2007, over 48,000 persons died in the United States from AIDS due to transmission through infected needles. Eric Sterling, "40 Years of Drug War Hasn't Worked; 'Time for a Change,' Says 9-Year Veteran," *Alternet*, June 15, 2011, available from www.alternet.org/story/151306/40_years_of_drug_war-hasn percent27t_worked percent3B_ percent22time_for_a_change percent2C percent22_says_9-year_veteran.

[158] William J. Clinton, "Press Briefing by Director of the Office of National Drug Control Policy General Barry McCaffrey, Deputy Director of the Office of National Drug Control Policy, Dr. Donald Vereen, and Chief of Staff of the Office of Drug Control Policy, Janet Crist," January 4, 2001, Peters and Woolley, *The American Presidency Project*, available from www.presidency.ucsb.edu/ws/?pid=47890.

[159] William J. Clinton, "Remarks Announcing the 1997 National Drug Control Strategy and an Exchange with Reporters," February 25, 1997, Peters and Woolley, *The American Presidency Project*, available from www.presidency.ucsb.edu/ws/?pid=53779. The annual federal drug budget for criminal justice tripled from $2.76 billion in 1989 to $8.45 billion in 1999.

[160] William J. Clinton, "Message to the Congress Transmitting the 1997 National Drug Control Strategy," February 25, 1997, Peters and Woolley, *The American Presidency Project*, available from www.presidency.ucsb.edu/ws/?pid=53780. One objective of supply-reduction efforts has been to reduce the availability of drugs sufficiently to create scarcity, which, at least in theory, should drive prices up and, thereby, make drug users unable or unwilling to continue their drug use. This proposition has been the subject of numerous studies, which have attempted to explain why, from 1981 to 2003, the prices of powder cocaine and heroin fell and the purity of these drugs increased, while their demand grew.

See Executive Office of the President, ONDCP, *The Price and Purity of Illicit Drugs: 1981 Through the Second Quarter of 2003*, November 2004, p. 70.

161 Michael Kramer, "Snow in August: Candidate George W. Tries to Stop the Cocaine Avalanche," *New York Daily News,* August 22, 1999.

162 Anne E. Kornblut and Glen Johnson, *The Boston Globe*, October 7, 2001, p. A6. Not surprisingly, the Gore campaign offered its own statistics, arguing that the number of drug users ages 25 to 34 had dropped 39 percent, and drug use by teenagers ages 12 to 17 had declined 21 percent between 1997 and 1999. Moreover, a Gore spokesman stated, "Al Gore and this administration proposed the largest antidrug budget ever."

163 Hutchinson would serve as DEA Administrator until January 2003, when he moved to the newly created Department of Homeland Security to lead the Border and Transportation Security Directorate, later renamed the Transportation Security Administration. Phillip Smith, "Bush's Drug Policy Troika," *Alternet*, May 14, 2001, available from www.alternet.org/story/10856/ bush's_drug_policy_troika/?page=entire. Hutchison co-sponsored the 2000 Methamphetamine Antiproliferation Act and advocated strongly against a medical marijuana initiative and needle-exchange programs in the District of Columbia. *Ibid*.

164 As Director of the Office of National Drug Control Policy (ONDCP), Drug Czar Walters was fond of military interventions and long prison sentences, and made only token efforts to address concerns that he would ignore the treatment and prevention components of drug policy. Phillip Smith, "Bush's Drug Policy Troika," *Alternet*, May 14, 2001, available from www.alternet.org/story/10856/bush's_drug_policy_ troika/?page=entire.

165 As Attorney General, Ashcroft's focus became the threat of terrorism after the attacks of 9/11. He played no significant role in the development of the national drug strategy. Peter Baker and Susan Schmidt, "Ashcroft's Complex Tenure At Justice," *The Washington Post*, May 20, 2007, available from www. washingtonpost.com/wp-dyn/content/article/2007/05/19/ AR2007051901275.html.

166 Phillip Smith, "Bush's Drug Policy Troika," *Alternet*, May 14, 2001, available from www.alternet.org/ story/10856/bush's_drug_policy_ troika/?page=entire.

167 *National Youth Anti-Drug Media Campaign: How to Ensure the Program Operates Efficiently and Effectively*, Testimony to Congress, August 1, 2001. Walters was so confident in the efficacy of the program that he invested $7 million a year in performance measurement-related spending to determine the effectiveness of the campaign. However, in 2002, a study commissioned by ONDCP reported that teenagers exposed to federal anti-drug ads were no less likely to use drugs for having viewed them, and some young girls said they were even more likely to give drugs a try. Walters blamed poor ads that failed to resonate with teenagers, and promised in 2002 Senate testimony that he would show results within a year or admit failure. Congress agreed to extend the campaign through 2003, while cutting funding for the ads from $170 million in 2002 to $150 million in 2003. An entirely new advertising campaign was created. Shawn Zeller, "Ads, Drugs & Money," *Government Executive*, September 19, 2003. In February 2005, a new research company hired by ONDCP and the National Institute on Drug Abuse reported that the government's ad campaign aimed at dissuading teens from using marijuana, a campaign that cost $1.4 billion between 1998 and 2006, did not work. "[G]reater exposure to the campaign was associated with weaker anti-drug norms and increases in the perceptions that others use marijuana." The research company was paid $42.7 million for the 5-year study. After the February 2005 report was received, the office continued the ad campaign, spending $220 million on the anti-marijuana ads in fiscal years 2005 and 2006. Ryan Grim, "A White House Drug Deal Gone Bad: Sitting on the Negative Results of a Study of Anti-Marijuana Ads," *Slate* magazine, September 7, 2006.

168 Jeff Zeleny, "Bush's Drug Policy Highlights Terror Link," *Chicago Tribune*, February 13, 2002, available from articles.chicagotribune.com/2002-02-13/news/0202130313_1_illegal-drugs-drug-control-prescription-drug-fraud. The budget request included $52 million in

DEA's budget to be used to fight terrorism. In 2004, DEA announced its participation in the U.S. Embassy Kabul Counternarcotics Implementation Plan, designed to reduce heroin production in Afghanistan, the world's leading opium producer.

169 Zeleny, "Bush's Drug Policy Highlights Terror Link." On February 13, 2002, Bush suggested that the 9/11attacks were made possible through the sale of illegal substances like heroin and other drugs. Nearly 70 percent of the world's heroin supply comes from Afghanistan, officials say. Even though the ousted Taliban regime had banned the production of opium poppies during its rule, Bush said the drug trade provided "a significant amount of money to the people that were harboring and feeding and hiding those who attacked and killed thousands of innocent Americans." *Ibid.* The President's remarks continued a theme the White House had launched during the February 3rd Super Bowl, with graphic television commercials linking drug sales to terrorism. *Ibid.*

170 For FY 2002 figures, see White House Office of National Drug Control Policy, "National Drug Control Strategy: FY 2003 Budget Summary," Washington, DC: Office of the President, February 2002, Table 2, p. 6. For FY 2003, CDSP Research Report, "Revising the Federal Drug Control Budget Report: Changing Methodology to Hide the Cost of the Drug War?" *Common Sense for Drug Policy*, Washington, DC, 2003. Beginning in FY 2004, ONDCP made significant changes in the way it computed the national drug budget. The new methodology was designed, according to ONDCP, so that the budget would reflect "only those expenditures aimed at reducing drug use rather than, as in the past, those associated with the consequences of drug use." Peter Reuter, "An Assessment of ONDCP's Budget Concept, Testimony presented to the House of Representatives Committee on Government," February 10, 2005. As a result, the FY 2004 budget request of $11.7 billion was touted as including an increase of $440.3 million over the FY 2003 budget, despite the fact that the FY 2003 budget was $19.2 billion. This feat of mathematical gymnastics was accomplished by retrospective application of the new budget accounting methodology to effectively reduce the FY 2003 budget total by approximately $75 billion by excluding, among other things, almost all costs associated with the prosecution and incarceration of federal drug prisoners—approximately $4.5 billion. On the other hand, the new drug budget approach expanded the amount of money reported for drug treatment spending by including hundreds of millions of dollars in alcohol treatment spending not previously included in the drug budget. For example, SAMHSA's full substance abuse treatment block grant funding will be included in the drug treatment budget report, including $55 million for alcohol treatment. This, despite a specific Congressional prohibition on ONDCP's involvement in alcohol abuse treatment matters. CSDP Research Report, "Revising the Federal Drug Control Budget Report: Changing Methodology to Hide the Cost of the Drug War?" *Common Sense for Drug Policy*, Washington, DC, available from *proxy.* baremetal.com/ csdp.org/research/ondcpenron.pdf. White House Office of National Drug Control Policy, FY 2003 Budget Summary Office of National Drug Control Policy, *National Drug Control Strategy, FY 2005 Budget Survey*, Washington, DC: March 2004, available from https://www.ncjrs.gov/pdffiles1/ondcp/203723.pdf. White House Office of National Drug Control policy, *National Drug Control Strategy, FY 2007 Budget Survey*, Washington, DC, February 2006, available from https://www.ncjrs.gov/pdffiles1/ ondcp/212977.pdf. White House Office of National Drug Control policy, *National Drug Control Strategy, FY 2008 Budget Survey*, Washington, DC, February 2007, available from https://www.ncjrs.gov/ pdffiles1/ondcp/216432.pdf. For 2009 figures, see U.S. Department of Justice, Bureau of Justice Statistics and Crime Facts: Drug Control Budget, available from *bjs.ojp.usdoj.gov/content/dcf/dcb.cfm.*

171 Maia Szalavitz, "Tearing Apart Bush's Drug Plan," *Alternet*, February 19, 2002, available from www.alternet.org/story/12439/tearing_apart_bush's_drug_plan/. Bush's plan promised to cut drug use by 25 percent in 5 years, unduly optimistic, but modest in comparison with Congress's 1988 plan, which had America entirely drug-free by 1995. *Ibid.*

[172] Nearly $1.6 billion has been pledged for treatment programs over the next 5 years, he said. Zeleny, "Bush's Drug Policy Highlights Terror Link."

[173] The administration's proposal drew criticism from treatment advocates, who argued that the drug problem would be solved only through health programs, not heightened law enforcement. Critics said the drug budget devotes two-thirds of its money to military-style enforcement, with the rest going to treatment and prevention programs. *Ibid.*

[174] Bush signed the Mérida Initiative in 2008, committing $1.4 billion to Mexico and other countries over 3 years to help combat drug trafficking and transnational crime. The funds were earmarked for military and law enforcement training and equipment, as well as technical advice and training to strengthen the national justice systems. Claire Suddath, "Brief History: The War on Drugs," *Time.com*, March 25, 2009, available from www.time.com/time/world/article/0,8599,1887488,00.html#ixzz17k4ZwMak; "Mexico's 2008 Defence Budget Goes Under Review," *Jane's Defense Weekly*, December 11, 2007, available from www.janes.com/news/defence/business/jdw/jdw071211_1_n.shtml; Politico.com, "Bush pushes Mexico money in Iraq bill," May 8, 2008, available from www.politico.com/news/stories/0508/10180.html. However, the flow of drugs across the U.S. Southwest border did not diminish.

[175] According to a study by the Rand Corporation, it would take 11 times as much money to reduce the demand for cocaine by 1 percent using interdiction, than it would to do so via treatment spending; similar figures are believed to apply for other drugs. C. Peter Rydell and Susan S. Everingham, *Controlling Cocaine: Supply Versus Demand Programs*, Prepared for the Office of National Drug Control Policy and the United States Army, Santa Monica, CA: RAND Drug Policy Research Center, 1994, p. xvi.

[176] "Public Views Clash with U.S. Policy on Cuba, Immigration, and Drugs," *Zogby International*, October 2, 2008, available from www.zogby.com/news/readnews.cfm?ID=1568.

[177] The Bush administration's 2002 goal of reducing all illegal drug use by 25 percent led to unprecedented numbers of marijuana-related arrests; however, marijuana use declined only by 6 percent, and the use of other drugs actually increased. Claire Suddath, "Brief History: The War on Drugs," *Time.com*, March 25, 2009, available from www.time.com/time/world/article/0,8599,1887488,00.html#ixzz17k4ZwMak.

[178] John Carnevale, "The Policy-Budget Mismatch," Carnevale Associates Policy Brief, Gaithersburg, MD: September 2009; CSDP Research Report, "Revising the Federal Drug Control Budget Report: Changing Methodology to Hide the Cost of the Drug War?" *Common Sense for Drug Policy*, Washington, DC, available from proxy.baremetal.com/csdp.org/research/ondcpenron.pdf; White House Office of National Drug Control Policy, FY 2003 Budget Summary Office of National Drug Control Policy, *National Drug Control Strategy, FY 2005 Budget Survey*, Washington, DC: March 2004, available from https://www.ncjrs.gov/pdffiles1/ ondcp/203723.pdf.

[179] Cortes, "Sketches of the Drug Czars," *Vanity Fair*.

[180] Katharine Q. Seelye, "Barack Obama, Asked About Drug History, Admits He Inhaled," *The New York Times*, October 24, 2006. As he revealed in his book, *Dreams from My Father*: "Pot had helped, and booze; maybe a little blow when you could afford it. Not smack though." Barack Obama, *Dreams from My Father: A Story of Race and Inheritance*, New York: Three Rivers Press, 2004.

[181] John K. Wilson, *Barack Obama: This Improbable Quest*, Boulder, CO: Paradigm, 2008, pp. 12-13.

[182] Candidate Obama had also insisted that medical marijuana was an issue best left to state and local governments, promising an end to the Bush administration's high-profile raids on providers of medical marijuana. Attorney General Holder vowed that Justice Department resources would not be used to circumvent state marijuana laws. However, the federal détente soon collapsed. Tim Dickinson, "Obama's War on Pot," *Rolling Stone*, February 16, 2012, available from www.rollingstone.com/politics/news/obamas-war-on-pot-20120216.

The public comments of Drug Czar Kerlikowske began to sound remarkably similar to those of his predecessors. "Marijuana is dangerous and has no medicinal benefit," see Cortes, "Sketches of the Drug Czars," *Vanity Fair*.

[183] B. Curley, "Obama's first drug budget fails to shift priorities," available from www.jointogether.org/news/features/2009/obamas-first_drug-budget.html.

[184] Cortes, "Sketches of the Drug Czars," *Vanity Fair*.

[185] Office of National Drug Control policy, "National Drug Control Strategy, FY 2011 Budget Survey," White House: Washington, DC, February 2010. In February 2011, ONDCP announced that it had once again restructured the Federal drug control budget "to more accurately represent the full range of federal spending, including costs associated with the consequences of drug use." According to ONDCP, "the new budget structure and framework prove[es] an inclusive and true description of the Federal contribution dedicated to the drug-control problem." The fact sheet does not provide a detailed explanation of the methodology; however, it does provide a list of new agencies and programs added to the FY 2012 National Drug Control Budge calculation, most of which appear to be traditional supply-reduction activities, Office of National Drug Control Policy, Fact Sheet: Changes to the National Drug Control Budget, February 2011. Under the "revised budget structure," ONDCP claims an increase of 100 percent in demand-reduction expenditures, as compared with an increase of only 50 percent in supply-reduction expenditures for FY 2010-12. Whether the change in methodology was designed to hide the true cost of the war on drugs or distort the ratio between supply/demand spending, it has that result. The figures used in the table were also included in the ONDCP fact sheet and described as computations made under the "previous budget structure." The figures clearly understate the totals expended; however, the percentages apportioned between demand-reduction and supply-reduction appear sufficiently accurate for comparison to the figures for earlier years.
For FY 2011 and FY 2012, see White House Office of National Drug Control Policy, The National Drug Control Strategy, FY 2011 Budget Survey, Washington, DC: February 2010, available from www.whitehouse.gov/sites/default/files/ondcp/policy-and-research/fy11budget.pdf. For FY 2013, see White House Office of Nation-al Drug Control Policy, The National Drug Control Budget: FY 2013 Funding Highlights, Washington, DC: February 2012, available from www.whitehouse.gov/ondcp/the-national-drug-control-budget-fy-2013-funding-*highlights*. Changes in accounting methodology create a misleading appearance of dramatic increases in both supply-reduction and demand-reduction spending. Phillip Smith, "What's in Obama's New Drug War Budget? Hint: Same, Old Broken Policies," *Drug War Chronicle*, February 18, 2012, available from www.alternet.org/story/154178/what percent27s_in_obama percent27s_new drug war budget_ percent28hint percent3A_same percent2C_old_broken_policies percent29.

[186] The $15.5 billion represents an increase of 3.5 percent over the 2010 budget; two-thirds of it is $9.7 billion for law enforcement and other supply-reduction efforts, and one-third, about $5.6 billion, for prevention and treatment. Phillip S. Smith, "Obama Wants More Money for the Failed Drug War," *Drug War Chronicle*, February 5, 2010, available from www.alternet.org/drugs/145563/obama_wants_more_money_for_the_failed_drug_war/?page=1. Yet, Drug Czar Kerlikowske called the imbalanced budget "balanced." "The new budget proposal demonstrates the Obama administration's commitment to a balanced and comprehensive drug strategy," said Kerlikowske. "In a time of tight budgets and fiscal restraint, these new investments are targeted at reducing Americans' drug use and the substantial costs associated with the health and social consequences of drug abuse." *Ibid.* The promise of a balanced approach is one that has been made by every administration since Nixon.

[187] In February 2011, ONDCP announced that it had once again restructured the Federal drug-control budget "to more accurately represent the full range of federal spending, including costs associated with the consequences of drug use." According to ONDCP, "the new budget structure and framework prove[es] an inclusive and true description of the Federal

contribution dedicated to the drug-control problem." The fact sheet does not provide a detailed explanation of the methodology; however, it does provide a list of new agencies and programs added to the FY 2012 National Drug Control Budge calculation, most of which appear to be traditional supply-reduction activities, Office of National Drug Control Policy, "Fact Sheet: Changes to the National Drug Control Budget," February 2011. Under the "revised budget structure," ONDCP could claim an increase of 100 percent in demand-reduction expenditures in the FY 2013 budget, as compared with an increase of only 50 percent in supply-reduction expenditures. Whether the change in methodology was designed to hide the true cost of the war on drugs or distort the ratio between supply/demand spending, it has that result. The figures used in the table were also included in the ONDCP fact sheet and described as computations made under the "previous budget structure." The figures clearly understate the totals expended; however, the percentages apportioned between demand-reduction and supply-reduction appear sufficiently accurate for comparison to the figures for earlier years.

[188] The proposed budget increases federal anti-drug funding by 1.6 percent over Fiscal Year 2012. Although funding for prevention and treatment would increase by 4.6 percent, some treatment and grant programs would be cut, while supply-reduction programs would see increases. The budget emphasizes drug courts and criminal justice-based drug treatment; it cuts SAMHSA, which provides treatment resources, but increases spending for prison-based treatment. The $364 million earmarked for SAMHSA's treatment programs is a $61 million reduction from FY 2012. Meanwhile, drug courts are in for a $17 million increase to $52 million, and BOP drug treatment programs would get a $16 million increase to $109 million. In sum, the 2013 budget request represents a 3 percent increase for treatment and an 11 percent decrease for prevention. Smith, "What's in Obama's New Drug War Budget?"

[189] Smith, "What's in Obama's New Drug War Budget?"

[190] *Ibid*. Those include operations for the Federal Bureau of Prisons, budgeted at $8.3 billion for 2011. Since more than half of all federal prisoners are serving time for drug offenses, the argument goes, the real cost of current drug policies should be increased by at least $4 billion. Only $79 million of the Federal Bureau of Prisons' budget is counted as part of the national drug strategy budget. *Ibid.*

[191] Office of National Drug Control Policy, Office of Public Affairs, *Fact Sheet: U.S. Drug Policy*, April 17, 2012; Zogby International., October 2008; *Zogby/Inter-American Dialogue Survey: Public Views Clash with U.S. Policy on Cuba, Immigration, and Drugs*, available from www.zogby.com/news/ReadNews.cfm?ID=1568.

[192] Remarks of ONDCP Director Gil Kerlikowske as Prepared for Delivery to the Center for American Progress, Washington, DC, May 1, 2012. Copy in author's files, available from www.c-spanvideo.org/ program/305743-1.

[193] The latest available federal data show that drug arrests during President Obama's first year in office are up compared to those during the first year of President Bush's administration. The arrest rate hasn't changed significantly, despite the White House's own admission that we cannot "arrest or incarcerate our way out of a problem this complex." Ending the Drug War: A Dream Deferred," *Law Enforcement Against Prohibition,* June 2011, p. 8, available from www.CopsSayLegalizeDrugs.com/40years.

[194] Although the Obama administration hasn't matched its deeds to its words with respect to a real shift in the drug-control strategy, the fault for our long-entrenched drug policies does not solely lie with this or any particular President. "Ending the Drug War: A Dream Deferred," *Law Enforcement Against Prohibition*, June 2011, p. 15, available from www.CopsSayLegalizeDrugs.com/40years.

[195] *Ibid*. "This is very much the same drug budget we've been seeing for years," said Bill Piper, national affairs director for the Drug Policy Alliance, DPA.

[196] In a February 2000 report prepared for the National Institute of Justice, a team of researchers concluded that a strategy based on supply-reduction simply cannot work:

> Given experiences since the beginning of the war on drugs, which initiated major expansions in expenditures on supply-based programs, it seems more reasonable to conclude that the Nation will not be able to have any large future influence on decreasing the availability and increasing the price of illicit drugs.

Abt Associates, Inc., "Illicit Drugs: Price Elasticity of Demand and Supply," February 2000, available from www.abtassociates.com/reports/20008744845311.pdf.

[197] Rydell and Everingham, "Controlling Cocaine," pp. xvi. The Rand Report analyzes the relative cost-effectiveness of four available drug interventions: 1) source country control; 2) interdiction; 3) domestic enforcement; and 4) treatment of heavy users. The first three focus on supply-control, whereby the cost of supplying cocaine is increased by seizing drugs and assets and by arresting and incarcerating dealers and their agents. The fourth is a demand-control program, because it reduces consumption directly, without going through the price mechanism. The Rand researchers confirm that the bulk of the drug budget, an estimated $13 billion in the year prior to publication is spent on domestic enforcement, and only a small percentage of the total budget is allocated to the treatment of heavy users. Given the high cost of supply control programs, treatment of heavy users may be a more cost-effective way of dealing with drug interventions. See also Peavie, "United States War on Drugs," p. 45.

[198] Fully 76 percent of the American people and 67 percent of chiefs of police have declared the drug war a failure, according to polls. "Ending the Drug War: A Dream Deferred," *Law Enforcement Against Prohibition*, June 2011, available from www.CopsSayLegalize Drugs.com/40years.

[199] Sterling, "40 Years of Drug War Hasn't Worked; 'Time for a Change,' Says 9-Year Veteran." The U.S. Department of Justice, National Drug Intelligence Center, "The Economic Impact of Illicit Drug Use on American Society 2011"; Peter Reuter, "An Assessment of ONDCP's Budget Concept," Testimony presented to the House of Representatives Committee on Government, February 10, 2005.

[200] Carnevale Associates, "Policy Brief."

[201] National Survey on Drug Use and Health, available from https://nsduhweb.rti.org/; FBI Uniform Crime Reports, available from www.fbi.gov/about-us/cjis/ucr/ucr. In 2010, 82 percent of high school seniors report that marijuana is easy to obtain—a decrease in perception of only 2 percent in 20 years. American Civil Liberties Union, "Feds Don't Walk Their Talk in Drug Control Budget," 2012, available from www. aclu-wa.org/blog/feds-dont-walk-their-talk-drug-control-budget.

[202] Claire Suddath, "Brief History: The War on Drugs," *Time.com*, March 25, 2009, available from www. time.com/time/world/article/0,8599,1887488,00.html#ixzz17k47wMak

[203] The rate has remained unchanged since 2002. Carnevale Associates, "Policy Brief: The Continued Standstill in Reducing Illicit Drug Use," Gaithersburg, MD: September 2009.

[204] *Ibid.*

[205] *Ibid.* The total number of drug offenders in the prison system, federal and state combined, is approximately one-half million, as large as the entire addict population of 1900.

[206] United States Department of Justice, National Drug Intelligence Center, *National Drug Threat* Assessment 2009, p. III.

[207] In his 1971 message, Nixon lamented 1,000 narcotics deaths in New York City, then the epicenter of the heroin addiction problem in 1970. At the end of 1979, the annual number of drug abuse deaths was 7,101. That number rose to 9,976 in 1986, the year basketball star Len Bias died from a cocaine-induced seizure. However, in 2007, there were an estimated 38,000 drug overdose deaths nationwide. The death rate has grown from 3.0 per 100,000 in 1980 to 12.8 in 2006. Sterling, "40 Years of Drug War Hasn't Worked." 'Time for a Change,' Says 9-Year Veteran."

[208] Liz Szabo, "Addicted infants triple in decade," *USA Today*, May 1, 2012, approximately 13,539 infants per year.

[209] Peter Reuter, "The Limits and Consequences of U.S. Foreign Drug Control Efforts," *The Annals of the American Academy of Political and Social Science*, Vol. 521, May 1992.

[210] The vast size of the drug market "has the power to negate all supply-side drug control efforts aimed at reducing the availability of illicit drugs to U.S. consumer." Wes Fryer, "U.S. Drug Control Policy: Where We Have Been," available from www.wesgryer.com/drugwar.html#past.

[211] Even if we are uncertain what shape the new strategy should take, we cannot continue to repeat the mistakes of the past. See, e.g., George Santayana, "The Life of Reason," Vol. 1, "Those who cannot remember the past are condemned to repeat it." This quote is not originally from the cited text.

[212] Nearly every administration has conceded, at least privately, that the best way to affect supply is to reduce demand for drugs. However, the rhetoric has never matched the reality. See e.g., *Szalavitz* , "Tearing Apart Bush's Drug Plan."

[213] See www.globalcommissionondrugs.org/wp-content/themes/gcdp_v1/ pdf/Global_ Commission_ Report_ English.pdf.

[214] The Commission includes the former Presidents or prime ministers of five countries, a former Secretary General of the United Nations, human rights leaders, and business and government leaders, including Richard Branson, George P. Shultz, and Paul A. Volcker. The report describes the total failure of the present global antidrug effort, with particular emphasis on America's 40 year "war on drugs." It notes that the global consumption of opiates has increased 34.5 percent; cocaine, 27 percent; and cannabis, 8.5 percent, from 1998 to 2008. *Ibid.*

[215] National Institute on Drug Abuse, "InfoFacts: Treatment Approaches for Drug Addiction," September 2009, available from www.drugabuse.gov/publications/infofacts/treatment Addiction need not be a life sentence. Like other chronic diseases, it can be managed successfully. Treatment enables people to counteract addiction's powerful effects on the brain and behavior and regain control of their lives. National Institute on Drug Abuse, "The Science of Addiction," National Institute of Health Pub Number 10-5605, rev'd August 2010; Caron Treatment Centers, "Relapse & Recovery: Behavioral Strategies for Change," pp. 15-17.

[216] The average cost for 1 year of methadone-maintenance treatment is approximately $4,700 per patient, compared with approximately $24,700 for 1 year of imprisonment. *Ibid.*

[217] In a study sponsored by ONDCP and the U.S. Army, researchers C. Peter Rydell and Susan Everingham compared the effectiveness of four types of drug-control programs: source-country efforts, interdiction, domestic law enforcement, and drug treatment. How much money, they asked, would the Government have to spend on each approach to reduce national cocaine consumption by 1 percent? Rydell and Everingham developed a model of the national cocaine market, then fed into it more than 70 variables, from seizure data to survey responses. Relying solely on domestic law enforcement, the Government would have to spend an additional $246 million to reduce U.S. cocaine consumption by 1 percent. Relying on interdiction, it would have to spend $366 million, and, on source-country programs, $783 million. Relying solely on drug treatment, however, the Government would only have to spend $34 million more. In other words, treatment was 7 times more cost effective than domestic law enforcement, 10 times more effective than interdiction, and 23 times more effective than attacking drugs at their source. C. Peter Rydell and Susan S. Everingham, *Controlling Cocaine: Supply Versus Demand Programs*, Prepared for the Office of National Drug Control Policy and the United States Army, Santa Monica, CA: RAND Drug Policy Research Center, 1994, p. xvi. In another study by the National Association of State Alcohol and Drug Abuse Directors, $1 in treatment brings a return of $11.54 for society. Harris, *Drugged America,* p. 154. The legal structure that is needed for increasing access has been in place since 1972. The Drug Abuse Office and Treatment Act was probably the most important statute enacted during the short era of enlightened and

progressive drug policy. Similarly, when effective pharmacotherapies emerge, we should also subsidize their use.

218 Examples of this type of treatment include Methadone and Levo-alpha-acetylmethadol (LAAM) for opiate withdrawal, benzodiazepine, and anti-seizure drugs for barbiturate withdrawal. To prevent relapses, other drugs, like Naltrexone and Buprenorphine/naloxone, reduce cravings and block the effects of opiates. Researchers continue to investigate effective treatments for cocaine and amphetamine addiction, and several drugs are currently in clinical trials. Doctors around the globe are exploring other promising addiction treatments. Ibogaine, a hallucinogenic drug used in some African religious rites, is an example of one such approach. Although the drug is illegal in the United States, between 20 and 30 ibogaine clinics operate in various countries to treat heroin addiction. "Addiction Treatments Past and Present," available from learn.genetics.utah.edu/content/addiction/issues/treatments.html; National Institute on Drug Abuse, "InfoFacts: Treatment Approaches for Drug Addiction," September 2009, available from www.drugabuse.gov/publications/infofacts/treatment-approaches-drug-addiction.

219 "Addiction Treatments Past and Present."

220 National Institute on Drug Abuse, "InfoFacts: Treatment Approaches for Drug Addiction," September 2009, available from www.drugabuse.gov/publications/infofacts/treatment

221 SAMHSA has estimated that about 1 in 10 people with serious substance abuse problems, 2.3 million of 23 million received treatment in 2005. Substance Abuse and Mental Health Services Administration, Results from the 2005 National Household Survey on Drug Use and Health: National Findings, DHHS Publication No. SMA 06-4194, 2006.

222 Over time, we ought to be able to reduce our reliance on the criminal justice system substantially. Richard J. Bonnie, "The Virtues of Pragmatism in Drug Policy," *Journal of Health Care Law and Policy*, The Stuart Rome Lecture, University of Maryland Law School, College Park, MD: November 7, 2008, Vol. 13, 2010, p. 7.

223 Treatment alternatives to criminal punishment were an important component of the strategy of the 1970s that eroded during the 1980s and early-1990s. Bonnie, "The Virtues of Pragmatism in Drug Policy." The establishment of more than 2000 drug courts since 1995 is a good step in that direction. *Ibid*. Conditional dispositions linked to drug treatment also remain available in many, ordinary criminal courts.

224 National Institute on Drug Abuse, "InfoFacts: Treatment Approaches for Drug Addiction."

225 Family members, friends, and employers regularly provide the same type of therapeutic leverage. *Ibid*. Also, as Bonnie, "The Virtues of Pragmatism in Drug Policy" suggests:

> Criminalization of consumption-related offenses is legitimate—as an instrument of deterrence and prevention for non addicted offenders, and, most importantly for our present topic, as an instrument of therapeutic leverage for addicted offenders.

Ibid. See also Redonna K. Chandler, Bennett W. Fletcher, and Nora D. Volkow, "Treating Drug Abuse and Addiction in the Criminal Justice System: Improving Public Health and Safety," *Journal of the American Medical Association*, No. 183, 2009, p. 301.

226 Although this is already occurring in several thousand state and local courts nationwide, there is no similar federal program. The Department of Justice recently changed its own policies, as codified in the U.S. Attorneys' Manual, to make alternatives to incarceration more available. In March 2011, DOJ expanded the permissible pretrial diversion programs "to include those that address addicted defendants through treatment and monitoring, rather than prosecution." Deputy Attorney General James M. Cole Speaks on Alternatives to Incarceration Programs: the Use of "Drug Courts" in the Federal and State Systems, New York, May 21, 2012, available from www.justice.gov/iso/opa/dag/speeches/2012/dag-speechEfforts to implement drug courts and other alternatives to federal incarceration have, thus far, been sporadic and largely dependent on the energy and initiative of individual U.S. Attorneys. Examples include the Central District of Illinois, where the Pretrial Alternatives to Detention Initiative (PADI), permits some defendants charged with felony drug offenses to be offered pretrial diversion and to have their charges reduced or dismissed upon

successful completion of rehabilitation. The Conviction and Sentence Alternative (CASA) program in the Central District of California and the BRIDGE court program in the District of South Carolina are similar programs, which provide diversion options for defendants with substance abuse problems. *Ibid.* Studies by the National Institute on Drug Abuse have confirmed the efficacy of such programs:

Combining prison- and community-based treatment for addicted offenders reduces the risk of both recidivism to drug-related criminal behavior and relapse to drug use, which, in turn, nets huge savings in societal costs.

National Institute on Drug Abuse, "InfoFacts: Treatment Approaches for Drug Addiction."

227 For 40 years, the budget trends have run counter to what research would otherwise suggest: efforts to reduce demand are best addressed through treatment and prevention rather than supply-reduction. *Ibid.* "The virtue of pragmatism in drug policy is that it focuses our attention on what works best." Bonnie, "The Virtues of Pragmatism in Drug Policy."

228 Massing, "The Fix," p. 272. Defenders of the current drug prohibition approach argue that the fall in drug prices following legalization or even after some slackening of enforcement would lead to a large increase in drug "abuse." This claim rests on the standard prohibitionist assumption that all use is abuse and the further assumption that price is a major consideration for most users or would-be users. Many researchers insist that drug prices directly affect the "bottom line"; that is, higher prices result in reduced use and fewer emergency room visits. Dhaval Dave, "The effects of cocaine and heroin price on drug-related emergency department visits," *Journal of Health Economics*, August 2005, available from www.appstate. edu/~whiteheadjc/eco4810/crap/jhe-drugs.pdf. However, in the view of other experts, personal preferences and social norms influence most people more than the price of drugs. Mary M. Cleveland, "Economics of Illegal Drug Markets: What Happens If We Downsize the Drug War?" available from www.mcleveland.org/ publications/Economics_of_Illegal_Drug_Markets.CV.pdf. In either case, we can be certain of one thing. An increase in the price of drugs will result in an increase in violent crime as hard-core users struggle to feed their habit. Higher prices require higher user income. If users cannot earn enough by legal means to pay higher prices, then they may be induced to engage in illegal conduct—theft, burglary, robbery—that they would not otherwise engage in. Mark H. Moore, *Buy and Bust*, Cambridge, MA: Lexington, 1977, Chap. 2. See also Llewellyn Hinkes-Jones, "How the Plummeting Price of Cocaine Fueled the Nationwide Drop in Violent Crime," *The Atlantic Cities*, November 11, 2011, available from www.theatlanticcities.com/jobs-and- economy/2011/11/cocaine-plummeting-price-nationwide-drop-violent-crime/474/.

229 John Carnevale, "The Failure of the Office of National Drug Control Policy," *The Huffington Post*, July 14, 2008, available from www.huffingtonpost.com/john-carnevale/the-failure-of-the-office_b_112693. html?view=p.

230 Wesley A. Fryer, "U.S. Drug Control in the Americas: Time for a Change," August 30, 1993, available from www.wesfryer.com/drugwar.html#conclusion. See also John Carnevale, "Is the Policy-Budget Mismatch to Blame," Carnevale Associates Policy Brief, Gaithersburg, MD: September 2009.

231 In the words of one anonymous wag: "The most powerful drug law is the law of supply and demand."

232 Even if we could, domestically produced marijuana, methamphetamine, and a host of illicit synthetic drugs would still be available to meet demand. Yet, for 40 years, successive administrations have annually sought additional funds to bolster supply-reduction efforts. The unspoken promise in each annual budget request has been: "With just a bit more money and a few more agents and prosecutors, the strategy is certain to succeed." The scene is reminiscent of a famous *New Yorker* cartoon, based on the well-known nursery rhyme "Humpty Dumpty" in which a crowned king, addressing his royal cabinet, declares: "Gentlemen, the fact that all my horses and all my men couldn't put Humpty together again

simply proves to me that I must have more horses and more men." Dana Fradon, *The New Yorker*, July 24, 1978.

233 We must ensure that the "cost" of manufacturing, importing, and distributing drugs in America remains painfully high and the potential "profit" unattractively low. Some administrations have adopted strategies promising to "take the profit out of drugs," by seizing the ill-gotten gains of traffickers, usually in the form of bulk cash and international currency transfers. Unfortunately, our success rate on seizing outbound dollars has been little more successful than our efforts to seize inbound drugs. Improved strategic intelligence and analysis could enhance our supply-reduction efforts. In the opinion of some experts, most of the advantages of prohibition can be attained with modest levels of overall enforcement, coupled with targeting of dealers whose behavior poses a particular risk to the community, e.g., use of juvenile distributors, violence against competitors. Tougher enforcement across the board does not appear to significantly raise drug prices or restrict availability; it imposes rather high individual and social costs. Jonathan P. Caulkins and Peter Reuter, "How Drug Enforcement Affects Drug Prices," August 26, 2010, available from www.publicpolicy.umd.edu/uploads/cms/faculty/reuter/Drug percent20Enforcement percent20and percent20Drug percent20Price.pdf. While it may be politically popular to have DEA Regional Enforcement Teams making street-level busts in Middle America, it does not reduce supply or demand; it produces only a temporary increase in the "cost of doing business" and a substantially longer-term increase in the federal prison population. Likewise, Foreign Assistance Support Teams (FAST) in places like Afghanistan have allowed DEA to claim a role in the war on terrorism and a share of the new budget dollars devoted to all-things counterterrorism. However, since very little Southwest Asian heroin ever reaches the United States, the efforts of these FAST teams would have no impact on the availability of drugs there.

234 Steve Chapman, "In the Drug War, Drugs Are Winning," *Reason.Com*, March 29, 2010, available from reason.com/archives/2010/03/29/in-the-drug-war-drugs-are-winn. "Iran has a repressive theocratic regime that imposes severe penalties for using and selling drugs—including death by hanging. Yet, Iran has one of the highest rates of addiction in the world." *Ibid.*

235 A survey of 17 countries published in 2008 found that, despite its punitive drug policies, the United States continues to have the highest levels of illegal cocaine and cannabis use. The study, by Louisa Degenhardt, University of New South Wales, Sydney, Australia and colleagues, is based on the World Health Organization's Composite International Diagnostic Interview (CIDI). "United States Has Highest Level Of Illegal Cocaine And Cannabis Use," *Science Daily*, June 30, 2008, available from www.sciencedaily. com/releases/2008/06/080630201007.htm. The authors found that 16.2 percent of people in the United States had used cocaine in their lifetime—a level much higher than any other country surveyed; the second highest level of cocaine use was in New Zealand, where 4.3 percent of people reported having used it. Cannabis use was also highest in the United States, with 42.4 percent, followed by New Zealand, with 41.9 percent. The authors also concluded that drug use "does not appear to be simply related to drug policy, since countries with more stringent policies towards illegal drug use did not have lower levels of such drug use than countries with more liberal policies." For example, in the Netherlands, which has more liberal policies than the United States, 1.9 percent of people reported cocaine use, and 19.8 percent reported cannabis use.

INDEX

#

A

D

E

F

G

H

I

J

K

L

M

P

Q

R

S

T

Y